nys

New York State

prime mover

robert a. slayton

Times Square in New York City, New York

Share Moments
share The Season
NEW YORK
Marriott
MARQUIS
AT&T Wireless
PIPER
MARQUIS
STOMP
maxell
MARQUIS THEATRE BOX OFFICE

Acknowledgments

The author wishes to thank, for all their help, Bobby Reiss, JoLaVerde, and the proprietors and staff of Westnap of Irvine, California. In addition, he salutes Margaret Martin, a fine editor, for her wisdom and patience.

Buffalo & Erie County Botanical Gardens in Buffalo, New York

Photo © James Schwabel/Panoramic Images

cherbo publishing group, inc.

president	Jack C. Cherbo
executive vice president	Elaine Hoffman
editorial director	Christina M. Beausang
managing feature editor	Margaret L. Martin
contributing editors	Erica Rheinschild Tina G. Rubin Penny Suess
senior profiles editor	J. Kelley Younger
profiles editors	Broos Campbell Liza Yetenekian Smith
associate editor	Sylvia Emrich-Toma
profiles writers	Broos Campbell Linda Chase Robynn Clairday Kathleen Gilbert Mary C. Marshall Beth Mattson-Tieg Tina G. Rubin Kristina Sauerwein Liza Yetenekian Smith Paul Sonnenburg Stefanie Spikell Penny Suess Jason Wroblewski Diane Ver Steeg-Anderson Stan Ziemba

art director	Peri A. Holguin
designers	Lucius Bryant III Joel Vendette Theodore E. Yeager
senior photo editor	Amy Juda
assistant photo editor	Walter Mladina
digital color specialist	Art Vasquez
sales administrator	Joan K. Baker
production services coordinator	Patricia De Leonard
production services assistant	Leslie E. Shaw
administrative assistant	Bill Way
eastern regional manager	Marcia Weiss
eastern development director	Glen Edwards
publisher's representatives	Steve Nafe Linda Sproehnle Kay Zeigler

Cherbo Publishing Group, Inc., Encino, California 91316

Printed by Friesens
Altona, Manitoba, Canada
Neche, North Dakota, USA

Library of Congress Cataloging in Publication data
Slayton, Robert A.
A pictorial guide highlighting 19th- through 21st-century
New York State economic and social history.
Library of Congress Control Number: 2004100705
ISBN 1-882933-58-3

Visit the CPG Web site at www.cherbopub.com.

Doubleday Field in Cooperstown, New York

Contents

Photo: © Carl Heilman II/www.carlheilman.com

Winter at Niagara Falls in Niagara Falls, New York

Photo: David Zimmerman/Masterfile www.masterfile.com

Jones Beach on Long Island, New York

Corporations and Organizations Profiled

The following corporations and organizations have made a valuable commitment to the quality of this publication. The Empire State Development Corporation gratefully acknowledges their participation in *New York State: Prime Mover.*

Brooklyn Bridge in New York City, New York

Dear Friends,

New York holds the promise of the American Dream. From the bustle of Times Square to the unparalleled beauty of Niagara Falls to the majesty of the Adirondacks, the Empire State's diverse natural, cultural, recreational, and commercial characteristics inspire New Yorkers and people from around the world.

We are home to the "City That Never Sleeps," suburban living at its best, spectacular wilderness settings, stunning beaches, and the best selection of theater, museums, art, sports, and entertainment in the world.

Long recognized as an industrial leader, New York pioneered the country's aviation industry, financial network, and the arts and entertainment world. Still on the cutting edge, today we are developing a Centers of Excellence network—a $1 billion high-tech collaboration among government, universities, and the private sector that will create a new economy for the 21st century.

I am proud of New York State's unparalleled heritage and its richness and diversity. *New York State: Prime Mover,* this visually appealing book, documents the culture, history, quality of life, and commercial achievements that help to define the State of New York.

I hope you enjoy this exceptional tribute to New Yorkers who strive to make the Empire State an ideal place to live, work, and visit.

Sincerely,

George E. Pataki
Governor

City Hall in Albany, New York

City Hall in Albany New York, New York

1693

1693 The first bookstore in New York City opens, run by William Bradford, who is also the official printer of the colony of New York.

1747 The oldest cattle ranch in the United States starts operations on Montauk on Long Island.

1754 King's College, later Columbia University, is chartered.

1768 The New York Chamber of Commerce is formed.

1789 James Fenimore Cooper is born. The author will live most of his life in Cooperstown (named for a relative) and write novels of life in the upstate districts, most notably, *The Last of the Mohicans*.

1807 Robert Fulton sails the first successful steamboat from New York to Albany.

1812 Citibank is founded in New York City as City Bank of New York.

1817 The New York Stock Exchange is organized by 28 local brokers in New York City.

1825 The Erie Canal opens, linking midwestern farmers to national and European markets through the Port of New York. By 1830, New York City will handle 40 percent of the country's foreign trade.

1836 Martin Van Buren of Albany is elected eighth president of the United States. His nickname, "Old Kinderhook," is the origin of the term "OK."

1836

1837

1837 Tiffany & Young opens in Manhattan; in 1853, the name is changed to Tiffany & Co.

1837 John D. Rockefeller is born in Richford, New York.

1842 The Broad Street Bridge in Rochester opens, enabling the Erie Canal to cross over the Genesee River.

1844–1849 Edgar Allan Poe lives intermittently in New York City and writes some of his greatest poems, including *The Raven* and *The Bells*.

1848 The first women's rights convention in U.S. history takes place at Seneca Falls.

1848 The first Ferris wheel built in the United States opens in Syracuse.

1850 Vice President Millard Fillmore, born in Locke, becomes the 13th U.S. president upon the death of President Zachary Taylor.

1851 *The New York Times* begins publication.

1851 The first Christmas tree retail lot is opened by Mark Carr in New York City.

1851

1853

1853 Niagara Falls Hydraulic Power and Manufacturing Company is chartered.

1857 The first safety passenger elevator in the nation, operated by Elisha Otis, begins service in a store on Broadway.

1858 Rowland H. Macy opens his first store at Sixth Avenue and 14th Street in Manhattan. The Herald Square store will begin operations in 1888.

1859 The Great Atlantic & Pacific Tea Company (A&P supermarkets) begins operations with one tea shop on Vesey Street in Lower Manhattan.

1859 Central Park opens in New York City.

1861 John Pierpont Morgan establishes J.P. Morgan and Company, which will become the most important financial firm in America by the turn of the 20th century.

1861 Vassar College opens near Poughkeepsie.

1861

1863

1863 New York City businessmen form the National Union Life and Limb Insurance Company, the predecessor of Metropolitan Life.

1863 Filled with animosity toward blacks, who are exempt from the draft because they are not considered citizens, whites take to Manhattan's streets in the Civil War Draft Riots, the worst riots in U.S. history, with nearly 1,000 killed or injured.

1867 Belmont Raceway holds its first race, with only four horses in the field. The winner, Ruthless, runs a mile and five furlongs in three minutes, four seconds.

1867

1870

1870 Syracuse University is chartered.

1875 Corning Glass Works, of Corning, is incorporated in New York State.

1875

Photo: © CORBIS

NYS Time Capsule

Carpe Diem

Ellis Island

Photo: © CORBIS

1878

1878 Rochester's Genesee Brewery, predecessor of High Falls Brewing Company, begins production of its namesake beer.

1879 Frank Winfield Woolworth opens the first five-and-dime store, in Utica.

1881 Chester Alan Arthur of New York City, vice president of the United States, succeeds James Abram Garfield when the latter is shot.

1882 Fiorello La Guardia, who will become the quintessential New York City mayor, is born in Manhattan.

1883 The Brooklyn Bridge opens.

1884 The first Dow Jones index of stocks appears.

1886 Dr. Josephine Walter of Mount Sinai Hospital becomes the first woman to complete an internship at an American hospital.

1886 The Statue of Liberty opens.

1888 George Eastman, of Rochester, sells his first camera.

1889 *The Wall Street Journal* begins publication.

1890 The Plaza Hotel opens.

1891 Carnegie Hall makes its debut.

1892 Ellis Island opens; more than 16 million immigrants will enter America through this gateway.

1892

1895

1895 The first cartoon in an American paper, *The Yellow Kid* by Richard Felton Outcault, appears in the *New York World*.

1896 Louis Henri Sullivan's Guaranty Building opens in Buffalo, one of the country's first skyscrapers.

1896 Buffalo's Ellicott Square Building opens; filling an entire city block, it is the world's largest commercial office building at the time.

1899 Construction of the New York State Capitol in Albany is completed.

1900 The Shubert Brothers move their theatrical organization from Syracuse to New York City and become a major force on Broadway, operating numerous theaters.

1901 President William McKinley is assassinated at the Pan-American Exposition in Buffalo. Vice President Theodore Roosevelt, a native of New York City, moves to the Oval Office.

1901 Thomas Alva Edison opens a film studio in New York, the first indoor, glass-enclosed movie studio in America. Two years later, the pathbreaking film *The Great Train Robbery* is filmed there.

1901

1903

1903 D. W. Griffith's Biograph Studios debuts in the Bronx.

1904 The New York City subway system is off and running.

1905 The Albright-Knox Art Gallery opens in Buffalo.

1907 Broadway impresario Florenz Ziegfeld produces his first *Follies*.

1909 The National Association for the Advancement of Colored People (NAACP) meets in New York City for the first time. W. E. B. DuBois edits its periodical, *The Crisis*, the first magazine devoted to black authors.

1910 Dr. Leo Hendrik Baekeland gets a patent for his new plastic, Bakelite.

1911 The Triangle Shirtwaist factory fire kills 146 workers and leads to fundamental reform of the New York Fire Code, which is adapted across the country by states and municipalities.

1911

1914

1911 In New York City, Rockefeller University scientists discover that cancer is caused by a virus.

1911 IBM is incorporated as the Computing-Tabulating-Recording Co.

1914 Ira Nascher, a Mount Sinai Hospital physician, writes the first textbook in the country on geriatrics.

1914 Charles Merrill and Edmund Lynch open their first office.

1915 Scientists at Corning, Inc., begin development of what will eventually be Pyrex.

1920s The Harlem Renaissance, a literary movement, holds sway in New York City.

1920

NYS Time Capsule

1922

1922 DeWitt and Lila Wallace publish the first volume of *Reader's Digest*, in Greenwich Village.

1923 Yankee Stadium opens.

1924 Simon & Schuster is founded by Richard Simon and Max Schuster; their first success is a crossword puzzle book.

1924

1925

1925 *The New Yorker* magazine makes its debut.

1926 the National Broadcasting Company is founded, followed by the Columbia Broadcasting System in 1928.

1927 Book publisher Random House begins operations.

1928 In Manhattan, Batten Co. merges with Barton, Durstine & Osborn to form BBDO, which will become one of the nation's leading advertising agencies.

1929 Work is started on Rockefeller Center.

1929 LeRoy Grumman founds Grumman Aircraft Engineering Company in Baldwin on Long Island.

1929

1931

1931 The Empire State Building opens; it will remain the world's tallest building for more than 40 years.

1932 Franklin Roosevelt, a native of Hyde Park, is elected president.

1932 Radio City Music Hall debuts, with Martha Graham, Ray Bolger, and the high-stepping Rockettes.

1933 The week ending July 21st is the worst in Wall Street history; the Dow drops 15.6 percent.

1933 The loafer-style shoe is patented by a Syracuse firm, the Nettleton Shoe Company.

1938 Action Comics introduces a new character, Superman, created by New York City residents Jerry Siegel and Joe Schuster; Superman lives in Metropolis, a thinly veiled version of his creators' hometown.

1938

1939

1939 LaGuardia Airport opens; it will be followed in 1948 by Idyllwild Airport (later John F. Kennedy International Airport).

1939 Savage Arms of Utica starts making Thompson submachine guns; the company will manufacture 68 percent of these firearms used during WW II.

1939 New York City hosts the World's Fair, using for the first time the Flushing Meadow site that will host another fair in 1964.

1942 Governor Thomas Dewey signs a bill authorizing planning for a cross-state superhighway; it will become the New York State Thruway.

1943 Rodgers and Hammerstein's *Oklahoma!*, the first of what would become a postwar boom in musical theater, opens on Broadway.

1945 Marvin Sands founds Canandaigua Wines in the Finger Lakes region.

1945

1948

1948 The State University of New York system begins operations.

1948 The law firm of Skadden, Arps, Meagher & Flom is founded.

1949 Construction begins in Manhattan on the United Nations headquarters.

1952 Lever House, corporate headquarters of Lever Brothers, opens in New York City and starts the nationwide boom in glassbox skyscrapers.

1959 Bristol Laboratories, in Syracuse, manufactures the first synthetic penicillin.

1959 Buffalo gets a football team, and team owners pick the name Bills over runners-up such as Bullets, Nickels, and Blue Devils.

1959 The Haloid Xerox Company of Rochester introduces the Xerox 914, the world's first automatic copier using plain paper.

1961 The first Marvel comic, *The Fantastic Four*, debuts; it is the first to feature New York City, instead of a fictional location, as the superheroes' home.

1961

1962

1962 The University of Buffalo joins the State University of New York and becomes the state's largest and most comprehensive private university.

1971 The National Association of Securities Dealers Automated Quotation (NASDAQ) begins trading.

1973 Secretariat runs the mile-and-a-half at Belmont in two minutes, 24 seconds, a world's record.

1975 *Saturday Night Live* begins broadcasting on NBC with the trademark line, "Live from New York...."

1976 The World Trade Center towers open for business.

1981 IBM introduces the PC desktop computer.

1981 Michael Bloomberg founds Bloomberg L.P. business-news service.

1982 *Late Night with David Letterman* begins broadcasting.

1982

1983

1983 William Kennedy, author of numerous works set in his hometown of Albany, wins the Pulitzer Prize for his novel *Ironweed*.

1993 Rudolph W. Giuliani is elected the 107th mayor of New York City.

1999 On December 31st, the Dow reaches 11,497, its highest point yet.

2001 The creation of the Centers of Excellence program is announced by Governor George E. Pataki.

2001 On September 11th, terrorists destroy the Twin Towers of the World Trade Center.

2002 The New York Stock Exchange trades 2,812,918,977 shares on July 24, a record.

2002

2003

2003 Rockefeller University scientist Roderick MacKinnon wins the Nobel Prize in Chemistry for work on the proteins that create nerve impulses.

2003 New York is plunged into darkness as the largest electrical blackout in history strikes.

2003 The 2002–03 Broadway season posts the highest box-office grosses in history, $771 million.

2004 Madison Square Garden hosts the 2004 Republican National Convention.

2004

NYS Time Capsule

Photo: © Jean Miele/CORBIS

Stissing Mountain farm in Pine Plains, Dutchess County, New York

Photo: © Carl Heilman II/www.carlheilman.com

Photo: © Carl Heilman II/www.carlheilman.com

Cloud Trail on Gore Mountain in Adirondack Park, New York

Photo: Chrysler Building at Grand Central Station. © Sitki Tarlan/Panoramic Images

PART**ONE**

Looking Ever Upward

The New York State of Mind

The Empire State

Quality of Life

Dynamic. Bucolic. Vigorous. Restful. Forward-looking. Historic.

CHAPTER**ONE**

New York State is full of contradictions, yet this seeming dichotomy is what gives it its strength and makes it a place where anything is possible.

William B. Harrison, Jr.
Chairman and Chief Executive Officer
J.P. Morgan Chase & Co.

The core of every JPMorgan Chase business includes our commitment to provide resources to help others do well and realize their aspirations. Beyond the balance sheet, that commitment is also evident in our development of community partnerships worldwide to support healthy, vibrant communities where we live and work. This is not a recent activity. We have long regarded these partnerships as a fundamental part of what we do and who we are around the globe.

Leadership in community partnerships is part of the enduring culture of this firm. Following the anticipated merger of J.P. Morgan Chase & Co. and Bank One Corporation in midyear 2004, the combined company will expand upon both companies' historic commitment to community development and philanthropy.

JPMorganChase

Since the first Europeans touched ashore in New York centuries ago and began exploring all the way to Niagara Falls, people have been settling in the Empire State. By 2003, there were an estimated 19 million people—or one-fifteenth of the U.S. population—making their home in New York. This was up .2 percent over the previous year and 5.5 percent since the 1990 census.

What draws them in such numbers? And what makes them stay?

There are plenty of reasons why so many millions of people have come to New York State, many of them based on the remarkable range of life choices and entrepreneurial opportunities that New York offers. Among the myriad reasons people come are a dynamic business environment, a productive workforce, unsurpassed educational opportunities, superior health care, and abundant arts and recreation.

Fifty-one Fortune 500 companies can't be wrong. That is the number of powerhouse corporations that have established their headquarters in the Empire State. Nearly 2,200 foreign companies have ties here, whether in property, employment, facilities, or equipment, making New York second only to California in foreign investment. *Site Selection* magazine ranked the state second in new business facilities and expansions for 2003, with 552 new facilities.

New York is second in the nation in the number of high-technology firms located here (approximately 16,700) and fourth in the amount of venture capital invested in this field, or $2.2 billion. Part of the reason for the state's success in this area is the Centers of Excellence and other state-sponsored programs that provide funding and other support to schools and businesses, encouraging their collaboration in research and entrepreneurial endeavors in new and emerging technologies.

With an annual Gross State Product of more than $800 billion, New York's economy is bigger than that of many countries. The state has 485,954 private businesses, or about one-fourteenth of all the private enterprise in the nation. Of these, 20 percent are minority owned, and 26 percent are owned by women. For 2003, the unemployment rate was 6.2 percent, up substantially from 4.9 percent in 2001, but that reflected the horrific impact of the events of September 11th. The labor force (those able to work), nevertheless, had grown, from 9.13 million to 9.36 million, and the number of employed individuals was also up, from 8.69 million in 2001 to 8.79 million in 2002.

And it is an industrious workforce. New York professional and managerial employees are 39 percent more productive than their national counterparts, while manufacturing employees outpace the rest of the country by 16 percent. Employee training and educational resources are greater than those of most other states. Fully one-quarter of all New Yorkers have four or more years of

continued on page 20

Photo: © Carl Heilman II/www.carlheilman.com

A source of inspiration and awe, Niagara Falls brings more than 18 million visitors to the region every year to bear witness to its stunning grandeur. Part of the Buffalo-Niagara metropolitan area, the U.S. side of the falls enjoys a thriving economy powered by tourism as well as trade, transportation, utilities, education, and health care.

© Ron Trinca Photography

Theodore M. Pasinski
President
St. Joseph's Hospital Health Center

St. Joseph's Hospital Health Center is proud to have called central New York State home for 135 years. Our hospital was Syracuse's first hospital and our growth has paralleled that of the city. The institution has evolved into a medical complex that, in addition to the hospital, includes a school of nursing, a psychiatric emergency program, and a physician's office building.

In central New York, our health care staff enjoy big-city living complete with cultural, sports, and recreational activities, without the crowds and crime. Housing and living costs are among the lowest in the country. Suburban and city schools are excellent, and there are many opportunities for higher education. St. Joseph's is pleased to be a part of central New York's history and its future, providing a higher level of care to the community.

ST. JOSEPH'S Hospital Health Center
A HIGHER LEVEL OF CARE

John V. Murphy
Chairman, President, and CEO
OppenheimerFunds, Inc.

After our nearly 600 employees were displaced by the events of September 11th, I am proud that we at OppenheimerFunds, Inc., were able to return to our roots in New York City's financial district by establishing headquarters in the World Financial Center. It is where we began, managing a single mutual fund in 1960, growing into a thriving asset-management company overseeing assets in excess of $160 billion, and ranking as the industry's eighth largest manager of mutual funds.

We now have the unique opportunity to be part of a historic revitalization as New York City rebuilds and renews. With the involvement of community, business, and government leaders, we are laying the foundation for what can be a better, stronger, and more vital lower Manhattan.

OppenheimerFunds®
The Right Way to Invest

Photo: Center, © John Gillmoure/CORBIS

Leonard Bernstein called New York City "Wonderful Town" in his 1953 musical. Whether in the 1950s or this current colorized version, the Manhattan skyline still represents the promise—and achievement—of success. For the millions who find their way to the city in pursuit of a dream, New York delivers—and then some.

David A. Caputo
President
Pace University

Rich diversity, abundant cultural opportunities, and international status as the world's capital of business and finance make metropolitan New York a prime location for a university. The city and its surrounding suburbs provide a laboratory for Pace students eager to put cutting-edge theory into practice through internships. A launching pad for careers in business, health care, education, law, communications, and computer information systems, the metropolitan area is home to thousands of Pace alumni who now hold leadership positions in these fields.

In turn, the contributions of New York's universities enhance business and the overall quality of life. Providing academic research and civic leadership through the Center for Downtown New York, the Center for Urban Education, the Center for Global Finance, and the World Trade Institute, Pace scholarship influences both local issues and global concerns.

PACE UNIVERSITY

Sanford A. Beldon
President and CEO
Community Bank, N. A.

Community Bank System has been meeting the banking needs of upstate New York communities since 1866. The hallmark of our banking philosophy is to provide a broad range of financial services to our customers through locally based decision makers, resulting in personal, responsive, and high value service to our customers. This philosophy, combined with a commitment to the outstanding upstate communities we serve, has been the foundation of our growth and success. We rank either first or second in deposit share in more than 70 percent of the places we do business, and our asset base has grown during the past 10 years from $700 million in 1993 to nearly $4 billion today.

Photos: Center, left to right, © Daniel Coyle Photography, Inc.; © Colgate College; © Robert Holmes/CORBIS

continued from page 16

college. The state awards more degrees than any other in medical, materials, and computer sciences; is second in bestowing biological sciences, mathematics, and electrical engineering degrees; and third in awarding mechanical and civil engineering degrees. It is not surprising, therefore, that more than 400,000 engineers and scientists make New York home.

Top of the Line

New York State has one of the best educational systems in the country,

Left: The Laboratory Institute of Merchandising brings the fashion business to students in the fashion capital. Center: A top liberal arts school, Colgate University sits on a scenic campus in the central New York village of Hamilton. Right: Legend among music students, The Juilliard School at Lincoln Center in New York City faces a reflecting pool containing sculptor Henry Moore's *Reclining Figure.*

capped by an extraordinary collection of institutions of higher learning. The state maintains a rigorous system of Regent's exams (implemented by the Regents of the State Board of Education), which mandates that every student in the state must pass a high level of competency in numerous fields before he or she can march down the aisle to a high school diploma.

Students who accomplish this task can choose from some of the best schools in America, without leaving the state. New York boasts two Ivy League schools—Columbia and Cornell—as well as many other outstanding institutions, such as New York University, Vassar, Syracuse University, Rensselaer Polytechnic Institute, Colgate University, the University of Rochester, the U.S. Military Academy at West Point, The Juilliard School, and the Culinary Institute of America. The State University of New York (SUNY) system of 64 campuses—offering a combined total of 6,688 degree and certificate programs—is made up of three tiers that cater to a variety of educational needs, including community colleges, State University Colleges (four-year institutions), and University Centers (doctoral-granting institutions).

In addition to educational opportunities, New Yorkers have access to some of the best medical care in the world. The state is renowned for its medical and research centers. The presence of such institutions as Rockefeller University, Mount Sinai Medical Center, New York-Presbyterian Hospital, NYU Medical Center, NewYork Weill Cornell Medical Center, Memorial Sloan-Kettering Cancer Center, and many others ensures quality health care for the state's residents.

New York is also in the vanguard of making sure access to health care is available to all through such programs as Healthy NY, Family Health Plus, and the Elderly Pharmaceutical Insurance Coverage Program. In addition, as a result of the Patient Health Care Improvement Act of 2000, residents now have access to information on physicians, health insurance providers, hospitals, and others via a Web site set up by the New York State Center for Consumer Health Care Information.

continued on page 24

Elizabeth S. Marcuse
President
Laboratory Institute of Merchandising

Laboratory Institute of Merchandising (LIM), The College for the Business of Fashion, offers its students a competitive edge by bringing them into one of the world's top fashion capitals. Manhattan provides LIM students with access to premier fashion companies, opportunities in both fashion retailing and fashion manufacturing, and the perfect place to experience some of the world's leading retail enterprises.

Since 1939, LIM has educated and trained its students in a real-world environment. Today, over 500 students pursue associate or bachelor degrees in Fashion Merchandising, Marketing, and Visual Merchandising. LIM's educational approach combines classroom instruction by professors who are leaders in their specialties and coveted internships that take students out into the field.

More than 90 percent of LIM students are placed in full-time jobs within three months after graduation. Manhattan is the perfect training ground for the fashion industry's leaders of the future.

LIM
LABORATORY INSTITUTE OF MERCHANDISING

Warren W. Heck
Chairman and CEO
Greater New York Insurance Companies

Greater New York Mutual Insurance Company was formed in 1914 by the Greater New York Taxpayers Association, a trade organization founded by a group of property owners on Manhattan's Lower East Side to insure tenement apartment houses.

From those modest beginnings, we have grown and prospered. We were the fourth largest writer of commercial multiperil business in New York State in 2002; we have been rated A+ by the A. M. Best Company, Inc., for many years; and for numerous years have been the largest writer of co-op, condominium, and apartment house business in New York State. Also, for the fourth consecutive year, in 2003, the Ward Group named us one of the 50 best property/casualty insurance companies out of 2,700 insurance companies in the United States.

Photos: Center, left to right, © Royalty-Free/CORBIS; © Yanick Wagner

Left: The face of New York health care, a resident at one of the state's renowned hospitals awaits the outbound subway, still smiling after a long day. Right: Known for fostering collaboration and interdisciplinary research, Rockefeller University is credited with groundbreaking advances in medicine, from discovering DNA's role as the building block of heredity to developing the "cocktail" drug therapy for AIDS patients.

Peter V. McGinn, Ph.D.
President and CEO
United Health Services

United Health Services traces its roots to the establishment of hospital care in Greater Binghamton in the 1880s. Today, we are the largest provider of health care services in the Greater Binghamton region.

Our members and affiliates include four hospitals, a geriatric campus, two home care agencies, a multispecialty medical group, and a foundation. Through major medical services, payroll, capital investments, and community outreach, our economic impact on Greater Binghamton is approaching $1 billion per year.

Locally owned and not-for-profit, United Health Services is proud to be part of a community known for its strategic location, rich ethnic and technological heritage, and high quality of community life.

United Health Services

Stuart Rabinowitz
President
Hofstra University

Long Island offers a rich array of resources and unparalleled access to coastline, commerce, and culture. Since our founding in 1935, Hofstra University has made a difference in the lives of our students by offering them a superb education, and in the Long Island community by working closely with local business leaders, community organizations, and K–12 students and educators. Our alumni, now nearly 100,000 strong, are leaders in business, education, communications, and other professions throughout New York and the nation.

Much more than a suburb of New York City, Long Island is home to growing biotechnology and other high-tech industries, a vibrant economy, and diverse businesses. It is also home to wild ocean beaches and estuaries, farmland, and vineyards. On Long Island there are hundreds of museums, historical sites, and cultural events—some of which we are proud to offer at Hofstra University.

HOFSTRA UNIVERSITY

continued from page 21

In addition to an exciting business environment, excellent education, and abundant health care, there are many other reasons to make New York home. New Yorkers are a diverse group, which contributes to the state's character: 16 percent are African American, 15 percent are of Latino descent, and 5.5 percent are Asian, according to the 2000 census. That year, the state had close to 7.7 million housing units, with a homeownership rate of 51 percent, and a median value of owner-occupied dwellings of $148,700, compared to $119,600 for the nation. Median household income was also strong: $43,393 compared to $41,994 for the nation.

New York boasts not one, not two, but three of the safest cities in the nation. Morgan Quitno Press, a publishing and research company, named Amherst the safest city in the nation in 2003 (the fourth year in a row Amherst has made the list). Colonie was ranked seventh, and Clarkstown eighth.

Residents enjoy one of the most extensive transportation systems in the world. Besides New York City's famous subway, there are commuter trains, ferries, ships, more than 112,000 miles of interstate highways, and 500 airports. New Yorkers also enjoy a superior telecommunications system and low rates on water, electricity, and gas.

Besides such practical advantages, New York has one of the world's richest arts, historical, and cultural scenes.

Inspired Living

New York City is the leading place in the world to experience great art; no other city can match its showplaces, although other spots in New York State give it a good run for its money.

The list of cultural attractions in the Big Apple includes many of the most famous museums on the globe. The city has not only the Metropolitan Museum of Art and the Museum of Modern Art but the Guggenheim, the Frick, the Whitney Museum of American Art, and the Pierpont Morgan Library. Science enthusiasts flock to the American Museum of Natural History and the Hayden Planetarium. Visitors may also tour the American Museum of Immigration at the Statue of Liberty, the Bronx Museum of the Arts, the Children's Museum of Manhattan, Grant's Tomb, the Museum of Colored Glass and Light, and the Jacques Marchais Museum of Tibetan Art, or take a stroll through a medieval monastery in the Cloisters.

Virtually every evening, there are musical, dance, and theatrical performances in the Big Apple. Tickets to a Broadway show are a must for any visitor to New York. Others may choose to attend a performance by the Metropolitan Opera, the New York Philharmonic, or the New York City Ballet at Lincoln Center or take in a concert at Carnegie Hall, while some flock to watch jazz legends at the Blue Note nightclub. In summer, the play's the thing as New Yorkers thrill to

continued on page 29

Photos: Center, left to right, © Patrick Batchelder; © Buffalo News/J. P. McCoy/CORBIS SYGMA; © www.scottbarrow.com

Left: Equestrians romp through Central Park, seemingly light years from frenetic Manhattan. Center: Being named the nation's safest city doesn't mean Amherst is snow free, as this resident knows. Right: The Lewis Miller Cottage was the home of the industrialist who cofounded the Chautauqua Institute, an educational center in southwestern New York.

Photo © Robert Bachrach

William F. Baker, Ph.D.
President and CEO
Thirteen/WNET New York

Location really is everything. As the flagship public television station serving the eclectic New York metropolitan area, we recognize the benefits of doing business here.

New York City is the media capital of the world, rich in resources and a constant inspiration for our work. As a producer, Thirteen/WNET New York enjoys access to preeminent talents and venues in many fields—right here at home—and exports them to the nation and the world through the magic of television.

That is one reason why New York is not just where we live and work—it is part of our name, part of our institutional identity.

thirteen
WNET NEW YORK

Photo: © Timothy Raab–Northern Photo

Louis S. Snitkoff, M.D., F.A.C.P.
Medical Director
Joan R. Hayner, C.P.A., C.M.P.E.
Chief Executive Officer
Capital*Care* Medical Group

When Capital*Care* Medical Group was established in 1997, the primary objective was to enable our health care practitioners to deliver high quality, patient-focused primary health care. The diverse resources in New York's Capital District have helped us achieve this goal. Our health care community has been proactive in the development of innovative quality-of-care initiatives involving physician groups, health plans, hospitals, and employers. Our teaching hospitals have been the source of many of our well-trained physicians. In addition, numerous colleges and universities offer forums for intellectual discourse, and opportunities for cultural and recreational activities are plentiful.

Capital*Care* is pleased to have a positive impact upon the economy and the quality of life in upstate New York and is well positioned to respond to the region's health care needs in the years ahead.

Capital*Care* Medical Group

Photos: Center, left to right, © Rudi Von Briel/Index Stock Imagery; © Julie Lemberger/CORBIS; © Bo Zaunders/CORBIS

Left: The Blue Note jazz club in Greenwich Village presents a roster of superstars any club owner would covet. Center: Members of the Alvin Ailey American Dance Theater polish the movements that earn the company critical acclaim. Right: The famed Metropolitan Opera House, now at Lincoln Center, has been synonymous with culture since 1883.

John F. Hennessy III, P.E.
Chairman of the Board
Syska Hennessy Group, Inc.

For more than 75 years, Syska Hennessy Group has been proud to call New York City and State our home and corporate center. Established in 1928 in New York City—where our main headquarters is still located—our firm has been honored to be a partner in the progress and growth of this great state.

At the turn of the century, Syska Hennessy Group was among the first engineering firms to specialize in the mechanical and electrical systems that revolutionized 20th-century building construction. For the 21st century, we are focused, among other things, on technically sophisticated energy-efficient designs—future-forward buildings born of a city and state that have always been ahead of the times. This spirit of innovation and world-class leadership, with its attendant responsibilities, invigorates the Syska Hennessy Group as it does New York City and State.

SYSKA HENNESSY GROUP

Charles G. Berg

President and Chief Executive Officer
Oxford Health Plans, Inc.

Oxford Health Plans, Inc., is committed to offering employers a wide range of health care benefits and services so businesses can provide their employees with high quality health care coverage at a reasonable price.

With regional offices located in New York City, Long Island, and Westchester County, Oxford provides benefits to more than 1.5 million members in the tri-state region.

Oxford's regional focus enables it to develop long-term relationships with some of the most respected and distinguished physicians and medical institutions in the country. By working collaboratively with them, Oxford has created a comprehensive range of clinical, preventive, and practical resources to help its members manage their health. At the same time, Oxford works diligently to reduce administrative burdens and costs for its constituents.

Oxford Health Plans®

Left: Visitors fill the galleries at the Frank Lloyd Wright–designed Guggenheim Museum, attesting to the artistic soul of every New Yorker, permanent or temporary. Right: A Picasso catches an art lover's eye at New York's Museum of Modern Art, one of the world's top repositories of 20th-century works.

Photos: Center, left to right, © Walter Bibikow/Index Stock Imagery; © Rudi Von Briel/Index Stock Imagery

continued from page 24

Shakespeare in the Park in Central Park. Many of the top dance companies in America, such as the Alvin Ailey American Dance Theater and the American Ballet Theatre, also make New York City their home.

On the other side of the state, Buffalo is also an important arts center. In fact, Buffalo was rated eighth in the country as an arts destination in 2003 by *AmericanStyle* magazine. The Buffalo Philharmonic Orchestra has featured soloists from Arthur Rubenstein to Jascha Heifetz to Van Cliburn and been led by great artists such as Igor Stravinsky and Leonard Bernstein. The Albright-Knox Art Gallery's permanent collection includes works by Picasso, Miró, Matisse, Mondrian, Moore, and Giacometti. Just outside Buffalo, in Lewiston, is Artpark, offering musicals, plays, and other visual and performing arts in a beautiful outdoor setting, the only state park of its kind in the country.

The Great Outdoors

New York State's majestic countryside has long been a source of inspiration for those seeking to experience its natural beauty in the moment or to translate its magnificence on canvas. The first American landscape artists—whose work was known as the Hudson River School—tried to capture what it meant to stand amid the Catskill or Adirondack Mountains, home to some of the most majestic vistas the New World had to offer. Not just artists, but poets and novelists traveled from far and wide to see, and attempt to describe, the grandeur of lush forests and proud native peaks. Artists like Thomas Cole, Asher Durand, and Albert Bierstadt drew vast panoramic landscapes, filled with unimaginable detail, helping to create a truly American art form.

continued on page 32

Anthony L. Watson
Chairman and CEO
HIP® Health Plan of New York

In our current annual report, we say that the future belongs to those with the vision to anticipate change and the strength to innovate with confidence. Those words reflect the kind of company HIP® Health Plan of New York has pledged to remain.

HIP has a special relationship with New York. We were founded here 57 years ago to provide access to quality, affordable health care. And what better place to be involved in the health care of more than 1.2 million people than in the capital of the world, where everything is possible?

HIP®
HEALTH PLAN OF NEW YORK

Left: Renewal comes with the crunch of leaves underfoot in one of New York's scenic state parks. About 65 million people take to the hills (and beaches and landmarks) every year. Center: With 90 miles of snowmobile trails to choose from, a rider in Allegheny State Park could stay all week. Right: The fish may be feisty, but they're biting—making this New Yorker one happy camper.

Photos: Center, left to right, © Conrad Zobel/CORBIS; © Royalty-Free/CORBIS; © Tom Stewart/CORBIS

John C. LaRosa, M.D.

President

SUNY Downstate Medical Center

"Brooklyn's Only Academic Medical Center" is more than a slogan at SUNY Downstate Medical Center. It is the essence of who we are.

Part of the State University of New York 64-campus system, we have given to New York State and the world advances in medical care and scientific research, and to Brooklyn its only Nobel Prize. Graduates of SUNY Downstate—physicians, nurses, allied health professionals, and scientists—can be found in hospitals, academic medical centers, and research settings across Brooklyn, the state, and the nation.

SUNY Downstate's interests also extend to the wellness of Brooklyn's economy. With the New York City Economic Development Corporation and Brooklyn leadership, we have created a comprehensive plan for developing the biotechnology industry in Brooklyn—and launched the city's first new biotechnology incubator in over a decade.

SUNY DOWNSTATE Medical Center

Tom Early
Executive Director
Health Plus, PHSP Inc.

New York State—and New York City, where Health Plus is one of the premier providers of access to quality health care for the uninsured—possess a diversity that may be unrivaled worldwide.

Doing business in New York, with its complex network of industries, resources, and multiethnic populations, is one of the most challenging and rewarding opportunities a company can have today. But at Health Plus, we cannot imagine a better place in which to pursue our goal: To work hard to ensure that every child and adult who qualifies has access to free or affordable health care. Health Plus has nearly 250,000 members among whom almost a score of languages are spoken and who have distinct cultural issues and concerns. And our company, which consists of over 600 employees of virtually every ethnicity, race, and religion, is a microcosm of the communities we serve. It is also, we believe, a microcosm of the great state, and city, of New York.

continued from page 29

The grandeur that drew Cole and Durand is still available to every American. The Adirondacks have 46 high peaks, all worth a good day's trek, plus 2,300 lakes and ponds and 2,000 miles of hiking trails. New York has 3.6 million acres of state forests and preserves, while 80 Wildlife Management Areas provide another 124,000 acres of upland and 53,000 acres of wetland. Deer are abundant, and the fishing is terrific. Musky and steelhead abound in the Niagara River, up by the Falls, while striped bass or coho or brook trout can be found in the mountain regions. In 2003, locals and visitors set a new state record for trout fishing, and possibly even a world record for coho.

Throughout the year, there are innumerable outdoor experiences. Winter means skiing, skating, snowmobiling, and cross-country skiing at Lake Placid and other resorts in the Adirondack, Catskill, and Allegheny Mountains. Jones Beach on Long Island offers more than six miles of sandy beach for summer recreation and has the world's largest surf-bathing facility.

New York State also boasts a large number of professional sports teams. Up in the northwest corner there's a team called the Buffalo Bills, football players who seem always to be bridesmaids, never brides wearing Super Bowl rings, but still beloved by the locals.

If fans want a winner, however, they have come to the right place. New York City has the grand champion of all time, a team so good, so loved—so hated—all because no one else in the history of team sports has ever come even close to its record of championships. This is the famed Bronx Bombers, of course. The New York Yankees still hold sway in their eponymous stadium where they draw loyal fans year after year.

While the Yankees are probably the most famous, other teams and sports have their followers, too. New York City has Mets baseball, Rangers hockey, and Knicks basketball, while Buffalo has the Sabres hockey team. Minor and independent league teams also liven the scene, competitors such as the Brooklyn Cyclones (baseball), the Albany Conquest (arena football), the Buffalo Bandits (lacrosse), the Rochester Raptors (women's football), and the Syracuse Salty Dogs (soccer).

The Empire State has it all. That is why, for centuries, people from all walks of life, of all backgrounds and interests, have chosen New York as their home—and will continue to do so.

Photos: Center, top left, © Ron Larson/Stringer/Reuters/Corbis; bottom left, © Reuters/CORBIS; right, © Marc Asnin/CORBIS SABA; far right, © Greg Fiume/NewSport/Corbis

Far left, top: Chris Drury of the Buffalo Sabres goes stick to stick with the Montreal Candiens' Saku Koivu in the first game of the 2003 NHL season. Far left, bottom: New York Giants tight end Jeremy Shockey's touchdown catch qualifies the team for the 2003 NFL playoffs. Left: The Yankees just have that effect on people—especially these boys, who watch the game close up from foul territory at Yankee Stadium. Below: Allan Houston drives the ball for the NBA New York Knicks in 2002, during the team's 57th season.

A Dynamic Convergence Doing Business in New York City

Doing business in New York City has always been unique and profitable. In the last few years, it has been a story of heroism and comeback.

There is no question of how badly the September 11th attacks hurt the local economy. Job losses between August 31, 2001, and mid-2003 totaled 170,000 with 155,000 of that in the private sector, a total decline of 4.6 percent. This represented a significant reversal: between 1999 and 2001, notwithstanding stock market woes, per capita personal income in Manhattan had risen by 16.5 percent.

And now, once again, the city, out of the ashes, is predicting better times. In the third quarter of 2003, Gross City Product was up 0.3 percent, compared to a decline of 0.9 percent in the second quarter, and analysts predict a 3.7 percent rise by 2006. By then, the city will be producing $430 billion in goods and services, more than most countries. Average annual salaries for all New Yorkers are expected to rise by more than 4 percent in 2004, with a similar increase every year through 2007. Job projections are for a modest 0.6 percent increase in 2004, then growth of over 1 percent a year through to 2007. Among the job sectors that made the biggest gains between 1999 and 2002—and are expected to continue on an upward path—were computer systems design (an increase of 125 percent), home health care services (94 percent), and colleges and universities (41 percent).

Wall Street profits for the period January–September 2003 stood at $11.9 billion, a vast jump from the $5.85 billion generated for the same period in 2002. Private-sector jobs in the city were up by 4,000 in October 2003. Hotel occupancy rates jumped to 80.2 percent in September 2003, up from 74.8 percent the same month a year prior, while building permits in September 2003 came in at 8,511, compared to 7,351 in September 2002.

New York City also has some unique attributes that are hard to quantify but make it one of the best spots in the nation to conduct business. Sociologist William H. Whyte in his 1990 book *City: Rediscovering the Center* found that New York's high density actually enhances its ability to serve as a business center. The close proximity of companies and people fosters face-to-face meetings, enabling executives to more easily work out deals, overcome obstacles, or simply maintain the business contacts that led to sales. In addition, executives enjoy the benefits of serendipity—the fortuitous occurrences when, for example, one encounters associates by chance, striking up conversations that may simply foster networking or be the start of important transactions. New Yorkers call this schmoozing, and Whyte comments favorably on its benefits, contrasting New York to suburban business campuses where no interaction occurs that is not previously scheduled.

In the long run, not just executives but Americans of all stripes choose New York as the place to be. In 2003, a Harris Poll reported that New York City was respondents' first choice of any place in the nation to live. In all fairness, this was not exactly news, as the city had earned that distinction for five years in a row. New York remains the place to work and live as humanity surges into a new century.

Such praise is well deserved. Throughout its history, New York City has been knocked down but it has always pulled itself up, smiled in the face of adversity, and looked to the future. As New York rebuilds its economy, so, too, does it rebuild the physical city. In December 2003, the first steel beam was raised for the new 7 World Trade Center; the previous building with that address was the last to fall during the attacks of September 11th. The 52-story skyscraper is expected to open in 2006. Nearby will be the Freedom Tower, which at 1,776 feet will be the tallest building in the world. Rising atop the tower will be a 276-foot spire, whose gleaming light will echo the torch of the Statue of Liberty, a symbol of hope to the world.

Photo: © S. Harris/Stock Image/Panoramic Images

PARTTWO

A Legacy of Innovation and Prosperity

New York Industries

Command Central

Headquarters to the World

CHAPTER**TWO**

Since the days of the 13 colonies, in all probability,

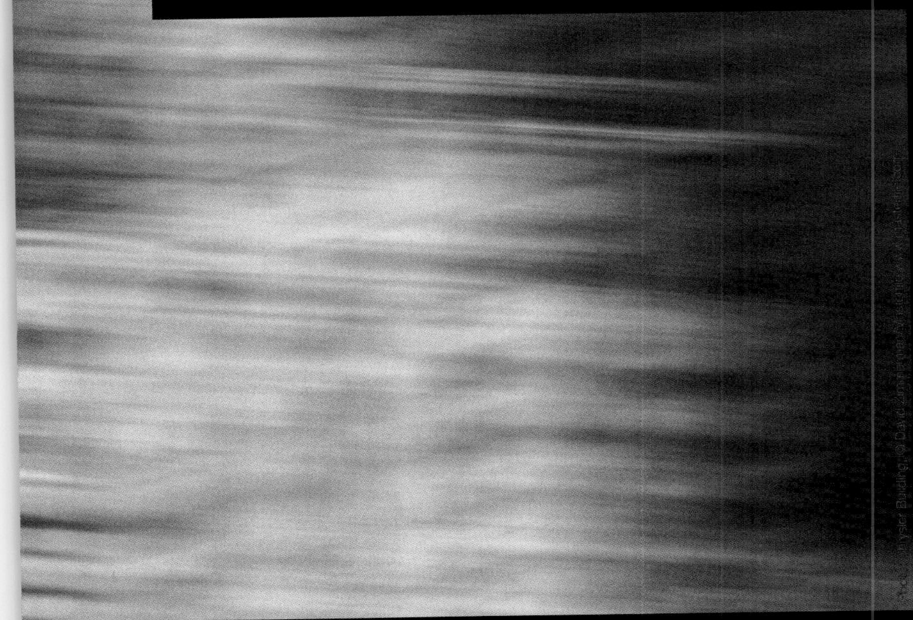

Chrysler Building, © David Zimmerman

New Yorkers have been accused of thinking that their home is the most important spot on the globe. The truth is, when it comes to worldwide business leadership, New York really has a right to crow.

Simply put, many of the world's greatest firms find New York State—and especially the Big Apple—the best place in the country to establish a command post for their global operations.

New York State has the second highest number of corporate headquarters of any state, with 51. California takes first place, but only by two, despite more than 15 million more residents. When it comes to cities, however, New York City blows away the competition, with 41 of these megaplayers making this special place their home. Houston is in second place, with only 19. New York City, in fact, had two of the top 10 companies on the *Fortune* magazine list of America's biggest and brightest. As one other indicator of just how strong New York is economically, the overall yearly revenues of all Fortune 500 corporations headquartered in the state in 2003 came out to an astonishing $1.1 trillion.

The companies operating from here are among the world's most powerful, with corporate trademarks familiar not only to Americans but to businesspeople and consumers in literally every inhabited region on Earth. The diversity of the industries they represent and, in many cases, their long association with the state attest to New York's importance on the world stage.

Pillars of Strength

New York is unquestionably the financial capital of the world. No fewer than 15 financial and insurance firms on the Fortune 500 list are headquartered in the state.

Among the oldest such firms is New York's first bank, The Bank of New York, which was established in 1784. Its charter was written by a young attorney named Alexander Hamilton, future secretary of the U.S. Treasury. In 1789, the bank issued the first loan to the newly created United States, for $200,000. In 2002, the bank made $34 million in loans.

Hamilton's nemesis, Aaron Burr, owned the Manhattan Company, founded in 1799, which would later become part of Chase National (later Chase Manhattan), at one time the nation's largest bank. In 2001, Chase bought J.P. Morgan, changed its name to J.P. Morgan Chase & Co., and became the second largest banking franchise in the nation. In 2003, the firm posted a net income of $6.7 billion.

Venerable New York–based financial powerhouses also include Citigroup; Morgan Stanley; Merrill Lynch; the Goldman Sachs Group; Lehman Brothers Holdings; and Bear, Stearns & Co.

Insurance companies also have a long tradition in New York. New York Life Insurance Company began operations in 1845. Today, it is the leading mutual life insurance firm in the country, employing more than

Photo: © James Leynse/CORBIS

The Bank of New York, the first to be established in the city, was founded in 1784, only months after the British departure. The bank's constitution was written by Alexander Hamilton, a New York attorney and secretary of the treasury in Washington's first cabinet. In the 1990s, the bank moved into its current home at One Wall Street.

Photos: This page, © James Leynse/CORBIS; opposite page, top, © Lee Snider/CORBIS; bottom, © James Leynse/CORBIS

From its headquarters in New York City, Pfizer discovers, develops, and markets pharmaceuticals for both animals and humans, including consumer products familiar to people worldwide. Some of the company's brands are Celebrex, for arthritis pain relief; the cholesterol-lowering medication Lipitor; and such staples as Visine and Rolaids.

12,000 people in the United States and throughout Asia and Latin America and posting more than $1 billion in net income in 2002.

American International Group (AIG), number 10 on the Fortune 500 list, had revenues of almost $68 billion in 2002. Its first U.S. office opened in New York City in 1926, and today the company is one of the world's leading insurers, serving 130 countries with commercial, institutional, and life insurance through its subsidiary firms. Its stock is listed on the New York, London, Paris, Switzerland, and Tokyo exchanges, and it is doing well: third quarter net income in 2003 was up by almost 27 percent over that of the previous year.

New York is also home to Fortune 500 listees Marsh & McLennan Companies, MetLife, and The Guardian Life Insurance Company of America.

Healing Powers

New York has long been a center for research, particularly in pharmaceuticals. Many of the medications that heal and cure people around the world are produced by New York–based companies, whose success has gained them a spot on the Fortune 500.

Pfizer, established in Brooklyn in 1849, helps in the effort to keep bodies strong and disease free by developing and selling some of the most important medicines available today. The company's 2003 revenues were more than $45 billion, and it spent over $7 billion of that on research. With its purchase of Pharmacia in 2003, Pfizer became the largest research-based pharmaceutical firm in the world. Its product line includes prescription drugs Lipitor, Viagra, and Zoloft, and over-the-counter remedies Listerine, Sudafed, Desitin, and Benadryl.

Excedrin, Enfamil, Pravachol, and Taxol are just a few of the drugs manufactured by the Bristol-Myers Squibb Company, another giant. The Bristol-Myers side of the company was founded in Clinton, New York, in 1887, while Squibb started out in Brooklyn in 1856. They merged in 1989, and today the company, headquartered on Park Avenue, has 44,000 employees worldwide and had a net income in 2002 of $2.1 billion.

Industrial Strength

Some of the oldest and best known manufacturing companies in the world have made New York their home since their founding.

One of the oldest manufacturers in the state, Colgate-Palmolive Company has been based in New York City since 1806, when it began as a soap and candle maker. Another venerable New York establishment, Corning Incorporated has had its head office in the town of Corning since the company's founding in 1851. Rochester has been the headquarters of Eastman Kodak Company since George Eastman opened his first manufacturing shop there in 1880, making dry plates for photography. Ninth on the Fortune 500 list, International Business Machines Corporation (IBM) traces its roots to late-19th-century New York and was officially incorporated in 1911. Today, the company oversees its worldwide operations from Armonk.

Headquartered on Long Island in Melville, Arrow Electronics began as Arrow Radio in New York City in 1935 selling secondhand radio equipment. Today, the firm sells and distributes electronics and computer equipment. Arrow

Left: Kodak's headquarters in Rochester is the company's largest manufacturing facility in the United States, as well as home to R&D and corporate services. Below left: The IBM logo greeting visitors to its Armonk home was designed in 1956 by Paul Rand, responsible also for the iconic UPS, ABC, and Westinghouse brands.

Right: Many New York–based companies, including L-3 Communications of Manhattan, provide satellite technology to the public and to private and government entities. Below: From its headquarters on Ninth Avenue in New York, Barnes & Noble oversees more than 800 stores in 49 states, such as this one near Lincoln Center.

had 2003 sales of almost $7.6 billion, making it number 238 on the Fortune rankings. Arrow's product line goes to original equipment manufacturers and other commercial customers through a network of over 200 sales facilities and distribution centers in 40 countries.

Relative newcomers find success in New York, too. Dover Corporation, for example, headquartered in the Big Apple since 1964, manufactures equipment for a variety of industries, from petroleum to automobile to food service and electronics. ITT Industries, of White Plains, an offshoot of International Telephone and Telegraph, was created in 1995 and produces electronics used in defense, fluid technology products, electronic components, and motion and flow components.

L-3 Communications, headquartered in the Big Apple, helps guard this nation by producing intelligence, surveillance, and reconnaissance systems, as well as secure telecommunications networks for military, civilian, and space projects. Founded in 1997, the company provides the communications systems for some of the most advanced ships afloat, including the Aegis missile cruisers, Arleigh Burke–class destroyers, and Trident nuclear submarines. For the Tridents, L-3 built the first computer-controlled communications center ever installed in a submarine. L-3 also created the communications system used on the Global Hawk Unmanned Aerial Vehicle. The firm's design of airborne dipping sonar, used by helicopters launched from U.S. warships to detect enemies beneath the sea, is the most advanced in the world. In space, three of the communications systems on the International Space Station are L-3 products.

Known by One and All

Consumers throughout the world use the products of the Colgate-Palmolive Company. Simply White toothpaste, Speed Stick deodorant, Irish Spring soap, and Science Diet pet nutrition products are just a few of the brands manufactured by the firm, which is number 196 on the Fortune 500 list. The company, whose roots in Manhattan go back nearly 200 years, saw a one-year increase in worldwide sales of 6.5 percent for 2003, with total sales of nearly $10 billion.

No less famous are the products of the PepsiCo family. Headquartered in Purchase, New York, since 1970 (where it moved from the Big Apple), the company is the world's second largest producer of soft drinks. Its product lines include Gatorade, Quaker Oats, Fritos, Lay's potato chips, and Tropicana juices. PepsiCo's

Photos: This page, © Jeff Christensen/Reuters/CORBIS; opposite page, top, © Brownie Harris/CORBIS; bottom, © Lynsey Addario/CORBIS

At the gleaming Park Avenue headquarters of The Colgate-Palmolive Company, executives guide the day-to-day operations of one of the world's largest manufacturers of toothpaste, soap, detergent, pet food, and other household and personal care products.

As dusk settles, the lights go on in Manhattan. Three of the state's largest providers of electricity—Consolidated Edison, KeySpan, and Energy East—are on the Fortune 500 list.

Photos: This page, © Joseph De Sciose/Agefotostock; opposite page, © James Leynse/CORBIS

2002 net income was $3.3 billion. The spin-off Pepsi Bottling Group, a Fortune 500 company in its own right, oversees 98 plants worldwide from its Somers, New York, headquarters, and employs some 65,000 people. Its 2003 net income was $4.1 billion.

Setting Up Shop

New York boasts some of the world's biggest retailers. Barnes & Noble (B&N), whose New York City roots date back to 1917, is the nation's number one bookseller. There are 630 B&N retailers throughout the United States, with 260 of its stores operating as Scribner's, B. Dalton, or Doubleday. The company also sells more video games, under various store names, than any other retailer.

Number one in athletic shoes is Foot Locker, introduced by F. W. Woolworth stores, of Utica. Foot Locker was founded in New York in 1974. Today the company has approximately 3,600 stores in North America, Europe, and Australia.

Avon is always calling. Established in New York City in 1886 as the California Perfume Company, Avon Products is the world's top direct seller of beauty products, boasting sales of $6.2 billion in 2002. This is accomplished through 3.9 million sales representatives working in 143 countries (the United Nations has 191 members, by way of comparison). Avon's commitment to women is more than just business-related; through fund-raising efforts such as the Avon Walk for Breast Cancer, the company has donated to women's health programs in 50 countries. Over the past 10 years, it has raised $250 million for breast cancer research alone.

Another cosmetics legend, Estée Lauder was founded in the Big Apple in 1946. The company sells its lines, including Clinique, M.A.C., Origins, and Bobbi Brown, through department stores, online, and in its own retail shops. It posted a net income for 2003 of nearly $320 million.

They've Got the Power

On the Fortune 500 list are three New York energy providers. At number 198 is Consolidated Edison, whose roots go back to 1823's New York Gas Light Company. Today, Consolidated Edison is a $658 million company with more than 14,000 employees. The former Brooklyn Gas Light Company, founded in 1825, is today's KeySpan Corporation. Still based in Brooklyn, KeySpan (Fortune's number 274) serves 2.5 million customers with natural gas and 1.1 million with electricity in three states. Energy East, headquartered in Albany, is 354th on the Fortune list and provides energy to parts of New York, Connecticut, Massachusetts, New Hampshire, and Maine. As a result of this widespread coverage, Energy East has tripled its customer base in the last three years; it now serves nearly three million people, with 1.8 million receiving electrical power and one million receiving natural gas.

Advantage: New York

Also on New York's roster of Fortune 500 designates are financial services giant (and the world's largest travel agency) American Express; the world's leading hotel franchisor, Cendant Corporation; advertising icons the Interpublic Group of Companies and the Omnicom Group; telecommunications giant Verizon Communications; and cable network and provider Cablevision Systems Corporation.

With its impressive list of advantages, New York State attracts the headquarters of the most powerful firms on the planet. The strength and talent these companies embody are among the reasons the Empire State remains such a vital force in business.

Verizon Communications, the country's largest local and wireless telecommunications provider, was formed by the 2000 merger of Bell Atlantic and GTE. The merger was one of the largest in U.S. business history. In 2003, Verizon had 37.5 million U.S. wireless customers and revenues of $67.8 billion.

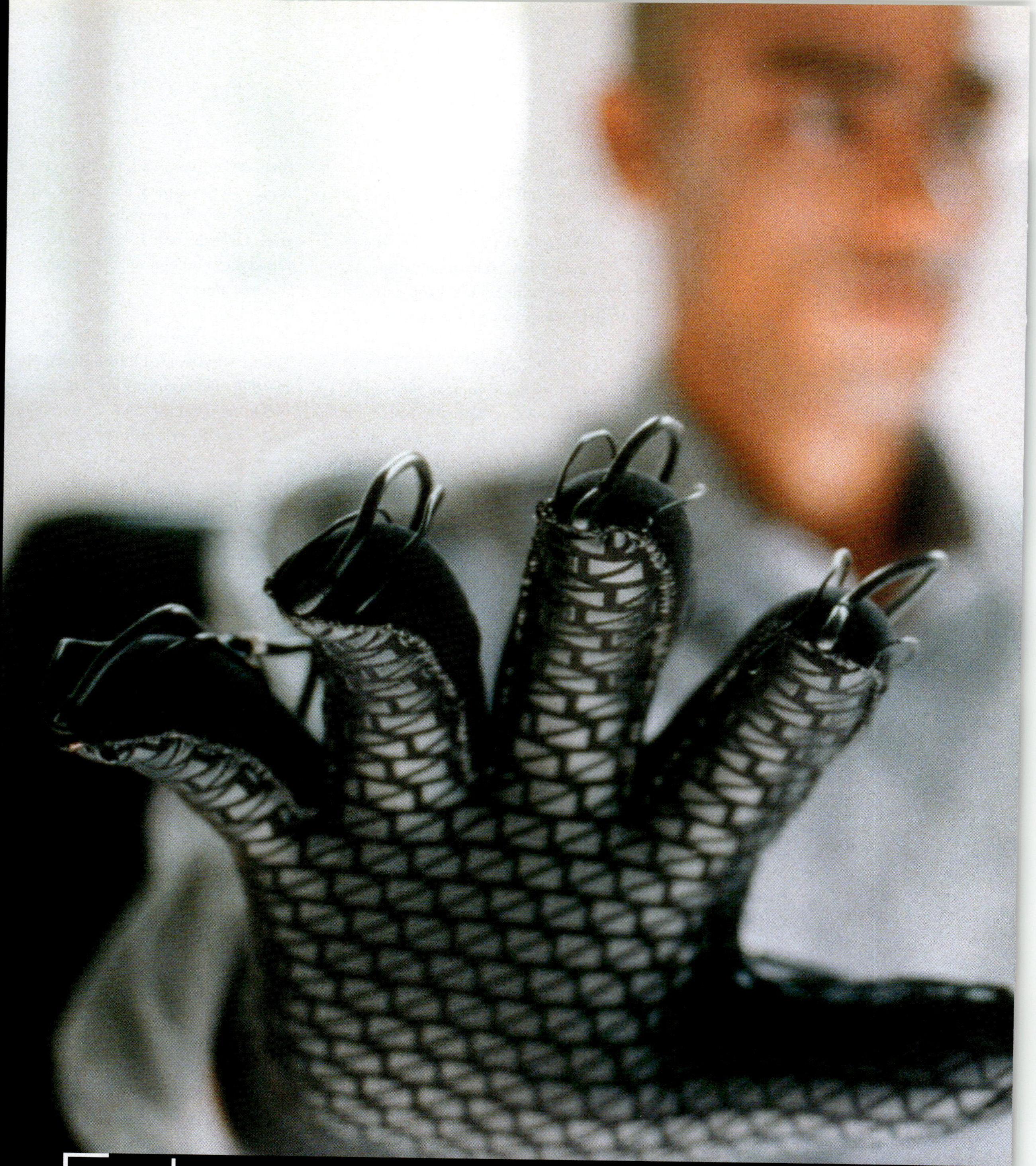

Inventing the Future

Emerging Technologies

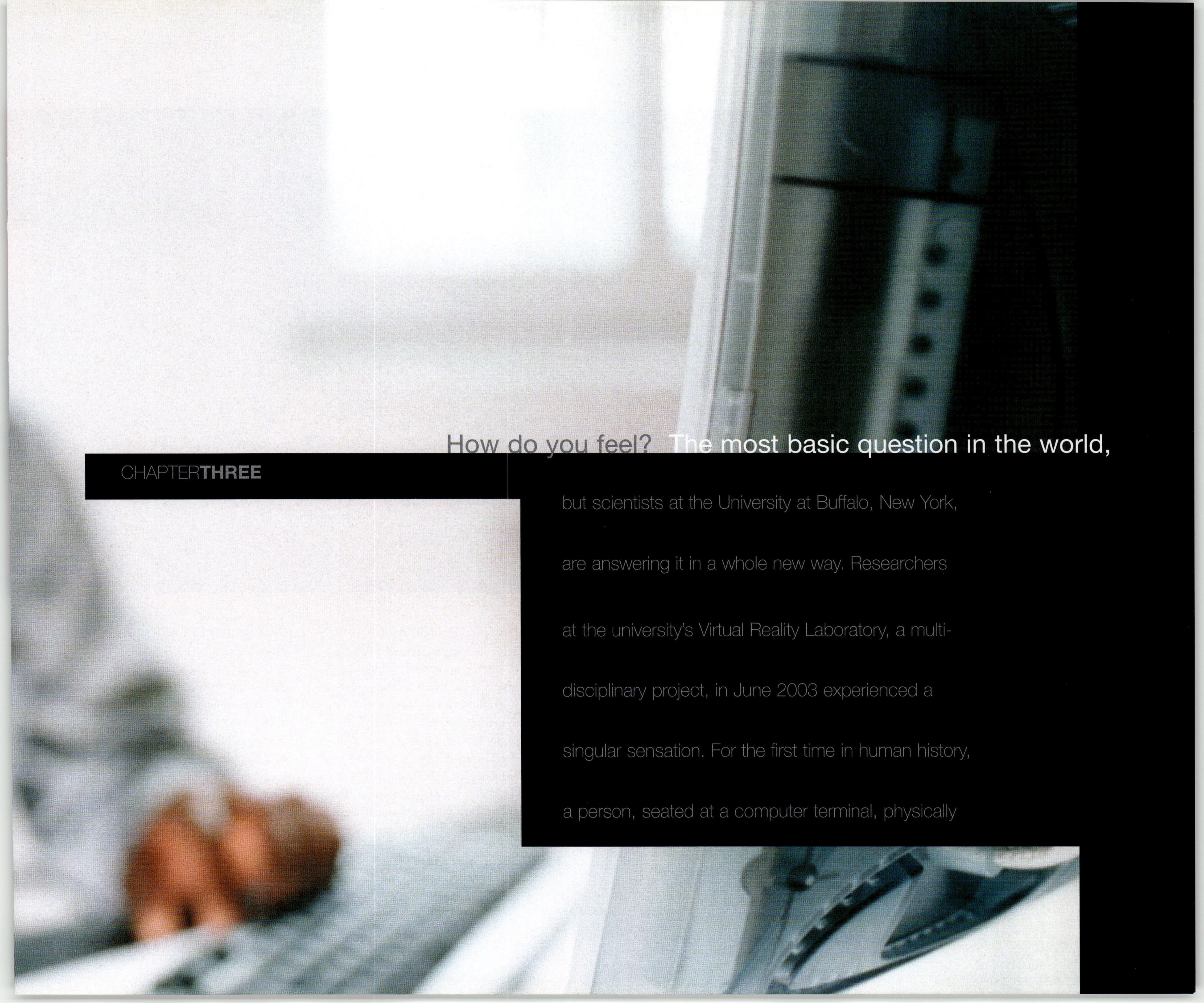

CHAPTER**THREE**

How do you feel? The most basic question in the world, but scientists at the University at Buffalo, New York, are answering it in a whole new way. Researchers at the university's Virtual Reality Laboratory, a multi-disciplinary project, in June 2003 experienced a singular sensation. For the first time in human history, a person, seated at a computer terminal, physically touched another person, sitting at another computer, by means of the Internet. This is the science of sympathetic haptics, and the University at Buffalo's is the only successful application of its kind in the world.

The implications here—for medicine, consumer technology, even the arts—are staggering. Using Buffalo's software, medical students of the future could feel the precise movements of a brain surgeon as she handles a tumor. A grandfather could purchase a pair of special gloves and be able to hold his grandson, even though he lives across the country. The subtle tactile movements of great artists could be passed along to other generations. Furthermore, since this knowledge is digital, it can be stored and used endlessly in the future.

High Tech in New York State

The Buffalo project is but one example of the many exciting discoveries taking place at New York institutions and companies that are making New York one of the nation's leaders in high tech. The American Electronics Association (AeA) ranks New York second among states in the total number of high-tech firms and third in high-tech employment. A report put out by the AeA and NASDAQ in 2000 placed New York first in photonics manufacturing, with 49,000 workers, and second in defense electronics, with 11,600 employees. It is also the nation's fifth largest high-technology exporter, having shipped $7.6 billion in electronics in 2000.

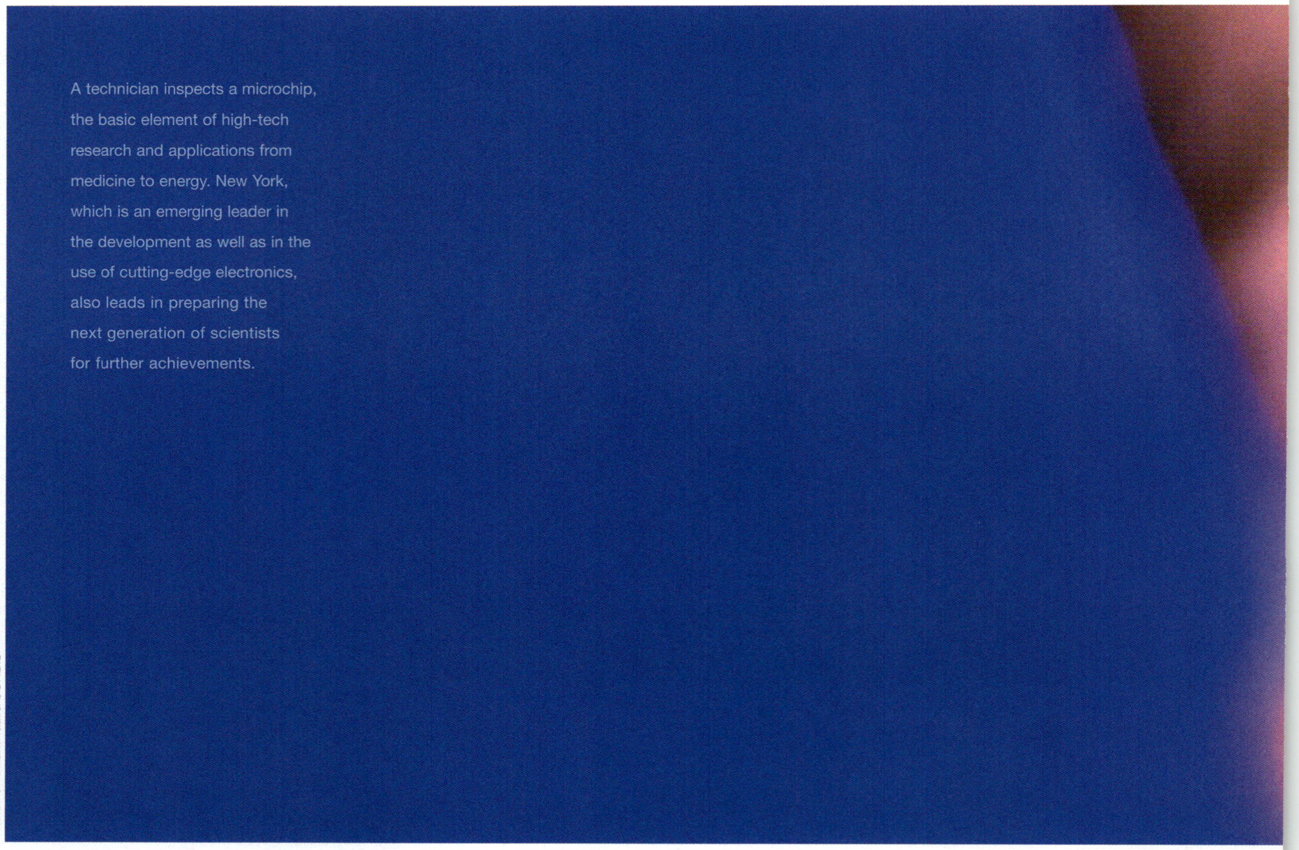

A technician inspects a microchip, the basic element of high-tech research and applications from medicine to energy. New York, which is an emerging leader in the development as well as in the use of cutting-edge electronics, also leads in preparing the next generation of scientists for further achievements.

Photo: © William Taufic/CORBIS

Much of New York's success in technology is the product of a superb educational infrastructure. In 2001, the state ranked second in the number of young scientists who won awards from the National Science Foundation (NSF). The year prior, 41 junior faculty members at New York schools received the NSF's Early Career Development Awards in science and engineering, almost double the previous year's figure. Not surprisingly, the state is second in the number of graduate students in these fields, and in 2003, four of the 10 winners of the Intel Science Talent Search—a nationwide competition—came from schools in the Empire State. There will be plenty of work for them, too: predictions of job growth for computer engineers in New York through 2008 are at an all-time high, at 7.3 percent. This makes it the fastest growing occupational category in the state.

Knowledge Is Power

All science starts with knowledge, and New York State has one of the nation's outstanding networks of research institutions in the high-tech field. Focusing on the strengths of New York's outstanding public and private universities, the state created a number of trendsetting programs to generate leadership in multiple industrial clusters. Among these programs, for example, are the eight Strategically Targeted Academic

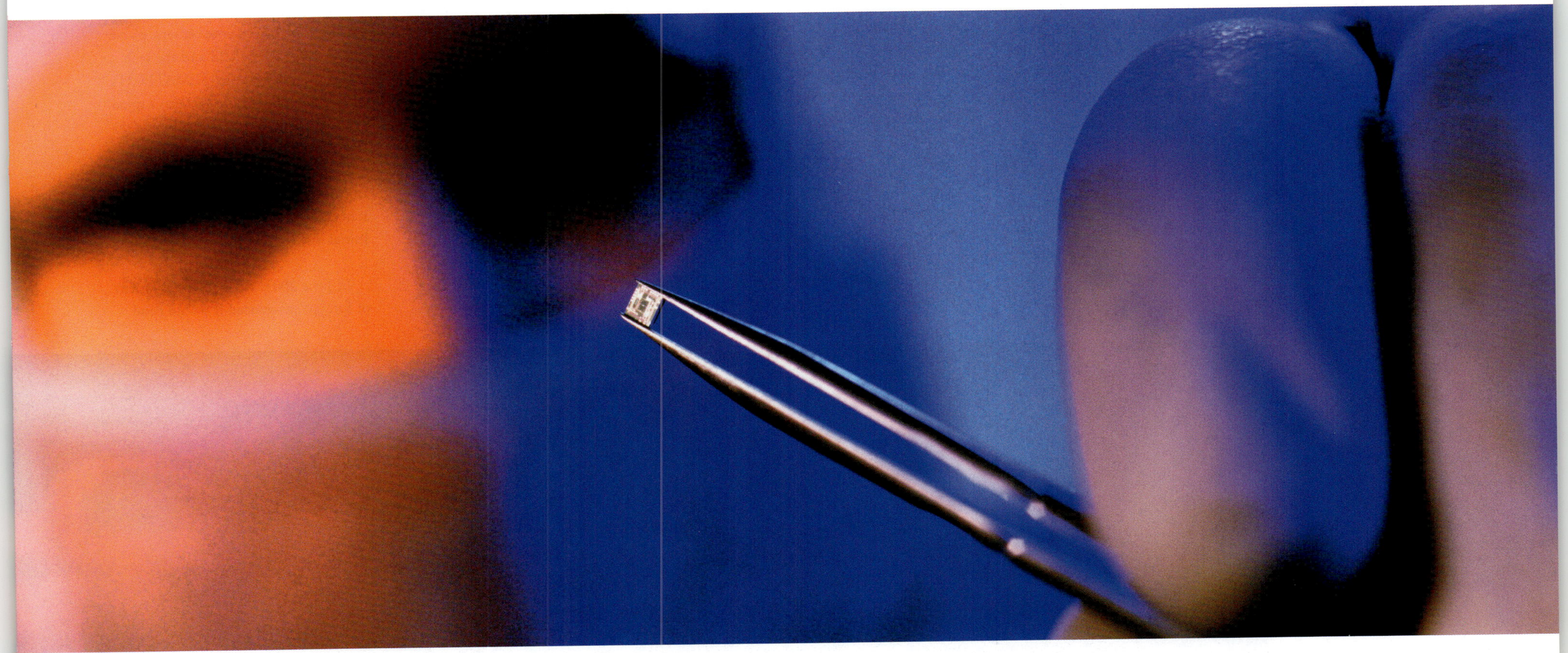

Research (STAR) Centers, which include the Integrated Imaging Center at Columbia University, the Genomic Technologies Center at Cornell University, and the Center for Environment Quality Systems at Syracuse University. There are also five Advanced Research Centers (ARCs), including the Center for Workforce Training at Alfred University, the Center for Pharmacogenomics at Albany Medical College, and the Center for Integrated Multilevel Analysis of Neuronal Plasticity at Mount Sinai School of Medicine.

The showpiece, however, is the Centers of Excellence program, a collaboration of academia, business, and government to forge a new $1 billion high-tech realm in New York.

A prime example is the Center of Excellence in Nanoelectronics at the University at Albany, New York. Nanotechnology is the seemingly incredible science of manipulating the atomic structure of materials. *Nano* means *one billionth*, and a nanometer is so small that only three to six atoms fit within one, depending on the composition of the individual atom. So far, for example, lithography produces printed circuits as small as one micron, enabling computer chip–makers to put millions of transistors on one small chip. A micron, however, still equals 1,000 nanometers. Nanotechnology, on the other hand, promises circuits far, far smaller—at the nano level—which means incredible speeds and incredible miniaturization. Moore's law claims that computers will double in speed every 18 months; nanotechnology promises a thousandfold increase just in the first efforts alone. Experts predict that nanotechnology will be a $1 trillion industry within a decade.

Leading this revolution is Albany NanoTech, a collaboration between the state, the University at Albany, and more than 100 companies around the world. It maintains one of the nation's premier state-of-the-art research labs—a one-stop center to assist companies with everything from technology incubation to prototype development to efficient production methods. With 70,000 square feet of existing space, including 10 clean rooms for chip manufacturing, and a new 25,000-square-foot facility under construction, Albany NanoTech has the tools to handle the job. It currently has net assets of more than $125 million, expected to rise to $500 million by 2005. The showpiece of the new, larger facility will be a 300-millimeter class 1 computer wafer pilot and prototyping facility, the only one of its kind in the world.

Recognition of Albany's importance as a center of high tech has come from a variety of sources. International SEMATECH, a 10-member computer-chip consortium, which includes on its roster such firms as IBM, Intel Corporation, Motorola, HP, and Texas Instruments, will fund research at the Albany site into advanced lithography, seeking to create faster and more powerful chips.

The SEMATECH development is particularly important because it puts Albany on a course to challenge America's high-tech core centers, places like Boston's Route 128 and the tech powerhouses of Austin. SEMATECH's first center, housed in the Texas capital city, opened in 1988 and employs 600 researchers. In Albany, it is investing $193 million for what is called International SEMATECH North, with the state putting up another $210 million. Initial hiring is for 250 researchers.

In June 2003, the U.S. Department of Energy announced it would fund

In a bit of scientific magic, a scrap of metal levitates above a superconductor. The natural phenomenon is the result of lowered electrical resistance due to adequate cooling, which allows a very powerful current to flow through a conductor. The resulting magnetic field created overhead is so strong that gravity is briefly overcome.

Photos: This page, © CORBIS; opposite page, top, courtesy, Charles River Laboratories; bottom, courtesy, International SEMATECH

seven proposals for research on high-temperature superconductivity electric wires. Albany received funding, but what was most important was the company it kept: other awardees included the Massachusetts Institute of Technology, Stanford University, and the University of Houston.

Albany is not the only place in New York where things are happening. Out on Long Island, the Center of Excellence in Wireless and Information Technology at New York's Stony Brook University, is also starting up, with $130 million in private investment plus $50 million from the state and another $50 million from the federal government. Long Island was a natural site for this project, given that it has more than 1,000 software companies already.

The state has also provided $37 million toward the $170 million Center of Excellence in Environmental Systems (CoE-ES), headed by Syracuse University. The center will study built and urban environments with the goal of improving air quality in homes, shopping centers, and commercial buildings, among other facilities. With the center's opening, Central New York lays claim to being the global leader in environmental technology.

Rensselaer Polytechnic Institute of Troy, meanwhile, has launched the Rensselaer Technology Park. This effort is designed to foster a wide range of technologies rather than focus on just one segment of the scientific or producer communities. To achieve this, the institute has set aside a vast site of more than 1,250 acres, encompassing facilities of more than one million square feet in 23 buildings. Among the more than 50 companies leasing space there are Charles River Laboratories, which creates DNA profiling technology; and Omnicare Clinical Research, an international contract research organization specializing in the areas of cardio-vascular, oncological, central nervous system, and infectious diseases.

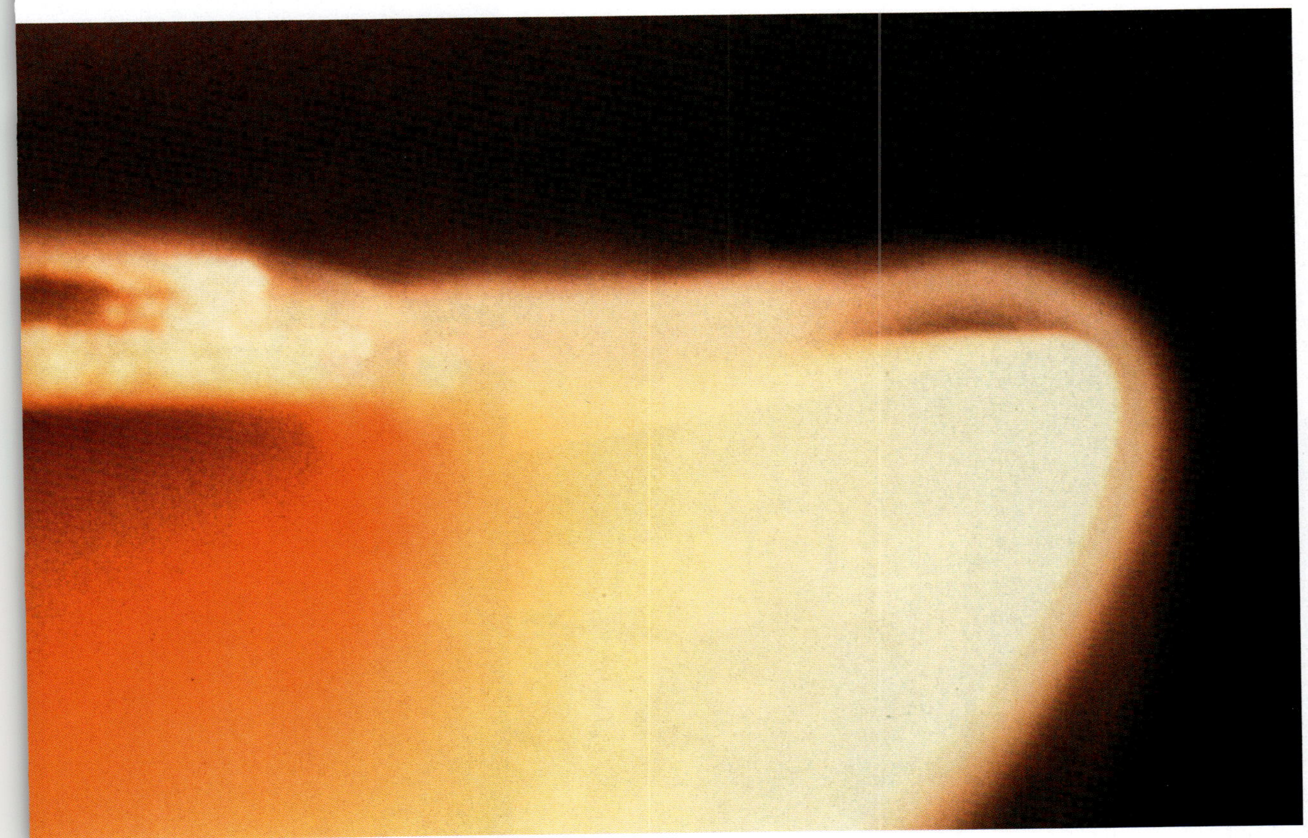

Private Initiatives

The high-tech companies of New York are creating the future. Leading the pack is the largest computer company in the world, IBM, which has been a New York firm since its incorporation here in 1911. Today, the company is headquartered in Armonk, New York, and maintains the Thomas J. Watson Research Center in two nearby facilities, one in Hawthorne and one in Yorktown Heights. IBM has eight such research centers in locations as diverse as San Jose, Austin, Beijing, Haifa, and Yamato, but none of these facilities has more than 400 employees (some fewer than 100), while the Watson Center, as headquarters of the IBM Research Division, boasts more than 1,000 researchers involved in everything from systems technology to physical and computer sciences to semiconductors. The firm also

Top: The nude mouse is born with neither hair nor a thymus, preventing it from mounting an immune response. Charles River Laboratories supplies these and other animals to biotech and pharmaceutical companies as research models. Bottom: An International SEMATECH worker inserts a quartz tube cleaner into a horizontal furnace, which dramatically reduces both the amount of chemicals and the time needed for maintenance.

constructed a new, $2.5 billion chip construction plant in Fishkill, benefiting from New York State assistance.

The figures on this international giant are staggering. IBM is the world's largest information technology company and the world's largest financier in this field. It ranks ninth on the Fortune 500 list of companies. In 2002, *BusinessWeek* ranked it the third most valuable brand name worldwide, after Coca-Cola and Microsoft.

One of the most exciting projects IBM is working on is taking place at its Yorktown Heights facility. The IBM Blue Gene is a supercomputer par excellence. When completed in 2005, it is expected to be one of the fastest, if not the fastest, supercomputer in the world, six times faster than current supercomputers. The name Blue Gene refers to the computer's intended use as a way to study how proteins work.

IBM is but one of a vast array of high-tech firms making their mark in the Empire State. Curtis Instruments began in 1960 with just 10 people in a rented storefront in Mount Kisco, producing electrochemical elapsed-time indicators. These devices soon led the industry because of their reliability, accuracy, and low power consumption and quickly became a fixture in every lunar landing module the United States sent to the moon. Today the firm operates worldwide, employs 1,000 people, and has a portfolio of more than 50 patents.

Sensis Corporation is in DeWitt, just outside Syracuse, and develops air defense systems for the U.S. military as well as air traffic–control systems for the civilian airline industry. Sensis created the radar surveillance system for Patuxent River Naval Air Station, home of the U.S. Navy's Air Warfare Center and a high-security site.

MapInfo of Troy is the world's premier generator of electronic mapping software, coming up with new ways to use location-based information. It has 600,000 customers and had 2002 net revenues of $92.6 million.

Well Connected

New York's telecommunications system is a study in entrepreneurship. Between

Bottom left: Ambuj Goyal and Paul Horn of IBM Research are involved with Big Blue's Blue Gene supercomputer, designed to help biologists model how a protein "folds." Bottom right: President and CEO Mark Cattini spearheads MapInfo's effort to provide its customers geographic software, information, and services.

Photos: This page, © Ron Watts/CORBIS; opposite page, left, courtesy, IBM; right, courtesy, MapInfo

Air traffic control, a sensitive issue in today's world, demands increased attention to safety, as well as capacity and efficiency, in the nation's airports. Sensis Corporation manufactures an array of low-cost surveillance sensors and real-time data communications products for accuracy in monitoring runways, tracking vehicles, and more.

TALK
2 abc
5 jkl
6
1
4 ghi

Instant Internet access via his laptop computer puts a smile on this employee's face. Opposite: Wireless technology has changed the way the world communicates. The telecommunications industry provides tens of thousands of jobs for New York's residents.

Photos: This page, © Royalty-Free/CORBIS; opposite page, © Ron Fehling/Masterfile

1997 and 2001, the number of Competitive Local Exchange Companies in New York grew from 13 to 46 (a 354 percent increase), and their market share climbed from 2 percent to 24 percent.

At the top of the telecommunications stack are companies like Verizon, with 2003 revenues of $68 billion, and 55 million access lines. Verizon provides both land-line and cellular service to six of the seven regions in the state and is part of the larger Verizon corporate structure. It has invested more than $10 billion to modernize its system and is now the largest private employer in the state, with 41,000 employees.

Verizon does not stand alone. Frontier Telephone of Rochester had 2002 revenues of $65 million and operates 106,000 lines in the Rochester metropolitan area, which covers seven counties. It is part of Citizens Communication, which provides service for 2.4 million customers in 24 states.

New York's expertise in telecommunications is just one example of how the state is at the vanguard in the development of new technologies. New York State will continue to foster an environment that promotes and encourages world-changing innovations.

Making It in New York

Manufacturing and Distribution

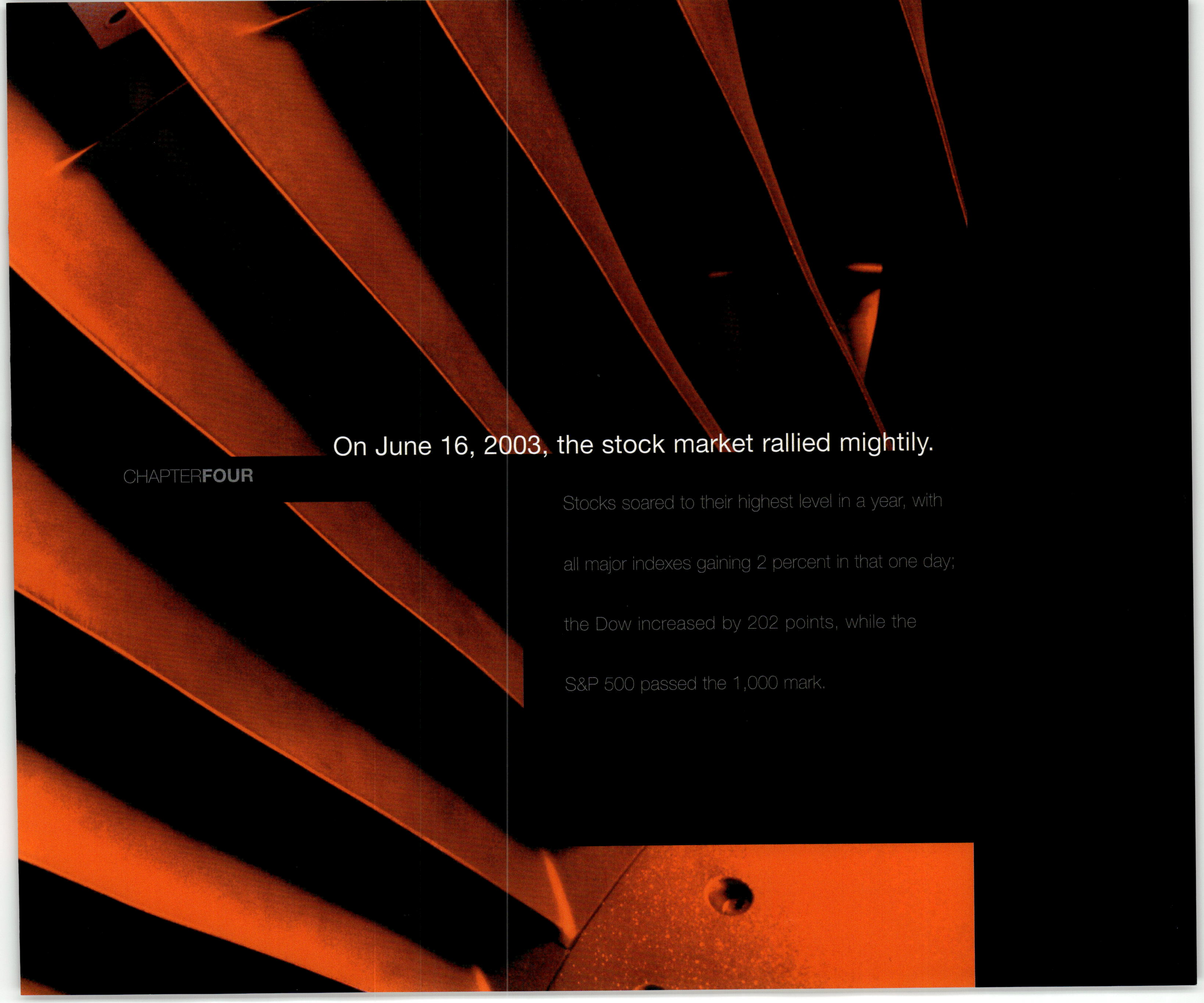

CHAPTER**FOUR**

On June 16, 2003, the stock market rallied mightily.

Stocks soared to their highest level in a year, with all major indexes gaining 2 percent in that one day; the Dow increased by 202 points, while the S&P 500 passed the 1,000 mark.

What kind of news could have sparked such a remarkable surge? The Federal Reserve Bank of New York had just released the Empire State Manufacturing Survey, a study in which manufacturers report on their activity and their predictions regarding the marketplace. As a general rule, figures above zero mean that more companies feel business conditions are improving than are reporting a decline. In this report, confidence skyrocketed, going from a figure of 10.6 that May to a June level of 26.8. It was the highest increase in the history of the Fed's survey. New York's manufacturing sector still has the power to move markets, quite obviously, in a big way.

The rally was also supported by other impressive numbers. Manufacturing had produced a $77.7 billion contribution to the Gross State Product in 2001. In September 2003, this sector employed 615,000 individuals, with 267,000 making nondurable goods and 348,000 making durable products.

Photos: This page, © NOGUES ALAIN/CORBIS SYGMA; opposite page, top, © Bill Varie/CORBIS; bottom, © Royalty-Free/CORBIS

The nation's security is in top shape with a fighting force that includes the Northrop Grumman–built surveillance vehicle, the Drone Global Hawk.

Systems That Safeguard

The manufacture of aerospace and defense products contributes not only to New York's economy but to the nation's security. Some of the largest such manufacturers make their home, or have a major presence, in the Empire State.

For decades, the U.S. Navy's carrier fleet won great naval battles with planes made by Grumman Aircraft in Bethpage, Long Island. These aircraft—so rock solid that aviators spoke with reverence of the "Grumman Iron Works"—included the F6F Hellcat, which downed 19 enemy aircraft for every one lost, a World War II record for American fighters.

The company merged with Northrop in 1994, but Northrop Grumman remains a critical presence on Long Island, with operations in the fields of electronics, information technology, and integrated systems. Among the projects these divisions take on are producing the Global Hawk Unmanned Aerial Vehicle (UAV); and building a new generation of E-2 Hawkeye surveillance aircraft for the navy, a $1.9 billion contract awarded directly to the Bethpage plant.

Northrop Grumman is not the only company doing exciting things on Long Island. Schweizer Aircraft in Horseheads is the oldest and largest privately owned aircraft company in the United States, building planes since 1930. It specializes in light utility helicopters that are rugged and inexpensive to operate, but it also builds special surveillance aircraft like the SA 2-37B. In September 2003, Schweizer received a contract to develop the Fire Scout RQ-8 Vertical Takeoff and Landing Tactical Unmanned Aerial Vehicle, which will provide sailors and marines with aerial surveillance and targeting data, for the first time in a heliborne mode, rather than using jet engines and a conventional runway.

Left: Lockheed Martin Systems Integration–Owego makes subsystems for the F-16 fighter. Below: Innovating with glass has been the hallmark of Corning since its founding in 1851. One such innovation, the photochromic lens, which automatically turns dark when exposed to light, was created in 1999.

In the state's Southern Tier is Lockheed Martin Systems Integration–Owego. Here, the aerospace giant manufactures subsystems for the F-16 and F/A-22 airplanes. This division oversees more than 60 programs, covering fields from defense to automotive and health care data technology.

BAE Systems is Europe's premier defense firm, and its North American division has facilities in 30 states. BAE's New York facilities include its Platform Solutions sector, headquartered in Johnson City. This division manufactures engine controls, inertial systems, and numerous other products that go into both military and commercial vehicles. BAE products are in the F-14 Tomcat and the H-60 Black Hawk, to name but two. BAE is expanding the facilities on its Greenlawn campus in Huntington, one of its Information and Electronic Systems Integration locations, a $19 million project that will add 148 new jobs by 2005. BAE also has facilities in Mount Vernon, Rome, Yonkers, and Syosset.

Molding the Future

Chemistry deals with the science of not just the physical properties of substance but their transformation. The chemical industry in New York State lives up to that definition, for it is helping the state's economy boom.

A pioneer in glass technology, Corning transformed itself from a kitchen glassware manufacturer to the world leader in fiber-optic cable, which it invented in the 1970s. The company created the first photochromic eyeglass lenses, in the 1960s, and, in 1999, introduced SunSensors, the first plastic photochromic lens. (Photochromic lenses change from transparency to a color when exposed to light and return to

transparency when the light source is dimmed or removed.) Corning also makes liquid crystal display components, semiconductor materials, cellular ceramics, and products for genomic laboratories. The company employs 6,000 people in New York State.

in Niagara Falls, where 300 workers make lithium and sodium products, and Rochester, where 18 individuals produce inks for ink-jet printers.

National Pipe & Plastics, a company that makes PVC pipe, meanwhile, is investing almost $13 million to establish its headquarters in Vestal. This project includes not only purchasing and rehabilitating a new facility but buying new equipment. The project created 45 new jobs, bringing the company's total employees in New York State to 225.

Top: DuPont Corian is one of the most popular materials for kitchen countertops and sinks, but 30 years of development have multiplied its applications to lighting, shelves, furniture, walls, windows, and many other products for both home and commercial use. Above: Plastic parts are inspected prior to final assembly.

E. I. DuPont de Nemours and Company is the second biggest manufacturer of chemicals in the United States, behind The Dow Chemical Company, with 2003 sales of $27 billion. Its Buffalo plant employs 700 people and manufactures Tedlar, a weather-resistant polyvinyl fluoride film, and Corian, a surfacing material used for applications such as countertops in homes and offices. The company also has plants

At its plant in Selkirk, New York, General Electric Company manufactures Noryl, a brand name for Polyphenylene Oxide (PPO). PPO is extremely versatile and can be injection- or blow-molded, or extruded into almost any shape. It is particularly useful for automotive parts (both exterior and interior), business and medical machines, plus telecommunications equipment. The Selkirk location is a GE Plastics Customer Innovation Center, one of six worldwide. Here, OEM marketers and designers meet with GE specialists who help them create custom-designed plastics.

GE has a long history on the local scene. Thomas Edison moved his Edison Machine Works, a GE predecessor, to Schenectady in 1887. Today, it employs 4,000 people at its Schenectady plant, where the company turns out power turbines.

The Wheels of Progress

Machines keep America's businesses operating, and New York State is part of that story. General Electric is just one of the big players in this sector. The Dresser-Rand Company, headquartered in Olean, builds energy conversion equipment, making compressors, turbines, expanders, and control systems for oil, chemical, gas, and general industrial operations. It has three manufacturing locations in New York—in Olean, Painted Post, and Wellsville—with a total of over two million square feet and employs more than 2,000 people. Pall Corporation on Long Island is a $1.6 billion firm, producing filtration, separation, and purification equipment. Its office on Long Island conducts research and development, while engineering and manufacturing take place at a center in Cortland. Pfaudler of Rochester is a major manufacturer of glass-lined equipment, while Xerox employs 8,900 people in the Rochester area, making fusers, photoreceptors, and systems and parts for its DocuColor iGen3 digital printer.

Pride in Production

New York State manufactures a great variety of products. Eastman Kodak Company, based in Rochester and long the leader in photographic film, is revamping its company with an eye to the future. The Fortune 500 company is focusing on the digital products market, manufacturing digital cameras, ink-jet printers, digital dental imaging products, picture archiving and communications systems, and much more.

Oneida Ltd. is located in the Central New York town of the same name, and manufactures stainless-steel and silver-plated flatware, as well as dinnerware, cookware, china, linens, glassware, and even picture frames. In 2003, it had sales of $480 million and employed 3,800 people.

Fashion *Is* New York

The Empire State is the fashion capital of America. More than 10 percent—almost 159,000—of those employed in the fashion, apparel, and textile industries work in New York, 80 percent of whom work in New York City. Among the New York brand names that have made American fashion famous in every part of the globe is Liz Claiborne, which

Photos: This page, © M. Thomsen/Masterfile www.masterfile.com; opposite page, top, © DuPont; bottom, © Roger Ball/CORBIS

In 1888, the Eastman Kodak Company gave the world the first camera simple enough for an amateur to operate. "As convenient as a pencil," went the advertising slogan. Today, after a world of innovation and a whole new way of capturing images, Kodak digital cameras still make picture-taking a snap for consumers like this woman.

Photo: © Reuters/CORBIS

Wearing spring creations by designer Vivienne Tam, models strut the runway during 7th on 6th Fashion Week, in Manhattan's Bryant Park. Founded in 1993 to showcase American couture, the semi-annual event draws buyers and the press from around the world.

This page: Oneida Ltd., of Oneida, is the world's largest manufacturer of silver-plated and stainless-steel flatware. The company, founded in 1880 as Oneida Community, Limited, also produces glass, crystal, and metal serving items. Opposite page: A worker uses a scanner to take inventory at a distribution center. New York State is home to many such centers for some of the nation's largest retailers.

Photos: This page, © Owen Edelsten/Masterfile www.masterfile.com; opposite page, © Royalty-Free/CORBIS

had revenues in the first three quarters of 2003 of over $3.2 billion, up from $2.7 billion for the comparable period in 2002. In the 14 weeks ending April 5, 2003, Claiborne's sales went up by 20 percent and net income rose 26 percent. Polo Ralph Lauren, another famed New York label, had 2002–03 fiscal year revenues of $2.4 billion, while New York's Kenneth Cole had revenues of $339 million for the first nine months of 2003.

Many other firms make up the New York fashion scene. In New York City, Bobby Reiss created World Wide Apparel Resources from scratch, and now does $120 million in annual sales, employing 42 people. His specialty is private-label garments, sold in chains such as Wal-Mart and Target, as well as the No Excuses line. Jacques Moret has 200 employees and handles activewear, including such labels as Jacques Moret, Jockey Activewear, Jockey Sport, and Spalding Activewear. Mamiye Brothers, also in New York City, sells a wide variety of children's clothing under such trademarks as Guess?, Lizzie McGuire, Mary-Kate and Ashley, Bubblegum, and Looney Tunes.

A specialty of New York State's fashion industry is leather goods. Lehigh Safety Shoes employs 75 at its factory in Vestal, a famous shoemaking town, where it manufactures boots and work shoes under 13 brand names, including Dr. Martens, Durango, Skechers, and Lugz. The G-III Apparel Group, based in the Big Apple, manufactures and sells leather outerwear and sportswear under the G-III name and makes

garments for Kenneth Cole New York, Nine West, Jones New York, Sean John, Timberland, and other design labels.

Distribution Centers

New York State is the hub for many discount operations' distribution centers. In the Florida Business Park just outside Amsterdam in Montgomery County, for example, Target is building a distribution center that will have 1.45 million square feet of space and will open in June 2005, bringing jobs to 695 workers in this small town near the Pennsylvania border in Orange County. Wal-Mart is investing $48.5 million in a distribution center in Wallkill, which will open in the fall of 2004 and employ 1,000 people. This is one of four distribution points that serve the company's New York State operations, which include 54 Wal-Mart stores, 23 Supercenters, and 18 Sam's Clubs, and employ 31,190 people. More than 630 people work at its Johnstown distribution center in Fulton County. In 2003, Best Buy opened a $45 million, 650,000-square-foot center in Nichols, in Tioga County. It is projected to employ more than 400 people by 2006.

Whatever the product, New York's manufacturers make it with care, with quality, and with pride.

Getting the Word Out

Advertising, the Media, and Publishing

CHAPTER**FIVE**

America gets most of its marketing plans and its corporate images, its entertainment and news, and its reading material from New York State. February 2004 employment in the state's information sector was 274,000, or 7 percent of all such jobs in the country, compared to New York State's 6.5 percent of the national population.

The Empire State is home to some of the most influential advertising, marketing, broadcasting, and publishing companies in the world.

Photo: © James Leynse/CORBIS

Selling the Product

New York State's command of the advertising field is the strongest of any branch of the communication industry. In early 2004, the industry employed more than 58,000 people. The top two ad organizations in the world—the Omnicom Group and Interpublic—are headquartered in New York City, as are 11 out of 12 of the top U.S. ad agencies. According to *Crain's New York Business* magazine, the top 25 agencies in the city billed $41.2 billion in 2001 out of their New York City offices alone.

The largest in Omnicom's network of agencies, BBDO dates back to 1890. Today, BBDO Worldwide employs 16,570 people in 345 offices in 76 countries, with $1.1 billion in sales in 2002, up by 34 percent from the previous year; its overall billings were $16.2 billion, of which $2.3 billion was generated by the New York City offices. It is the number three advertising agency in billings globally, and in 43 different countries ranks in the top five. BBDO's client list includes such famous names as Visa, Pizza Hut, Campbell's Soup, DaimlerChrysler, FedEx, and Pepsi.

Advertising firms thrive outside the Big Apple as well. Eric Mower and Associates, headquartered in Syracuse, has offices in Buffalo, Albany, and Rochester; in Portsmouth, New Hampshire; and Atlanta, Georgia. The largest ad agency in upstate New York, Eric Mower had billings of $130 million in 2002, 200 employees, and was ranked 73rd largest of all U.S. agencies by *Adweek* magazine.

Positive Impressions

New York firms also help companies, not-for-profits—even countries—handle their public image. The Ruder Finn Group, based in Manhattan, specializes in the fields of health care, technology, corporate, consumer, arts and culture, and travel and tourism, and delivers services that range from crisis communications to reputation management to advertising. It has offices in five U.S. cities, plus Beijing, Hong Kong, London, Paris, and Jerusalem, among other locations. Among its clients are Target, Bank of America, Matsushita Electric Corporation of America, the Guggenheim Museum (New York), and Skidmore, Owings & Merrill. *Crain's New York Business* ranked it second in fee income in 2001 with $58.8 million generated.

Ogilvy Public Relations Worldwide, headquartered in the Big Apple and whose clients include Bayer and Merck, was ranked number 11 by *Crain's*. Its fee billings were $22 million in 2001. Even more notable, Ogilvy's "America Responds to AIDS" campaign was named by *PRWeek* news publication as one of the 30 greatest public relations campaigns of all time. Its "Heart Truth" campaign, warning women about heart disease, won *PRWeek*'s Public Sector Campaign of the Year for 2003.

From its Times Square headquarters, media giant Viacom is reaching people around the world. The company owns CBS Television Network, the most-watched network in the country, and MTV, the world's most widely distributed cable-television network. Its motion picture studio, Paramount Pictures, has produced more than 2,500 films.

Media Giants

Broadcasting is a vital part of the New York State economy, employing 24,000 people in September 2003. Employment alone gives only a partial indication, however, of what a major role the Empire State plays in creating the country's media offerings.

Times Square is home to the corporate headquarters of Viacom. This is the second largest media firm in the United States, according to *Advertising Age* magazine, with 2002 sales of $16.3 billion domestically and $24.6 billion worldwide. The former figure was up 5.1 percent from the year prior, the latter was up by 6 percent. Viacom owns not only the CBS Television Network but Paramount Pictures Corporation; MTV Networks, BET, Nickelodeon, Showtime Networks, and Comedy Central on cable; 39 local television stations and Infinity Broadcasting Corporation, with over 180 radio stations; plus publisher Simon & Schuster and the Blockbuster chain of video-rental stores. In 2002, it had 120,000 employees around the globe.

Rupert Murdoch's News Corporation has its U.S. headquarters in New York City. This influential media conglomerate owns the Fox Entertainment Group as well as 20th Century Fox Studios, HarperCollins Publishers, and much more. In 2002, *Advertising Age* ranked it the seventh largest media firm in the United States, with domestic sales of $6.6 billion. Worldwide in 2003, the News Corporation took in $20.1 billion (an increase of 23 percent from the previous year) and employed 37,000 people.

Mention William Randolph Hearst and many Americans think of Hearst Castle, his ranch in San Simeon, California. The headquarters of The Hearst Corporation, however, are on Eighth Avenue in New York City. This firm owns 12 daily newspapers that span the continent—papers like the *San Francisco Chronicle* and the *Houston Chronicle*, plus weekly papers and magazines. It has a major stake in the cable networks Lifetime, A&E, and ESPN, and even manages the King Features syndicate, which provides cartoons for

many of the nation's papers. *Advertising Age* ranked Hearst the 15th largest media company in the nation, with 2002 domestic revenues of $4.2 billion.

Cablevision of Bethpage broadcasts the NBA Knicks and NHL Rangers through its MSG (Madison Square Garden) Network, and services three million customers throughout the New York metropolitan area. The company, which employs 21,000, ranked 17th on *Advertising Age*'s list of largest media firms, with 2002 sales of $4 billion.

Westwood One, based in New York City, runs the largest radio network in the United States, with over 7,700 stations. Its programming ranges from news to sports to talk to weather and includes such media stars as Dan Rather and Don Imus. The firm saw its sales in 2002 climb by 6.8 percent from the previous year, to $551 million. It has 2,800 employees.

Sirius Satellite Radio is not a giant yet but it is on its way to becoming one. This Manhattan-based firm is pioneering in a new media format and has a nationwide network that beams 60 channels of commercial-free, CD-quality music directly to car radios, plus another 40 channels of news, sports, and talk. A start-up company, Sirius had 2002 sales of only $800,000, but by the third quarter of 2003 it was up to 150,000 subscribers (a jump of 42 percent from the previous quarter). In December 2003, The Hertz Corporation announced that it would offer the Sirius service in 29 vehicle models available at Hertz car rental operations in 53 major airports.

It's on the Air

The best indication of New York City's importance to broadcasting is geographical: the headquarters of the four top broadcasting networks are all within 20 blocks of each other, in a zone only a fraction of a square mile in size. Fox Entertainment Group had sales in 2003 of $11 billion, an increase of 13.1 percent. ABC's (American Broadcasting Company) sales in 2003 were also at $11 billion, up 12.4 percent. The CBS (Columbia Broadcasting System) Television Network reported 2003 sales of $7.8 billion and one-year growth of 3.6 percent. NBC (National Broadcasting Company) brought in $6.7 billion in 2003, approximately 4 percent less than the previous year.

New York City is also the most powerful local television market in the country. According to the Nielsen Media Research Local Universe Estimates, during the 2003–04 season, the Big Apple was number one among 210 Designated Market Areas (DMA), with 7.4 million TV households, 6.8 percent of the U.S. total. The leading station in the city is WNBC followed by WABC, WNYW/Fox, and WCBS.

Buffalo is an up-and-coming market. In 2001, Nielsen ranked it as number 47, but by the 2003–04 listings, it was up to 44th, with 648,000 households and a 0.6 percent share of the national total. Albany was the 55th biggest market at 543,000 or 0.5 percent, and Rochester placed 75th, with 395,000 households, or 0.4 percent of the national figure.

Top and above: Television reporters in the state cover the latest local, national, and international news. Right: Programs such as *NBC Nightly News*, *Saturday Night Live*, *Dateline*, *Late Night with Conan O'Brien*, and *NBC Sports* are filmed at NBC's New York City studios in Rockefeller Plaza.

Photos: This page, top, © Marc Asnin/CORBIS SABA; middle, © John Lund/CORBIS; bottom, © Jeff Christensen/Reuters Newmedia Inc/CORBIS; opposite page, © Mark Peterson/CORBIS

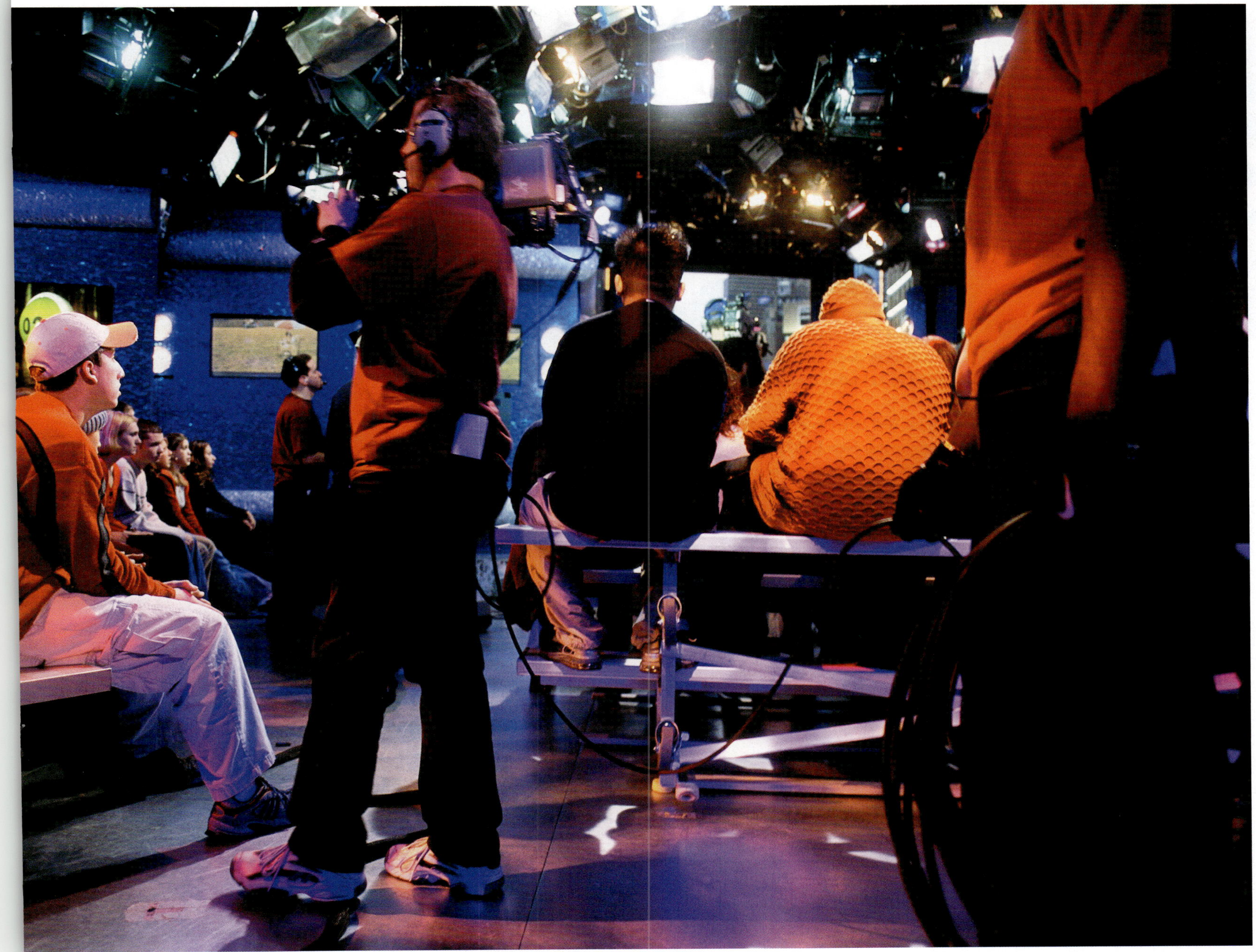

More than a million people tune in to MTV's wildly popular *Total Request Live (TRL)* each day. Host Carson Daly and the rest of the crew film the show before a live audience in MTV's New York City studio overlooking Times Square. *TRL* features a top 10 video countdown list along with appearances by bands and celebrities.

Getting the News

New York City produces the second and third highest circulation daily newspapers in the United States, *The Wall Street Journal* and *The New York Times*, with respective 2002 circulations of 1.8 million and 1.1 million. The *Times* also has the highest readership of any Sunday paper in the country: 1.7 million.

The Wall Street Journal is the most influential business publication in the world, with editions for Asia and Europe. The combined daily circulation of the paper's international editions is 175,000. In addition, the *Journal*'s Web site has the largest number of paid subscribers of any site on the entire World Wide Web, with 686,000 individuals paying to read this critical source online.

The New York Times Company publishes not only its flagship paper but the *International Herald Tribune* and *The Boston Globe* and owns eight network-affiliated television stations and over 40 Web sites. The *Times* has been honored with 89 Pulitzer Prizes, far exceeding that of any other newspaper, with some of the latest awards coming for its coverage of September 11th.

Supplying news to such papers as the *Times* and the *Journal*—as well as much of America's newspaper industry—is a New York–based institution known as the Associated Press. AP, with its 242 bureaus across the country and the world, provides content to 1,700 newspapers and 5,000 radio stations in the United States alone, and has 8,500 subscribers in 121 other countries.

With Wall Street so close, it is not surprising that New York City companies, many dating back to the 19th century, would also specialize in business and financial reporting. Ordering a *D&B Report* from Dun & Bradstreet has been one of the staples of American business for decades, and Moody's Investors Service, which began its newsletter more than a century ago, monitors more than $30 trillion worth of debt in 136,000 corporate and government securities, 67,000 public finance obligations, and 100 independent nations.

In 1882, three young reporters, Charles Dow, Edward Jones, and Charles Bergstresser, joined forces and began issuing handwritten newsletters with news and analysis about the stock market and financial and business conditions. They called these early reports

This page: The vast majority of newsstand magazines are published by New York companies. Firms such as Time Warner, Advance Publications, and Reader's Digest dominate the industry. Opposite page: *The Wall Street Journal*'s global network includes more than 575 reporters and editors stationed worldwide.

Founded in 1801, the *New York Post* in New York City is the country's oldest continuously published daily newspaper. It is also one of the fastest growing, with a circulation that exceeds 652,000. The *Post* is one of more than 175 newspapers owned by News Corporation, whose U.S. headquarters are in New York City.

Photos: This page, © Roger Tully; opposite page, left, © Mark Peterson/CORBIS; right, © Najlah Feanny/CORBIS SABA

"flimsies." Their first stock indicator, an index of railroad stocks, appeared in 1884, and today there is nothing flimsy about the Dow Jones Averages, the most watched market index on the globe.

On the Newsstand

Some of the most famous magazines are published in New York City. Headquartered here is Time Warner (formerly AOL Time Warner), the largest media company in the world and, according to *Advertising Age*, the top magazine publisher of 2002. Its *Time* division puts out 140 different periodicals, including the signature title and *People*, *Entertainment Weekly*, and *Sports Illustrated*. It also manages the publishing operations of American Express, producing such well-received forums as *Travel + Leisure* and *Food & Wine*.

Advance Publications comes in at number 11 on the *AdAge* list. The firm owns 25 newspapers around the country and publishes the *Parade* Sunday insert. Its Condé Nast division brings out *Allure*, *Glamour*, and *Vanity Fair*, and its Fairchild Publications is in charge of *Women's Wear Daily*.

Just outside New York City, in Pleasantville, is Reader's Digest, publishers of the world's highest circulation monthly magazine, selling 11 million copies an issue in the United States and 23 million worldwide, seventh on *AdAge*'s list. The *Digest* appears in 48 editions in 19 languages, reaching readers in 60 countries.

A Good Read

New York City is also the heart of American book publishing. The five largest trade publishers in the United States are headquartered in Manhattan. These companies had combined worldwide sales in 2002 of $5.7 billion and North American sales of $4.1 billion.

Random House is at the top of the list, and has over 100 imprints in 16 countries, including such lines as Bantam Dell, Doubleday, Alfred A. Knopf, and the parent imprint. Its authors include such luminaries as Toni Morrison, John Grisham, Danielle Steel, and John Updike. Random House publishes 8,000 new titles a year and handles 50,000 more in backlist. The company's latest endeavor, AtRandom.com is the first dedicated e-book line from a major publisher.

The Penguin Group comes in second, and its list of imprints covers not only its signature line but also New American Library, G. P. Putnam's Sons, and Viking Press. Its Penguin Books for Young Readers ensures that children are still thrilled by Watty Piper's *The Little Engine That Could*—just as previous generations were—and brings them the Nancy Drew and Hardy Boys series. Penguin Putnam publishes the works of best-selling authors Tom Clancy and Patricia Cornwell.

New York State is the home to ideas and dreams and visions, expressed in everything from a corporate ad campaign to Pulitzer Prize–winning books.

Above left: Children eagerly read the latest Harry Potter book at a Manhattan bookstore. The series is published by Scholastic Corporation in New York City. Above right: First published in 1922, *Reader's Digest* is now read by almost 100 million people each month. The company's headquarters are in Pleasantville.

Investing in the Future

Finance and Insurance Services

When it comes to money, New York State is the center of the known universe.

CHAPTER**SIX**

It is the heart and soul of the country's—and the world's—economy, the wellspring of capitalism. State employment in finance and insurance in September 2003 was 519,000, and in 2001 this industry cluster added $166 billion to the Gross State Product.

Photos: Left, © www.scottbarrow.com; right, © Charles O'Rear/CORBIS

The world's largest finance and insurance companies are either headquartered in the Empire State or have a presence here. The industry is a major contributor to the state economy, providing $81 billion in annual payroll in 2001.

In 2002, the state employed 527,000 people in the finance and insurance industry, or 8 percent of the national total for these sectors, an impressive amount considering that the state's population is 6.7 percent that of the entire United States. Not surprisingly, New York City led the field, with 331,000 people, or 63 percent of all statewide employment in these sectors. Long Island came in second, with 64,400, or 12 percent of the state total, followed by the Albany-Schenectady-Troy metropolitan area, with 20,200, or 4 percent. All told, these figures represented approximately 28,000 businesses statewide.

New York State's influence on the financial industry can be summed up in the answer to a simple question: Is there any business community in the world that does not watch the New York Stock Exchange, the most important and powerful securities market in existence? The Exchange—also known as the Big Board—states its mission simply and clearly: to provide "the highest quality and most cost-effective self-regulated marketplace for the trading of financial instruments."

The organization of the Stock Exchange formally began on March 8, 1817, when 28 brokers agreed to a governing constitution and membership rules. The Exchange did not do well at first: in 1830 it hit a Big Board low, when traders handled only 31 shares. Volume did not hit one million shares until 1886, and the Dow Jones Average did not exceed 100 until 1906. But things have picked up since then. The highest volume day—so far—was July 24, 2002, when the Exchange handled 2,812,918,977 shares, and on December 31, 1999, the Dow climbed to 11,497.

Another institution that brings New York to the attention of the world is the Federal Reserve Bank of New York. The Federal Reserve system was created to manage the nation's monetary policy and provide an elastic currency as well as to supervise and regulate banks within its jurisdiction. The New York chapter—one of 12 regional Reserve Banks—is far and away the most important because

On the 36,000-square-foot floor of the New York Stock Exchange, the traders are a blur of buying-and-selling activity. Opposite: Investors hoping for good luck in the market rub this bronze bull sculpture, located in the Financial District's Bowling Green Park. Created by sculptor Arturo DeModica, *Charging Bull* weighs 7,000 pounds.

it oversees the banking activity of the nation's financial hub. The New York Fed—besides storing billions in gold—also handles all U.S. transactions with foreign central banks and is responsible for maintaining the value of the dollar on the world's exchange markets.

It's in the Bank

New York City is a landscape of financial giants, of names known to every American and familiar all over the globe. Citigroup Inc., the world's largest financial services firm, started as City Bank of New York in 1812 with $2 million in capital and paid its first dividend a year later. In 1919, it became the first U.S. bank to have $1 billion in assets, and in 1929 the largest commercial bank in the world. By then, it had offices in places as disparate as Argentina, Belgium, and Indonesia. Today, Citigroup is the largest credit card issuer on the planet, with 200 million customers in over 100 countries and assets of more than $1.1 trillion. In New York State, the diverse firm has more than 300 offices, including retail and Salomon Smith Barney branches, employing almost 32,500 people.

The year 2000 saw the merger of Chase Manhattan and J.P. Morgan, two of the most famous names on Wall Street. J.P. Morgan Chase & Co. is now the second largest banking franchise in the nation. The institution builds on both Chase's consumer and middle-market businesses and Morgan's record as the world's financial leader. The founder of the latter firm, J.P. Morgan, was the greatest banker of his age—or any other—given that in his era he assumed many of the duties of the present-day Fed, personally deciding credit terms and the flow of money for the country. Today, JPMorgan Chase employs approximately 100,000 people worldwide—30,700 in New York State alone, where it has 431 locations—and had 2003 assets of over $1.1 trillion.

These preeminent U.S. companies are joined by many of the world's most dynamic financial institutions. The Credit Suisse Group is based in Zurich, has over 70,000 employees worldwide, and boasts roughly $1 trillion in assets. Its American branch, the New York City–based Credit Suisse First Boston, handled over $200 billion in public debt and equity offerings in 2001, making it the city's third biggest investment bank, according to *Crain's New York Business 2003 Book of Lists*. Japan's Nomura Group has an office in New York City that handles over $1 billion in capital, while the Israel Discount Bank of New York is the seventh largest commercial bank in the New York City metropolitan area, with assets in 2002 of $7.1 billion.

New York City is also home to the world's major brokerage firms and investment bankers. Merrill Lynch & Co. handles client assets of approximately $1.1 trillion. Its 2002 sales were $28.3 billion. In 2001, it handled $321.3 billion in public offerings. *Crain's New York Business* ranks the Goldman Sachs Group as the fifth largest investment bank in New York City on the basis of the $198 billion in public offerings it shepherded in 2001. Its 2002 sales reached almost $22.9 billion. Lehman Brothers came in sixth, with $189 billion in public offerings. Its 2002 sales were almost $4 billion.

High Finance in New York State

Not all of New York's money power rests in Manhattan, however. Buffalo's M&T Bank Corporation traces its roots in that city back to the mid-19th century. The firm now employs 9,200 people in 700 branches in five states and the District of Columbia. Sales in 2002 were $2.35 billion. Long Island has institutions like Astoria Financial Corporation, parent of Astoria Federal Savings. With assets of $22.5 billion, it is the second largest thrift in the New York City area and the fifth largest in the country. Approximately 2,100 people worked for Astoria in 2002, and sales came to $1.4 billion. The Capital Region is also a financial powerhouse. The First Albany Companies is an investment banking and capital markets boutique, handling institutional trades of corporate, government, and municipal securities and employing 445. By 2002, sales were up to $183 million.

Planning for the Future

Insurance is a crucial part of the financial sector in New York State. Employment among insurance carriers, brokers, and agents was 152,000 in September 2003, while the industry's contribution to the Gross State Product in 2001 was $19.2 billion.

For many Americans, Manhattan-based MetLife (formerly Metropolitan Life Insurance Company) is best known for the use of *Peanuts* characters in its commercials. Yet the company also stands out as the largest insurer of life in the nation, a position it has held since 1909. Throughout its history, MetLife has been an innovator, believing that insurance could be a force to improve the lives of all Americans. In 1909, the

Photos: This page, © Peter Morgan/Reuters NewMedia Inc./CORBIS; opposite page, © Tom Stewart/CORBIS

This page: A family enjoys a hike on a brisk autumn day. Many of New York's insurance firms have provided coverage and security to families like this one for more than a century. Opposite: The J.P. Morgan Chase & Co. headquarters on Park Avenue in Manhattan is home to one of the largest financial services firms in the world.

Photo: © Mark Peterson/CORBIS

Originally built for Pan American Airways in the 1960s, the MetLife Building is an icon of the New York skyline almost as recognizable as the Chrysler Building, at the right of the photo. MetLife, which purchased the building in 1981, follows Pan Am, Barclays Bank, and other companies with headquarters at 200 Park Avenue.

This page: New York's many qualified financial advisers help clients choose the investment and insurance products that are right for their personal needs. Opposite: The four office towers of the World Financial Center, with their distinctively shaped rooflines, reflect the rays of the setting sun from across the Hudson River.

company began sending employees to some of the city's poorer quarters to distribute pamphlets about combatting tuberculosis. Around the same time, it started the Metropolitan Life Visiting Nurse Service to help seriously ill policyholders. Almost a century later, in 2002, *Working Mother* magazine named MetLife one of the "100 Best Companies for Working Mothers" for the fourth year in a row, while the Minority Corporate Counsel Association gave the insurer's law department an Employer of Choice Award. In 2001, MetLife became the first insurance institution to set up a financial holding company with a nationally chartered bank and established MetLife Bank, a retail firm. MetLife had 2002 revenues of $33.1 billion, up 6 percent over the previous year, and 48,500 employees.

Also based in New York City, MMC—the Marsh & McLennan Companies—is number 169 on the Fortune 500 and provides risk and insurance services worldwide, as well as investment management and consulting; it is now the world's largest insurance brokerage firm. In 2002, its sales exceeded $10 billion, nearly 6 percent over the previous year, and it had almost 60,000 employees.

Throughout the state, there are important insurance companies. In New Hartford, the Utica National Life Insurance Company is one of the nation's 25 largest mutual insurers, with 2002 sales of $643 million and 1,500 employees. The firm has four offices in New York State with 1,100 employees. Unity Mutual Life Insurance Company got its start in Syracuse in 1903, when the Imperial Order Tycoons, a local organization, created a benefit society to help members' families get past tough periods due to sickness, accident, or death. In 2001, Unity had income of $55.5 million and 100 employees. Swiss Re, based in Zurich, is one of the world's largest reinsurers; it posted 2002 sales of $24.8 billion. This global concern has a U.S. office in Manhattan at Liberty Plaza, but also runs a subsidiary, Swiss Reinsurance America Corporation, from Armonk. The total number of Swiss Reinsurance employees in New York State is 1,800.

Photos: This page, © Jose Luis Pelaez, Inc./CORBIS; opposite page, © www.scottbarrow.com

In the long run, the success of New York's financial and insurance industries, for all their power, rests on values. As has always been true, these firms remain dedicated to providing the consumer—both individual and corporate—with the highest level service in every kind of transaction. Their ability to do so, and the trust this has created, is why the entire world looks to the Empire State for leadership in these sectors.

Expert Support

Professional and Business-to-Business Services

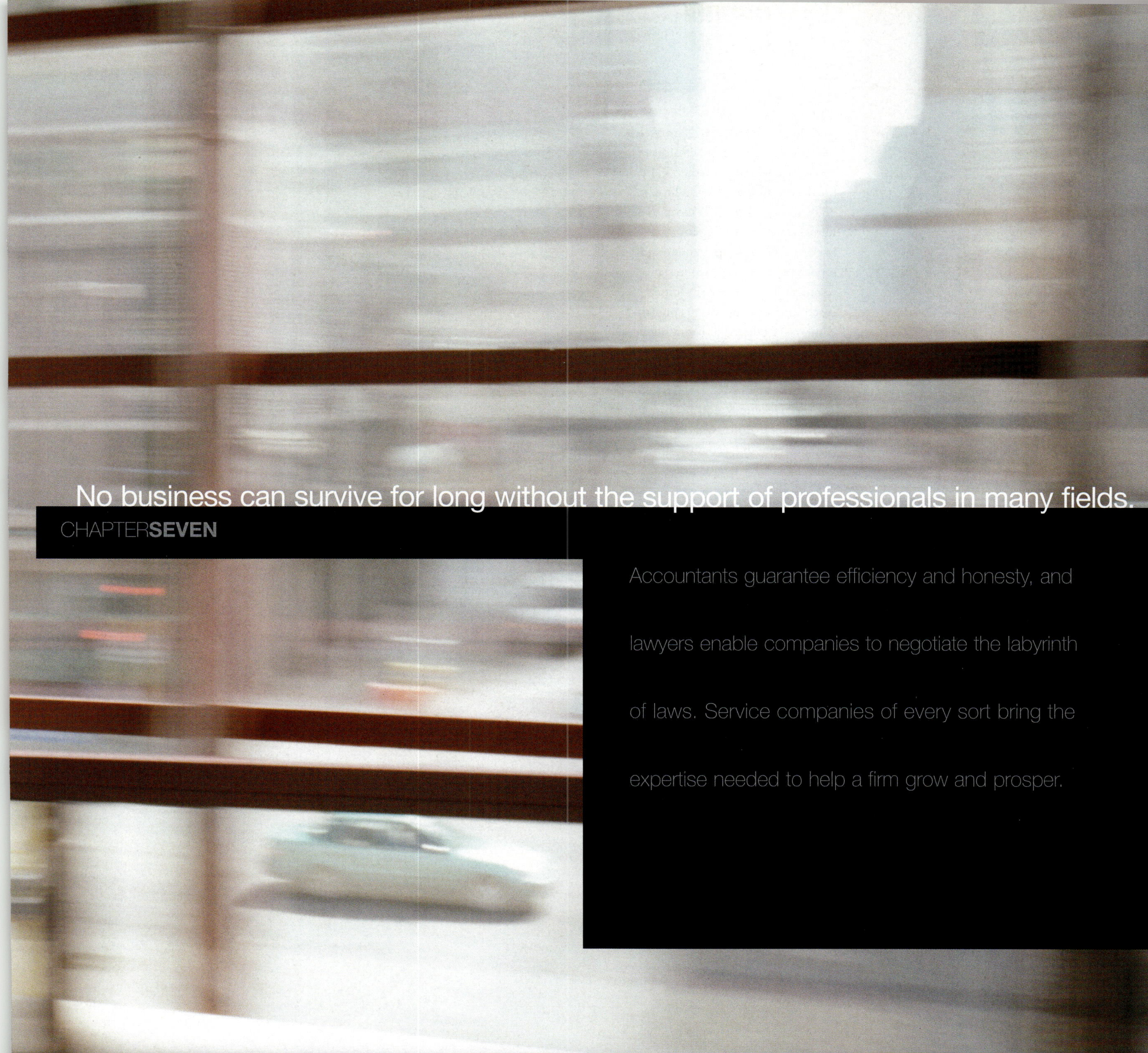

No business can survive for long without the support of professionals in many fields.

CHAPTER**SEVEN**

Accountants guarantee efficiency and honesty, and lawyers enable companies to negotiate the labyrinth of laws. Service companies of every sort bring the expertise needed to help a firm grow and prosper.

New York State is a power in all these fields, with many of the nation's most important firms located here. February 2004 employment in professional services was 1,025,000. New York City had the highest concentration of the state's professional services jobs with 52 percent, followed by Long Island with 14 percent. When it came to growth, however, the Hudson Valley dominated, Greene and Putnam Counties producing job increases of 17 and 10 percent respectively over the previous year, followed by Wyoming County in western New York, with 9 percent. In 2001, business services contributed $40.4 billion to the state's economy; legal services another $21.5 billion.

Columns of Figures

The New York State business landscape includes the corporate offices of 51 Fortune 500 companies. With this kind of heft, it is no surprise that the Big Four accounting firms—Deloitte, PricewaterhouseCoopers, Ernst & Young, and KPMG—are all headquartered in New York City.

Deloitte's founder, William Welch Deloitte, was one of the creators of modern accounting, the first individual hired as an independent auditor, in 1849. Today, Deloitte is the nation's number one accounting firm and handles every kind of accounting service from tax advice to human resources management. Deloitte's parent firm operates in 40 countries, employs 119,000, and had 2003 sales of $15.1 billion. Growth from the previous year was 21 percent, the 10th consecutive annual increase. Its U.S. division, Deloitte & Touche, had sales of $5.9 billion in 2002, with 28,000 people working around the country. *Working Mother* magazine named Deloitte one of its "100 Best Companies for Working Mothers," the only Big Four firm to make the list seven years in a row (1997–2003), while *International Securitization & Structured Finance Report* (the leading publication in its field) claimed Deloitte was the number one securities accounting firm in Europe, North America, and Asia Pacific. Deloitte has three offices in New York City, and in 2001, 5,400 professionals worked in its metropolitan area branches.

The second biggest accounting firm in terms of revenue has the longest name of the four. PricewaterhouseCoopers specializes in three areas: tax and legal, business advisory, and corporate finance. Its 2003 sales reached $14.7 billion, backed by 122,800 staffers. Its New York City operations include six local offices and 5,600 professionals in the Tri-State area.

Photos: Left, © Steve Cole/Masterfile; right, © David P. Hall/Masterfile

This page: A lawyer reviews his e-mails and voice messages updating him on the latest developments in his client's case prior to entering the courthouse. Opposite: Online stock market reports help chart a profitable course for securities firms.

Financial services firm Ernst & Young's headquarters are located at 5 Times Square in Manhattan. The company—with Deloitte, Pricewaterhouse-Coopers, and KPMG—is one of the Big Four, the largest accounting firms in the nation.

Photos: Left, © James Leynse/CORBIS; right, © Rick Gomez/Agefotostock

The third member of the quartet, Ernst & Young had 2003 sales of $13.1 billion—up 29.8 percent over 2002—and 103,000 employees. In 2002, *InformationWeek* listed it as one of the top 500 most innovative firms in the nation for its use of technology, and *Fortune* named it one of the "Top 100 Companies in the U.S. to Work For." Ernst & Young has one office in New York City and others on Long Island and in New Jersey, which employ a total of 2,500 professional staff.

KPMG is a Dutch firm with 98,000 employees worldwide, but its U.S. operation is run from an office on Park Avenue. Its 2002 U.S. sales came in at $10.7 billion. Residents of New York City can go to any of KPMG's three offices, but there are more throughout the New York City metropolitan area, and these sites employ a total of more than 2,300 people.

These firms are joined by a network of smaller but just as ambitious accounting firms, both in New York City and throughout the state. Grant Thornton, based in Manhattan, specializes in middle-market clients, both in this country and overseas, and had 2003 revenues of $485 million domestic and $1.84 billion worldwide. Its four New York State offices have 362 employees. In Buffalo, Freed Maxick & Battaglia employs more than 200 personnel and offers services in a wide variety of areas, including pension, health care, construction, manufacturing, and much more. Kruth, Stein, Squadrito & Liberman is a major Syracuse firm with 23 CPAs and accountants.

Justice Served

September 2003 employment in the legal field in New York State was 125,000, and the state bar association had over 70,000 members, making it the largest state lawyers organization in the nation. In 2001, the profession contributed $21.5 billion to the state economy, and New York City had 34 of the top 100 law firms in the country. It is talent like this that defines the term *power lawyer*.

Among the world's preeminent law firms is Skadden, Arps, Slate, Meagher & Flom, which has headquarters in Manhattan and roughly 1,750 attorneys. In 2003, of the top 25 companies in the Fortune 500 ranking, Skadden represented 15 from the domestic list and 11 from the global list. Its handling of the $11.8 billion acquisition of TRW by Northrop Grumman earned Skadden the M & A (Merger and Acquisitions) Deal of the Year Award from *Investment Dealers' Digest*. At the same time, Skadden worked on IBM's acquisition of PwC Consulting from PricewaterhouseCoopers, a $3.5 billion project that earned notice from that same investment publication as Technology Deal of the Year. *Chambers Global: The World's Leading Lawyers* picked Skadden as the "USA Best Business Law Firm" and recognized it with the publication's prestigious Devereux Chambers award for North American Law Firm of the Year in

On his way to a meeting with a client, an investment broker checks stock market action via his phone. In February 2004, approximately 176,000 people in the state were employed in securities, commodities, and other related financial positions.

2002. Skadden's New York City–area operations employed 797 lawyers and total staff of over 2,100 in 2002.

There are other heavy hitters here as well. Shearman & Sterling represented the Bank of China in the $2.7 billion IPO for its commercial bank in Hong Kong in 2002, BOC Hong Kong (Holdings) Limited. The law firm was also in charge of WestLB AG's financing for the new Wembley Stadium in London, a $1 billion project cited by Project Finance International as one of the top 10 deals in 2002. Shearman & Sterling's New York City office has 562 lawyers and almost 1,400 total staff.

Proskauer Rose is a New York institution; one of its earliest partners was Joseph M. Proskauer, a renowned judge.

Photo: © Tom & Dee Ann McCarthy/CORBIS

In February 2004, professional services employment in New York State stood at 1,025,000, with 52 percent of such workers located in New York City, home to many top suppliers of legal, accounting, and other services. Greene, Putnam, and Wyoming Counties rated highest in the number of jobs created in the professional services sector.

Besides corporate finance, taxation, real estate, and litigation, the firm specializes in intellectual property law. Its clients range from AT&T to Arista Records, from UPS to Major League Baseball. It is the 11th biggest law firm in New York City, with 458 lawyers in 2002 and 1,000 total staff.

There are major law firms outside New York City as well. Albany, for example, enjoys the services of Whiteman Osterman & Hanna. The city's largest practice, it has more than 50 attorneys, of which one-third are female, as are seven of the 23 partners. Not surprisingly, given the location, the company specializes in lobbying at the state capitol, and among its clients are national firms like American Express, Bristol-Myers Squibb, and Hertz, as well as New York–based entities such as the Metropolitan Museum of Art and Syracuse University. Solomon and Solomon, the capital city's leading firm in debt collection and litigation—and one of the biggest firms practicing this specialty in the country—has seven lawyers and over 200 staff, many working in collections.

Buffalo's largest law firm, Hodgson Russ, has 190 attorneys and is the 200th largest law firm headquartered in the United States, covering all branches of the law, from labor to taxation, estates and trusts to litigation. In 2003, the editors of *American Employer Digest* chose Hodgson as one of the country's most admired employers, and *Corporate Board Member* magazine recognized it as the top law firm in Buffalo.

Another prestigious New York firm is Nixon Peabody. Its Rochester headquarters office features 120 lawyers and 250 total staff, specializing in business services and litigation and tax.

Supporting Players

New York State brings a wealth of knowledge to help guide business; 17 of the top 40 management consulting firms are located here. One of them, Blasland, Bouck & Lee (BBL), is an environmental consulting and engineering firm based in Syracuse and with offices in five other New York cities. Nationwide, BBL has 35 offices and 650 employees. Yearly sales average between $100 million and $150 million. In 2003, the firm was ranked 11th by *Engineering News–Record* magazine on its list of the top 20 environmental science firms in the country.

MasterCard International has 4,000 employees worldwide, 1,100 of whom work at the headquarters in Purchase. In 2002, the company handled $1.14 trillion in transactions worldwide—up 15.2 percent from the year prior—and had revenue of $1.9 billion.

Zogby International, of Utica, is a public-opinion research firm that conducts telephone polls and handles public relations, fund-raising, and telemarketing. Its clients range from Microsoft to the U.S. Census Bureau, from Reuters to the United Nations. Zogby has 50 full-time and 300 part-time employees (who conduct the phone surveys), and had 2002–03 sales of $5 million.

In Buffalo, Capital Management, which provides collection services, in 2002 invested $1 million to expand its facilities, a move that will add almost 700 new jobs by 2005 to the 150 already in place. Capital will receive a $300,000 grant from Empire State Development, and another $94,000 for training programs, as it opens a new 30,000-square-foot facility.

New York State does more than just support business. Its remarkably diverse economic infrastructure helps companies grow and thrive, guiding them to greatness. New York is where America's businesses come not just to survive but to triumph.

Photos: Left, © James Leynse/CORBIS; right, © Ron Fehling/Masterfile

Management consultants often meet in the field to get the best feel they can for a client's business. Opposite: This sign indicating the headquarters of MasterCard International, in Purchase, New York, displays the company logo, well known to consumers in 210 countries. MasterCard processes as many as 32 million transactions a day.

Modern Medicine

Health Care and Biotechnology

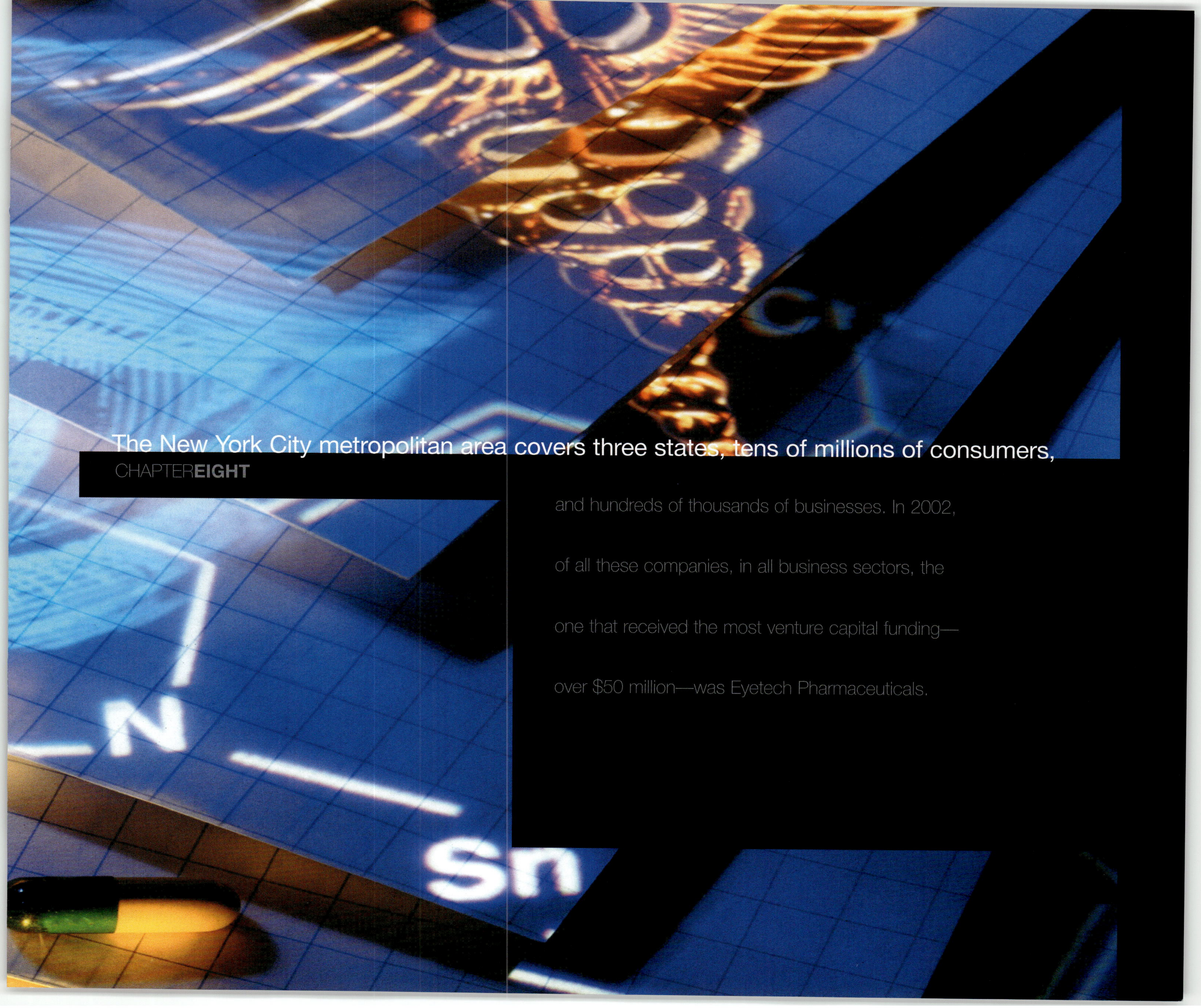

CHAPTER**EIGHT**

The New York City metropolitan area covers three states, tens of millions of consumers, and hundreds of thousands of businesses. In 2002, of all these companies, in all business sectors, the one that received the most venture capital funding—over $50 million—was Eyetech Pharmaceuticals.

Starting operations in 2000, Eyetech is a newcomer but a powerful one. Its mission is to discover, develop, and market drugs to combat eye disease and reduce and block vision loss, with special emphasis on age-related macular degeneration. Eyetech's current team of ophthalmologic researchers comes from world-famous institutions such as Columbia University, Harvard Medical School, Stanford University, the University of Chicago, and the Johns Hopkins University. At present, Eyetech's top product is Macugen, a path-breaking aptemer. Aptemers are RNA or DNA molecules that have a unique ability for binding together other molecules, proteins—even microscopic organisms. In this case, the aptemer creates an element that blocks abnormal blood-vessel growth in the eye, the leading cause of vision loss among the aged and diabetics. Macugen is currently in Phase II/III testing (the final stage before being approved for the consumer marketplace) at over 100 medical centers worldwide.

Eyetech is typical of companies in the thriving biotechnology sector of New York State's economy. September 2003 employment in the field was 1.2 million, and this area contributed $7.6 million to the 2001 Gross State Product. In New York City alone, employment in health care jobs has grown consistently from 1998 to the present, without a single downward period, and this pattern is predicted to continue into the immediate future. The reason for this growth is clear: the enormous strength of the hospitals and medical schools, the health care plans, and the private companies in biotechnology in the Empire State.

New Discoveries: Medical Research in Hospitals and Universities

In the quality of its research institutions and hospitals, New York leads not only the country but also the world. The Rockefeller University in Manhattan, for example, helped solve the secret of DNA, discovered that a virus causes cancer, linked cholesterol and heart disease, and developed the program that uses methadone as a maintenance drug for heroin addicts. Since its founding, the Rockefeller University has benefited from the sheer brainpower of 23 Nobel Prize winners, 19 Lasker Award honorees, five MacArthur Fellows, and 12 recipients of the National Medal of Science, the highest award for scientific achievement given by the United States. As of 2003, 34 members of the faculty were members of the National Academy of Sciences. In fall 2003, these great minds were joined by Professor Roderick MacKinnon, who won that year's Nobel Prize in Chemistry for his work in studying the proteins that create nerve impulses, which generate all movement and thought. This came on the heels of his colleague Robert Roeder's taking the 2003 Lasker Award for work on how human genes operate. At roughly the same time, Sir Paul Nurse, 2001 Nobel Prize winner for his work on cancer cells, assumed the reins as president of Rockefeller University.

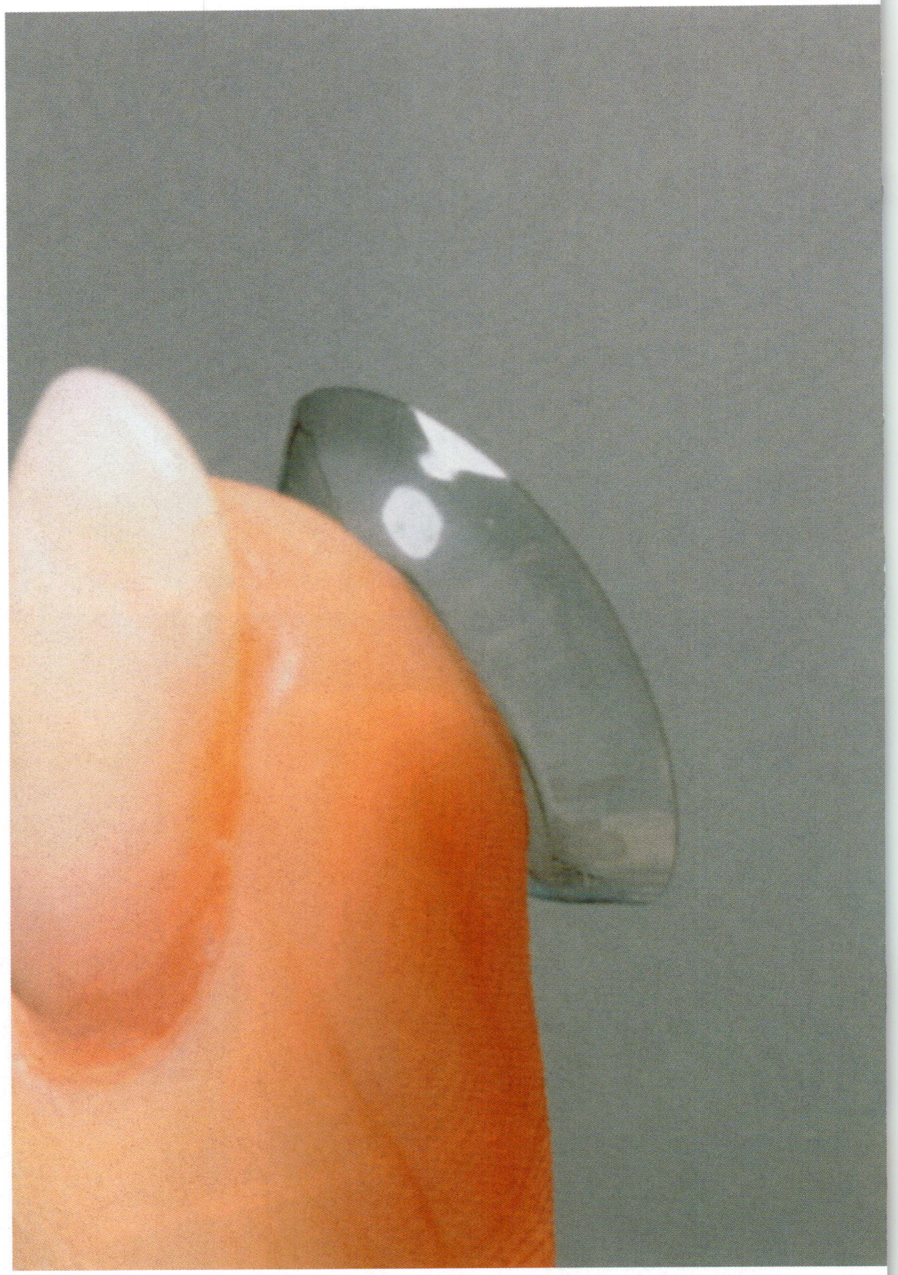

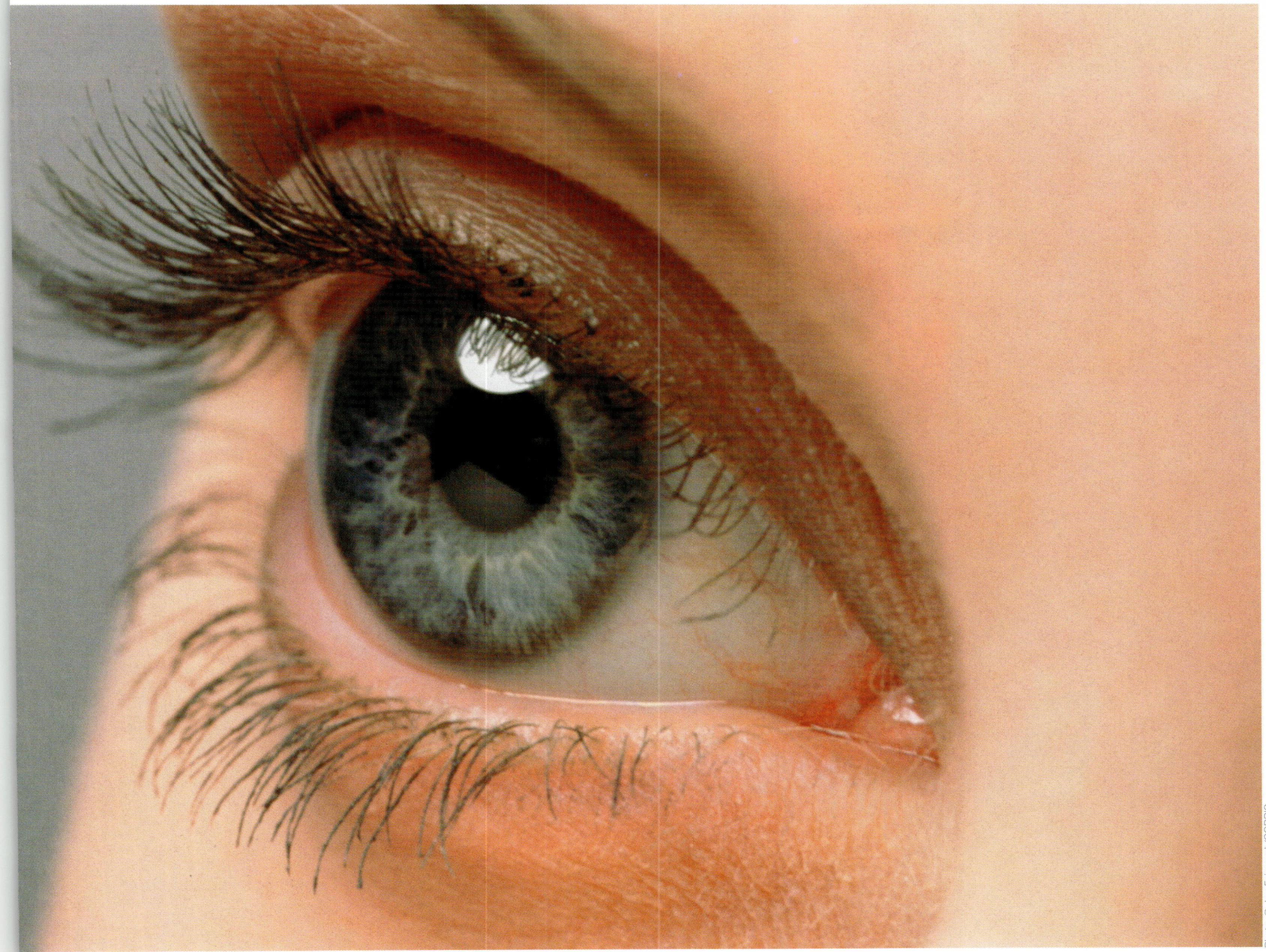

Photo: © Jon Feingersh/CORBIS

A woman applies a soft contact lens to correct her myopia. One of the world's leaders in vision care products—from contact lenses to surgical tools and pharmaceuticals—is Rochester-based Bausch & Lomb. The company posted 2003 sales of more than $2 billion.

This page: A researcher, indicating some DNA coding of interest on her screen, is using a computerized sequence database to analyze a particular genome. Opposite: Patients such as this man rely on their hospital system not only for diagnosis and treatment of disease but also for the basic research that makes possible advances in both.

Photos: Left, © Andrew Douglas/Masterfile www.masterfile.com; right, © Orbit/Masterfile www.masterfile.com

The Rockefeller University is hardly an isolated case when it comes to the New York research environment. Another source of leadership is the University at Buffalo's Center for Excellence in Bioinformatics. Bioinformatics is a new field, but a critically important one. It combines computer science with biology in an effort to use modern technology to help reveal the secrets of nature's most complex creation, the human gene sequence. Only massive computing speed—combined with the insights of biological researchers—can unlock these secrets.

Thus, the mission of the center is to use computers to help discover what proteins do and how they interact with each other and outside elements, and to design drugs using this knowledge in the quest to fight disease. Initial funding was $200 million. One-quarter of this came from the state, with another $62.5 million from Veridian Corporation, $42.6 million from Compaq Computer Corporation, and $20.8 million from InforMax. The federal government has also appropriated a crucial $3.1 million in start-up funds.

This money will go into setting up a 150,000-square-foot facility with research and computer labs, three-dimensional visualization capabilities, and workforce training facilities. Plans are to have this all completed by 2005. The bioinformatics center will employ 500, although within five to 10 years 4,000 to 10,000 jobs will be created by nearby companies making use of the discoveries coming out of these labs.

Supporting endeavors like this is a network of hospitals and affiliated medical and research institutions throughout the state. NewYork–Presbyterian Hospital has 2,395 beds, more than 13,000 employees, and an annual revenue flow that hit $1.8 billion in 2001. Its physicians performed the first laser surgery, in 1961, and the first successful heart transplant in a child, in 1984. Its patient care, furthermore, is nationally recognized. Castle Connolly Medical surveys 250,000 physicians annually to determine the best in their fields, then publishes the results in a volume titled *America's Top Doctors*. In 2003, more doctors from NewYork–Presbyterian made the list than from any other hospital in the country.

The Mount Sinai Medical Center is another pioneer. In 1886, Josephine Walter finished its house staff program and became the first woman to complete an internship in an American hospital. Doctors at this hospital and medical college authored the first American textbook on geriatrics, in 1914 (a Mount Sinai physician actually coined the term in 1909), and one on thoracic surgery. Today, Mount Sinai has 1,406 beds, 8,500 employees, and annual revenue of $1.1 billion.

In 1982, the hospital created a separate Department of Geriatrics and Adult Development, the first full academic geriatrics department in the United States and still one of only three in the country. Medical researchers in fiscal year 2001 achieved over $121 million in National Institutes of Health (NIH) grants alone, placing Mount Sinai 24th among the nation's 125 medical schools in funds granted for research. As a result, in 2003 the hospital had under way clinical trials for treatments of ailments ranging from asthma to multiple sclerosis, from acne to prostate cancer.

Buffalo's Roswell Park Cancer Institute has been designated by the National Cancer Institute as a comprehensive cancer center. In 1995, one of its researchers, Dr. Thomas Dougherty, gained U.S. Food and Drug Administration approval for the drug Photofrin. This is the first photodynamic treatment so authorized and treats esophageal cancer. In 1998, Roswell acquired a Leksell Gamma Knife, used for noninvasive

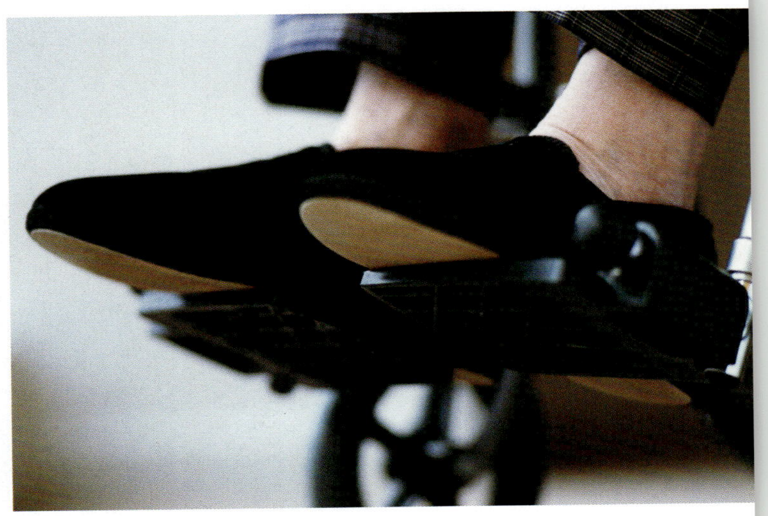

Photo: © L. Langenmeier/Masterfile www.masterfile.com

A doctor strides briskly along a hospital corridor, dressed in green scrubs and sneakers. Through licensing of innovative technology, his medical facility is likely to contribute millions to the state economy. In 2002, the Sloan-Kettering Institute, in New York City, led the nation in licensing income, with $54.4 million.

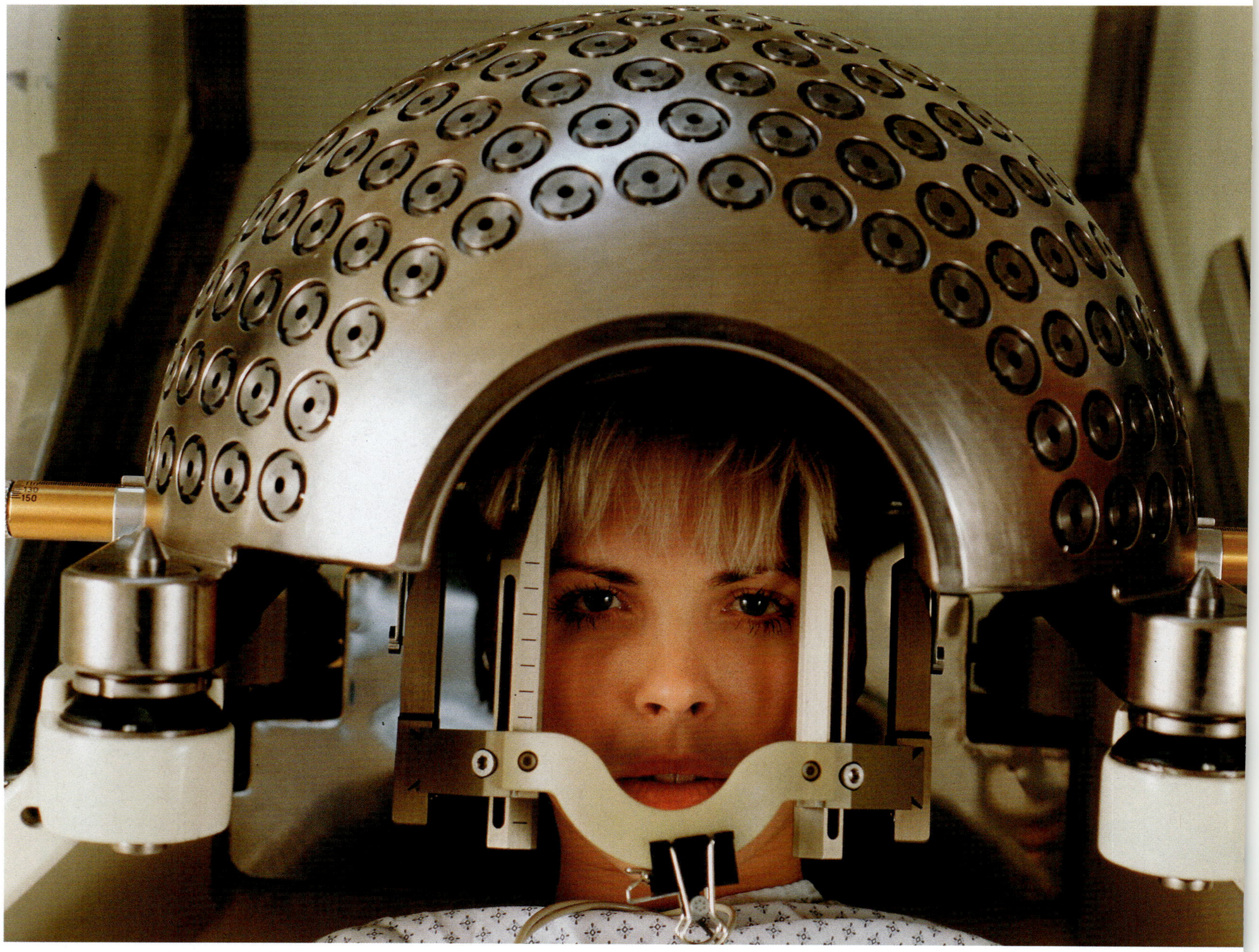

A nurse demonstrates a Gamma Knife radiosurgery helmet, which is used in brain surgery. The noninvasive procedure involves beaming concentrated doses of cobalt-60 through holes in the helmet to a precise location in the patient's brain, destroying abnormal tissue. The Roswell Park Cancer Institute in Buffalo acquired a Leksell Gamma Knife in 1998.

brain-tumor radiosurgery, making Roswell one of only 47 locations in North America with this equipment. Following up its work with Photofrin, in September 2003 Roswell researchers received a $10.9 million National Cancer Institute grant to pursue photodynamic therapy.

Health Plans

New Yorkers benefit not only from the presence of these renowned institutions but from some of the nation's best health plans. The biggest HMO in the state is Oxford Health Plans, which, in New York, covers New York City, Westchester, Long Island, and the Hudson River Valley. Systemwide, the plan has more than 1.5 million members and provides access to 60,000 primary care physicians and specialists.

HIP® Health Plan of New York, on the other hand, is the largest HMO in New York City, according to *Crain's New York Business.* It covers 1.2 million people in the New York City metropolitan area and has affiliations in that zone with 21,000 doctors at 32,000 locations. *InformationWeek*'s annual survey of technology innovators recently ranked HIP number one nationwide, especially for the company's advanced use of the Internet. Besides speeding up member care, HIP became the first health care company in the country to provide a Web site with English, Spanish, and Chinese editions.

Photos: Left, © Roger Ressmeyer/CORBIS; right, © Antigenics

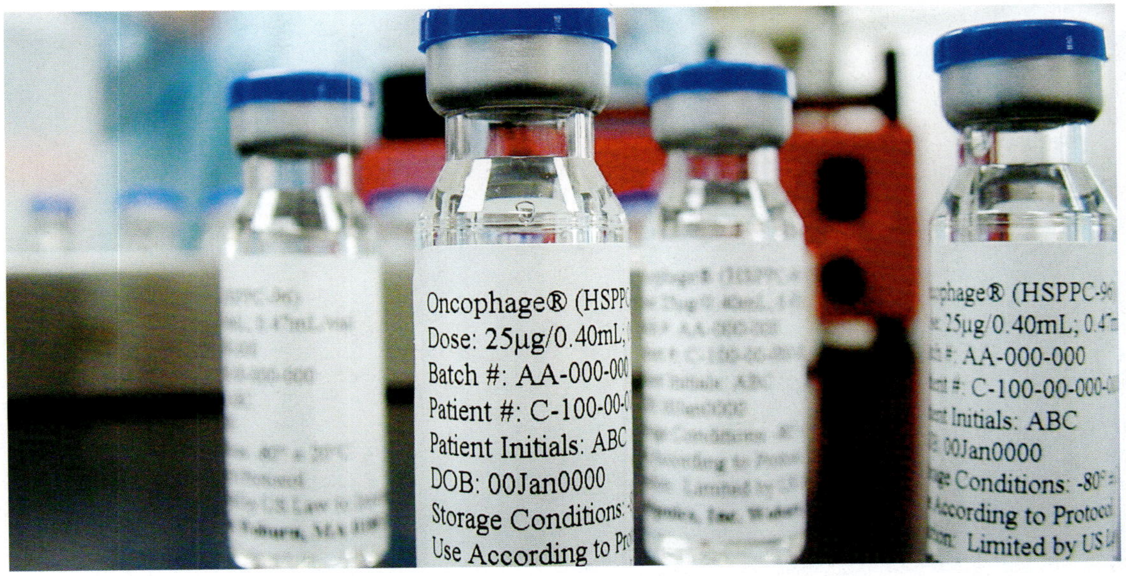

Antigenics, based in Manhattan, produces Oncophage cancer vaccine, which is derived from patients' own tumor cells through heat shock protein technology, a proprietary process that "fingerprints" the cells' unique antigens. Each person's initials and identifying number are carefully noted on the vial label.

Upstate, the leaders are Excellus BlueCross BlueShield, which covers the Hudson River Valley up through Albany and Watertown, plus Utica, Syracuse, and Rochester; and Univera Healthcare, in Buffalo, Syracuse, and Rochester. Each serves more than 680,000 members.

Booming Private Sector

New York State companies big and small are leading the way in creating a revolution in medicine. Bausch & Lomb's Rochester roots go back to 1853, when John Jacob Bausch, a German immigrant, opened an optical store, later partnering with his friend Henry Lomb. In 2002, the company they started had $1.8 billion in sales, growing 6.1 percent from the prior year. Its surgical division is a leader in making lasers for eye surgery, while its pharmaceuticals wing develops prescription eye treatments.

Antigenics, headquartered in New York City, had 2002 sales of $3.4 million and is working simultaneously on more than 20 programs to combat cancer as well as immune and degenerative disorders. Its flagship product is Oncophage, which aims to reprogram the body's immune system while leaving healthy tissue unaffected, and thus eliminate harmful drug side effects. While Oncophage has the capability of treating all forms of cancer, the versions targeting kidney cancer and melanoma are in Phase III trials.

Albany Molecular Research is a pioneer in the development of new drugs, especially those using small-molecule technology. Total revenue in second quarter 2003 was up over the same period of 2002 by 70 percent, while contract revenue over the same period grew by an astonishing 118 percent, or more than double. With results like that, it is no surprise that Albany Molecular ranked 67th in *Forbes*'s 2003 list of the "200 Best Small Companies in America" for the fourth consecutive year in a row, the same year *Fortune* listed it as one of the "100 Fastest Growing Companies in America" for the second consecutive year. Albany Molecular has 850 employees and is building a $40 million research facility in its home city.

New York State is a powerhouse in medical research and treatment. Its scientists and care providers are blazing new trails that will make life better, not just for residents of the state but for people everywhere on the globe.

Top of the Class

Education in New York State

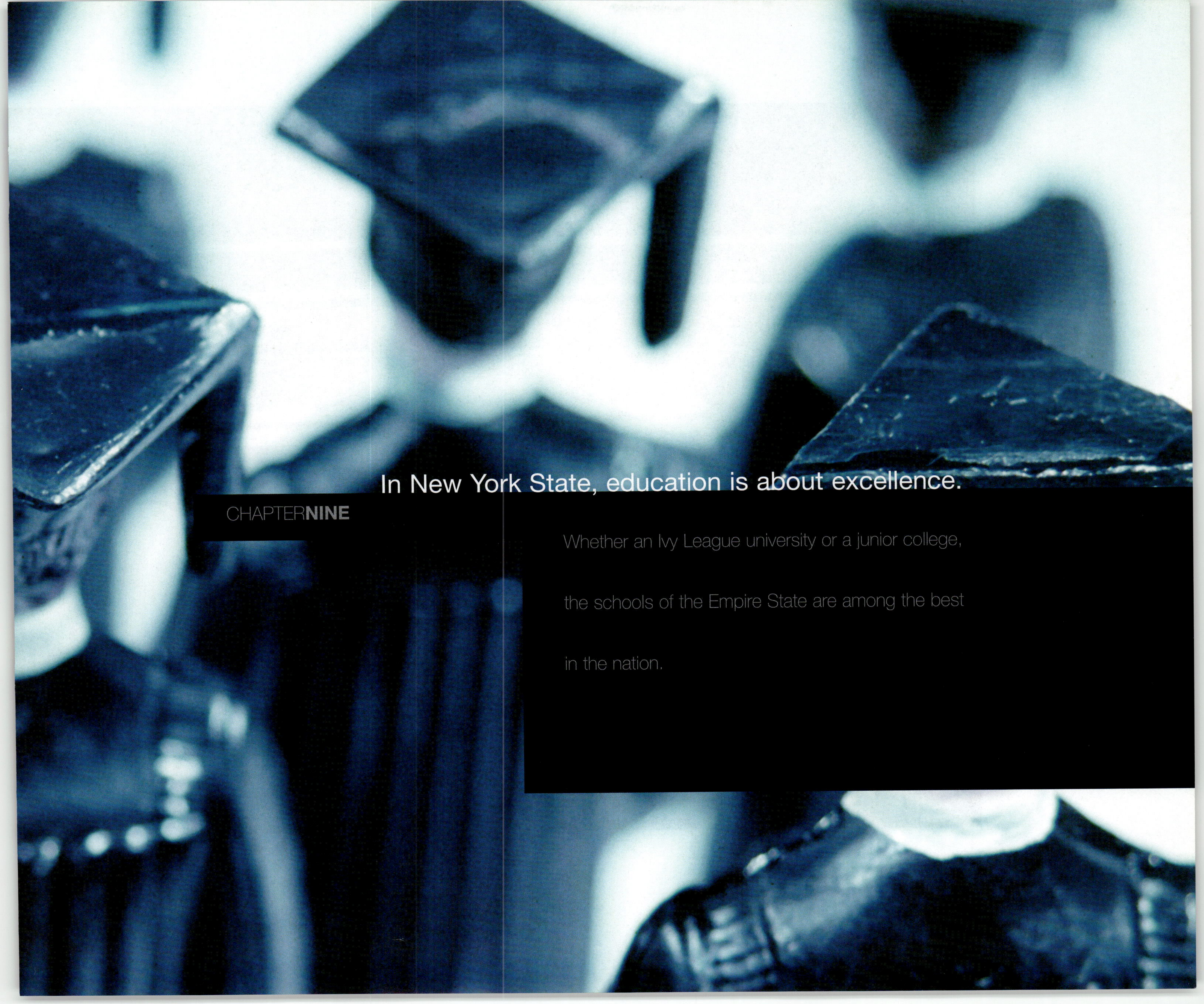

CHAPTER**NINE**

In New York State, education is about excellence.

Whether an Ivy League university or a junior college, the schools of the Empire State are among the best in the nation.

This page: These gates admit students to Barnard College, a women's liberal arts college founded in 1889 and now one of four undergraduate schools within the Columbia University system. Opposite: A film student works in an editing room at one of several universities in the state offering top-ranked film and television courses.

Photos: Left, © Lee Snider/CORBIS©; right, © Lonnie Duka/Index Stock Imagery

Private-University Leadership

World-class education abounds in the state. Columbia University in the City of New York is one of the finest universities in the world. Its faculty members and alumni have won 69 Nobel Prizes, 19 MacArthur Foundation Awards, and seven National Medals of Science. In 2002, the university received grants and other sponsorships worth over $400 million. In addition, its law and business schools are ranked in the top 10—and, in many cases, the top five—by professional and educational organizations.

One of the factors that keeps Columbia at the top is its remarkable library resources, capped by the recently renovated Nicholas Murray Butler Library. The system's total holdings include 7.5 million printed volumes, 5.5 million microforms, 28 million manuscripts, 500,000 rare books, 190,000 government documents, and 135,000 maps and map-related materials. The university subscribes to approximately 50,000 journals and magazines.

Columbia remains one of the most competitive schools in the country in terms of admissions, and is becoming more so over time. In 1995, 8,714 candidates applied and only 2,045 were admitted, for an acceptance rate of 24 percent, but by 2002, out of 14,135 applicants, only 1,641 received acceptance notices, a rate of only 12 percent.

Joining Columbia in the Ivy League is Cornell University, situated in a picturesque valley in Ithaca. Founded in 1868, Cornell now has 260 buildings on 745 acres, as well as one of the best faculties in the nation. Among the projects Cornell researchers are working on are a computer simulation model, developed in the university's Joan and Sanford I. Weill Medical College, to create emergency responses to bioterrorism, and studies in the School of Industrial and Labor Relations' Smithers Institute on the work, mental health, and quality of life of New York City firefighters, both before and after September 11, 2001. Cornell graduate students also won the 2003 Collegiate Inventors Competition, beating out over 150 other entrants from schools across the globe. Cornell's team received this award for developing a generator that is 100th the thickness of a human hair and can be used to speed up computational machines.

These researchers and educators work not only in the usual colleges of arts and sciences but in some unique professional institutions, as well. They include Cornell's College of Agriculture and Life Sciences, known worldwide for its Agricultural Experiment Station, and the School of Industrial and Labor Relations, which was the first of its kind in the United States. The School of Hotel Administration is the world's most sophisticated, the choice of those who wish to become the top hospitality professionals. Its roster of 60 full-time faculty is the largest on the globe for hotel schools, and the school boasts undergraduates from 42 countries. Participation in its graduate and executive programs is even more extensive, with participants from 90 nations, demonstrating the global reach of this institution.

Another world-class institution, New York University (NYU) was founded in 1831, and from its earliest days had a powerful research component. Samuel Morse worked in one of the labs in the main building. Since then, the faculty has gone on to win two Nobel Prizes, three Pulitzers, and seven Lasker Awards. NYU has been the recipient of 137 Guggenheim Fellowships and a dozen MacArthur Foundation Awards. Some of this may be due to the magnificent setting of the main Washington Square campus in the heart of Greenwich Village, with its heady intellectual and artistic atmosphere that helps the human mind thrive and create.

In New York State's abundant world of educational excellence, technology flourishes. Researchers at Rensselaer Polytechnic Institute, for example, just outside Albany, recently created a microsensor to detect gases at the nano level. Other researchers at the school pioneered the use of radiation to detect small defects in space shuttle foam, thus helping solve the riddle of the *Columbia* space shuttle disaster, while the faculty's Ravi Kane is working on molecules that will defeat an HIV infection.

Among the top small, undergraduate liberal arts colleges is Vassar College, founded in 1861, a coeducational school located in the Hudson River city of Poughkeepsie. Average class size is 16; faculty-to-student ratio is one to nine. Roughly two-thirds of Vassar's students come from public high schools, one-third from private institutions. In choosing the Class of 2006, Vassar accepted only 31 percent of applicants, an all-time low.

Another gem is Hobart and William Smith Colleges, located in Geneva, in the Finger Lakes region. Over 75 percent of the school's roughly 1,900 students either conduct independent research or work with faculty mentors on research projects, and most participate in one of 29 off-campus programs that carry them to destinations on six continents. Hobart and William Smith also created the first men's studies minor in the nation; three men and two women were the first to graduate with this minor.

The State University of New York

New York also provides the most comprehensive state system of higher education in the United States. The State University of New York (SUNY) has 64 campuses and a total enrollment of over 400,000, and offers 6,400 different courses each year.

SUNY has four tiers. There are four University Centers—at Albany, Binghamton, Buffalo, and Stony Brook—that are major research institutions and award all levels of degrees, including the doctorate. Thirteen university colleges provide 973 baccalaureate and 350 master's level curricula that cover every area, from the liberal arts and sciences to professional disciplines. Technology colleges—there are eight of them—feature hands-on training in fields ranging from agriculture to engineering, medical science to computers. These schools offer the widest range of programs in the SUNY system, from vocational certificates to associate degrees, from bachelor's of science to technology diplomas. Thirty community colleges, meanwhile, cover the state, offering a gateway to four-year schools.

The opportunities at SUNY are boundless, dreams fueled by the enterprise and inspiration of students. A prime example is the University at Buffalo. The school began as a small private medical college in 1846 and merged into the state system in 1962. This provided a massive influx of funds, and as a result UB, as everyone calls it, is now the state's largest and most comprehensive public university. Its Center for Computational Research is a world leader in high-performance computing sites; the *Wall Street Journal* ranked its School of Management on

Photos: This page, © University of Buffalo office of Creative Services; opposite page, top, courtesy of © Hobart and William Smith Colleges; bottom, © Royalty-Free/CORBIS

This page: The University at Buffalo's Center for the Arts includes three theaters and a large screening room. Opposite page, top: The Melly Academic Center, at Hobart and William Smith Colleges, is a state-of-the-art information and instruction facility. Opposite page, bottom: Students check out their school's Web site at a campus computer center.

Photo: Courtesy, SUNY Oswego

A group of students at the State University of New York (SUNY) at Oswego enjoy a social moment in one of 12 residence halls on the campus, which occupies 700 acres on the shore of Lake Ontario in central New York. SUNY is the largest university system in the United States, generating eight dollars in state spending for every dollar it takes in.

The U.S. Military Academy at West Point graduates more than 900 new officers, such as this smiling cadet, every year. Women make up approximately 15 percent of the student body, and were admitted to the USMA and other service academies beginning in 1976. Cadets may select from 31 fields of study along with the core curriculum.

At the the Culinary Institute of America (CIA), immaculately attired chefs-in-training observe as one of the school's 130 international instructors demonstrates his technique. Both bachelor and associate degrees are offered by CIA, which is the only residential college in the world dedicated solely to the culinary arts and baking and pastry arts.

Photos: Left, © www.stockbarrow.com; right, © Eric Futran

the list of top 50 business schools in the world in 2001, 2002, and 2003. It also has the region's most modern performing arts complex, including a $50 million Center for the Arts. More than 6,400 employers—national and international—recruit at SUNY Buffalo each year.

Cayuga Community College, a unit of SUNY, may not be that big, but it offers opportunities that are just as important, just as special. Besides curricula in business, computer technologies, studio art and design, criminal justice, and mechanical and electrical technology, it has a program in geospatial information technology (GIT). This makes it the only community college in the United States with a NASA regional application center, specializing in GIT, global positioning, and remote sensing.

Unique Institutions

New York State's educational roster also includes institutions that have no parallel anywhere else. Among these is the United States Military Academy at West Point. Since Thomas Jefferson signed the establishing legislation in 1802, West Point has trained young men and women to become commissioned officers in the U.S. Army. Over and over, in generation after generation, the academy has turned out officers who have led this country to greatness. Pre–Civil War alumni included both Ulysses S. Grant and Robert E. Lee, plus Thomas J. "Stonewall" Jackson, William T. Sherman, and Oliver O. Howard, who founded Howard University. The late 19th and early 20th centuries saw a new burst of heroes, including not only John J. Pershing, who led U.S. forces in World War I, but George W. Goethals, architect and chief engineer on the Panama Canal. Generals Douglas MacArthur, George S. Patton, Omar N. Bradley, and Dwight D. Eisenhower were West Point alumni as are astronauts Edwin E. "Buzz" Aldrin Jr., Michael Collins, and Frank Borman.

Not far from West Point is the Culinary Institute of America (CIA), which began in 1946 as a vocational training school for World War II veterans and is now one of the world's premier cooking schools. Located in Hyde Park, it has an international student body of approximately 2,300. In 1999, CIA student chefs were part of the team that won the grand prize at the Coupe du Monde de la Boulangerie (the World Cup of Baking).

In every field of endeavor, New York State educates students for excellence. It is where tomorrow's leaders are taught.

Climbing to the Sky

Real Estate, Development, and Construction

New York State is a land of builders.

CHAPTER**TEN**

In September 2003, the construction industry provided 347,000 jobs to the state, and in 2001 added 27.4 billion to the Gross State Product.

This industry, however, has had its rough moments. It would be folly to argue that September 11th did not impact the New York City real estate market. Downtown vacancy rates dropped but then stabilized at around 11.1 percent. Asking rents in midtown averaged $52.26 a square foot in early 2003, down from a high of $56.56 in 2000.

But that is only part of the picture. As Marilyn Jordan Taylor, chair of the New York Building Congress, so eloquently put it, "We must remember that what is right about New York is much greater than what is wrong."

Start with the greatest real estate market in the world. The demographics are staggering, and in time, will always create a winner. New York is not only the most populous city in the country by a long shot—it now tops eight million residents, an all-time high—but the island of Manhattan alone contains roughly 10 million people on any given working day. It is also the most crowded city in the country, with 26,000 people per square mile, and one of the most popular: the Big Apple gained 685,714 people in the 1990s, the most of any U.S. city. These figures indicate a need for a lot of office space, a lot of industrial and warehouse buildings, and constant pressure on the residential market.

In fact, there are signs that New York is undergoing a building revival.

Showpieces

Part of this revival is the new 7 World Trade Center. The original building at this address collapsed due to fire caused by the September 11th attacks. Its replacement was designed by Skidmore, Owings & Merrill and is being built by the Tishman Construction Corporation. The new building incorporates "green" guidelines, reflecting New York City's environmental awareness policy.

Another bright spot on the city's horizon is the new headquarters of a local paper called the *New York Times.* The *Times* gave its name to the square where it opened its headquarters in 1904, but since 1913 it has been housed mostly in a nearby location, on West 43rd Street. Increasingly, this facility has become outdated and overcrowded, with staffers forced to decentralize at seven additional locations.

In response to these conditions, the New York Times Company followed a bold path. First, it chose a location and structure that would enable it to consolidate operations. The new headquarters will rise on Eighth Avenue between 40th and 41st Streets, across from the Port Authority Bus Terminal, and will be 52 stories tall and contain 1.5 million square feet, including the shops on the ground floor. The project will create 3,500 construction jobs and 3,500 permanent positions, mostly for building and maintenance workers and retail employees. This effort is solidly supported by New York State, which put up $26 million worth of incentives, from sales tax exemptions on building materials to reduced electrical rates.

What makes this such an important addition to the city is the striking architecture. The Times Company picked Renzo Piano as lead architect, and he delivered a postmodern masterpiece. Piano, the Pritzker Award winner who also designed the Pompidou Center in Paris, made clear his intentions: "I prefer things that are light." In order to accomplish this, he created a design that sheathes the building in 250,000 white ceramic rods, $1^{5}/_{8}$ inches in diameter, which change color as the sun shifts and the weather changes, capturing nuances of the moment. On the roof, next to a conference room, will be a grove of maples and a lightweight mast. This last item is not a broadcasting antenna, nor will it serve any other technical function; it is merely there to show the breeze, to remind one of the joy of wind. At this peak, the building will stretch 1,142 feet tall, almost 100 feet taller than the Chrysler Building.

On 57th Street and Eighth Avenue, the Hearst Corporation is also pulling the strands of its publishing empire together into one building in a project that combines the old with the new. The company now occupies a six-story building erected in 1927, as well as offices across the city for various of its 17 major publications. Instead of tearing down the central structure, Hearst is building on top of it, capping the older design with a new 48-story tower that will bring the total to 54 stories. This innovative approach was the brainchild of its architect, Sir Norman Foster, another Pritzker winner, who completed reconstruction of the acclaimed Reichstag in Berlin in 1999.

Buffalo is also experiencing exciting new construction projects, such as the three-building research complex going

This page: Architect Renzo Piano's airy *New York Times* headquarters is his first major project in New York City. Piano calls the building, a collaboration with Bruce Fowle of Fox & Fowle Architects, "an expression of love" for New York. Opposite: The pizazz and energy of New York City nightlife come together on 42nd Street, where Forest City Ratner developed this entertainment, retail, and hotel complex to match the area's vitality.

The 599-seat Judy and Arthur Zankel Hall occupies renovated space below Carnegie Hall's Isaac Stern Auditorium. It was once used for recitals, then a cinema. Opposite: Radio City Music Hall underwent a renovation in 1999 that restored its art deco beauty. The project, led by the New York City architecture firm Hardy Holzman Pfeiffer Associates, received a 2000 National Preservation Honor Award from the National Trust.

up on the Buffalo Niagara Medical Campus. This $150 million project will eventually house 550 scientists and support workers, and will include facilities for the University at Buffalo's Center for Excellence in Bioinformatics, the Roswell Park Cancer Institute's Center for Genetics and Pharmacology, and the Hauptman-Woodward Medical Research Institute.

New Rochelle is also enjoying the results of new construction. In 1999, New Roc City, a retail and entertainment center, opened. The overall facility—including offices and condos—has 1.2 million square feet, while the retail and entertainment section alone is 447,000 square feet and is valued at $105 million. Attractions include the Tower Space Shot Ride, bowling alleys, an NHL-size ice skating rink, an IMAX theater, and an 18-screen Regal Cinemas megaplex. Given these attractions, it makes sense that three million visitors show up each year.

Albany saw the completion of a new headquarters for the state Department of Environmental Conservation in 2001, located in the downtown district, with 400,000 square feet of space. Also opened in 2003 in the Albany metropolitan area was Southgate Commons, a 350,000-square-foot retail complex with a Wal-Mart and a Loews multiplex.

Hammer and Nails

The state's construction industry is among the nation's most formidable. The Syska Hennessy Group, based in New York City, is one of the premier builders in the country, with 2002 revenues of $100 million. Its projects include such revered structures as the Lincoln Center for the Performing Arts and the Chrysler Building. In 2004 alone, the firm won three awards for its U.S. Embassy building in Istanbul, Turkey. In 2003, it achieved one of the highest certifications ever by a U.S. building in the Leadership in Energy and Environmental Design rating system for its design of the Santa Monica, California, headquarters of the Natural Resources Defense Council.

Foreign builders also see the possibilities in New York. Skanska started in Sweden in 1887 making cement products and is now an international firm with projects in places ranging from Scandinavia to Poland, from Argentina to India. Revenues in 2002 were $18 billion. Skanska USA Civil is headquartered in Queens and has handled the magnificent reconstruction of City Hall Park, built a new state-of-the-art student center for Columbia University, and

Photos: Left, courtesy, Tishman Construction Corporation; right, © Rolf Bruderer/CORBIS

redeveloped Rockefeller Center. One of its divisions, Slattery Skanska, has a bonding capacity of $4 billion and 300 staffers. Among its projects is the new John F. Kennedy International Airport Light Rail System, a $1.2 billion project.

All across the state, there are quality building firms handling big projects. In 2002, *Engineering News–Record* ranked Welliver McGuire of Montour Falls among the top 200 construction firms in America and among the top 25 nationwide for educational ventures. The company's projects range from renovating the Chemung County Jail to building the Corning Museum of Glass to constructing a chemistry building for the State University of New York's Upstate Medical University in Syracuse.

Benderson Development Company of Buffalo constructs and owns shopping centers and now has a portfolio of 40 million square feet of real estate, including plazas in Albany, Batavia, Utica, Rochester, and Syracuse. Cappelli Enterprises of Valhalla has developed over four million square feet, ranging from residential to mixed-use to retail to office space. The company is constructing the City Center at White Plains, a $320 million project that will provide 1.1 million square feet of usable space. This combined entertainment and retail center will include a 150,000-square-foot Target store and a 15-screen National Amusements multiplex, as well as two 35-story residential structures.

Filling the Room

It is never enough just to put up new structures; any building of size has to be managed by firms that know how to run large office, residential, or commercial properties, as well as marketing them to ensure full occupancy.

Vornado Realty Trust of Manhattan owns or manages 75 million square feet of space, including 21 office buildings in New York City alone. The firm is also a major presence in what is arguably the

The fondest dream of many an aspiring home owner looks just like this New York charmer: a split-level Colonial-style house, surrounded by spacious green lawns and trees. Obliging builders are happy to throw in traditional white paint, a broad front porch, and plenty of room for the whole family to gather over the holidays.

choicest real estate in the nation, the only full block available for development in Manhattan: from Lexington to Third Avenues, 59th to 58th Streets (the site of the former Alexander's store across from Bloomingdale's). Vornado has a one-third interest in Alexander's, the former retail chain-turned-REIT that owns this site. A 1.3 million-square-foot mixed-use building is under construction there, to be completed in 2005; 695,000 square feet have already been leased to the Bloomberg company.

Another giant, Rudin Management Company, oversees 7.5 million square feet of office space in 14 New York buildings (boasting an overall occupancy rate of 98 percent), plus 22 luxury apartment buildings with 3,500 units and 15,000 rooms. Among those who have chosen to lease from Rudin are the Consul General of the United Kingdom, Bristol-Myers Squibb, both Bank of America and UBAF Arab American Bank, plus the Weather Channel.

Living Space

According to the 2000 census, New York State had 7.7 million housing units and a home ownership rate of 53 percent. New York City had 3.2 million of these units, Buffalo 146,000, Rochester 100,000, Syracuse 68,000, and Albany 45,000. The median value of owner-occupied domiciles was $149,000, compared with $120,000 for the nation as a whole. Median monthly mortgage costs, by county, ranged from a low of $734 in Allegany County to a high of $3,615 in New York County.

The state is also experiencing considerable construction activity in the residential sector. In 2002, the various jurisdictions issued 49,280 housing unit building permits, with 21,531 of these coming from the New York City metropolitan area, 3,295 from the Albany-Schenectady-Troy cluster, 3,091 from Rochester and surrounding suburbs, 2,960 in the

"Walk-up" apartment buildings such as these are a typical sight in Manhattan, though not all of them have facades as colorfully painted. Such masonry row houses, known as tenements, were erected in the 19th century for the burgeoning population of immigrants entering the country through Ellis Island. Renovation makes them desirable today.

Photos: Left, © Patrick Batchelder; right, © Albanese Organization

Buffalo–Niagara Falls vicinity, and 2,083 permits in and around Syracuse.

Not surprisingly in a state this big, there is an enormous variety in housing prices. The New York State Association of REALTORS reported that the October 2003 statewide median price for an existing single family home was $206,000, up 25 percent from the year prior. The National Association of REALTORS' study of metropolitan area prices for the third quarter of 2003 found that Nassau/Suffolk had the highest median housing price, at $374,000, followed by greater New York City at $367,000. Albany was next, with $149,000, followed by Rochester at $106,000 and Syracuse at $105,000. Buffalo–Niagara Falls had a median home price of $91,000, the lowest in the nation.

New York State generates excitement when it comes to housing. The Solaire is the first new residential construction in Lower Manhattan since September 11th, and is already making headlines. Developers set out to create one of the nation's premier "green" buildings, and the design features a number of advanced environmental features. This 27-story building recycles wastewater for toilets and air-conditioning systems, and its facade includes photovoltaic panels that generate 5 percent of the energy used by the structure. The rooftop has a pesticide-free garden and stores rainwater for irrigating plants and flowers. The overall design is 33 percent more energy efficient than required by code.

"Green living" features of The Solaire, a luxury high-rise on the Hudson in Battery Park, include electricity from photovoltaic panels, storm- and wastewater reclamation systems, and filtered fresh air and drinking water. The Solaire, which opened in late 2003, is Lower Manhattan's first new residential construction since September 11th.

The Solaire is not the only innovation going on in New York State. In Buffalo, Ellicott Development Company took over the former L.L. Berger department store downtown and turned it into the Belesario, which opened in 2003. The building space includes several loft units and features restored hardwood floors and fireplaces plus a gated parking lot and easy access to mass transit. In 2003, Ellicott also opened Cazenovia Commons Apartments, with 12 units, and Lakefront Commons, which added eight town houses to the Waterfront Village district.

The Empire State is booming. Recovered from the tragedy of September 11th, New York is seeing dramatic new buildings going up all over the state. Local developers pioneered the building of skyscrapers, and in a new millennium, the state is still reaching for the stars.

Photo: Rockefeller Center's *Prometheus*, by Paul Manship. © Macie/age fotostock

Where the World Comes to Play

Tourism, Hospitality, and Retail

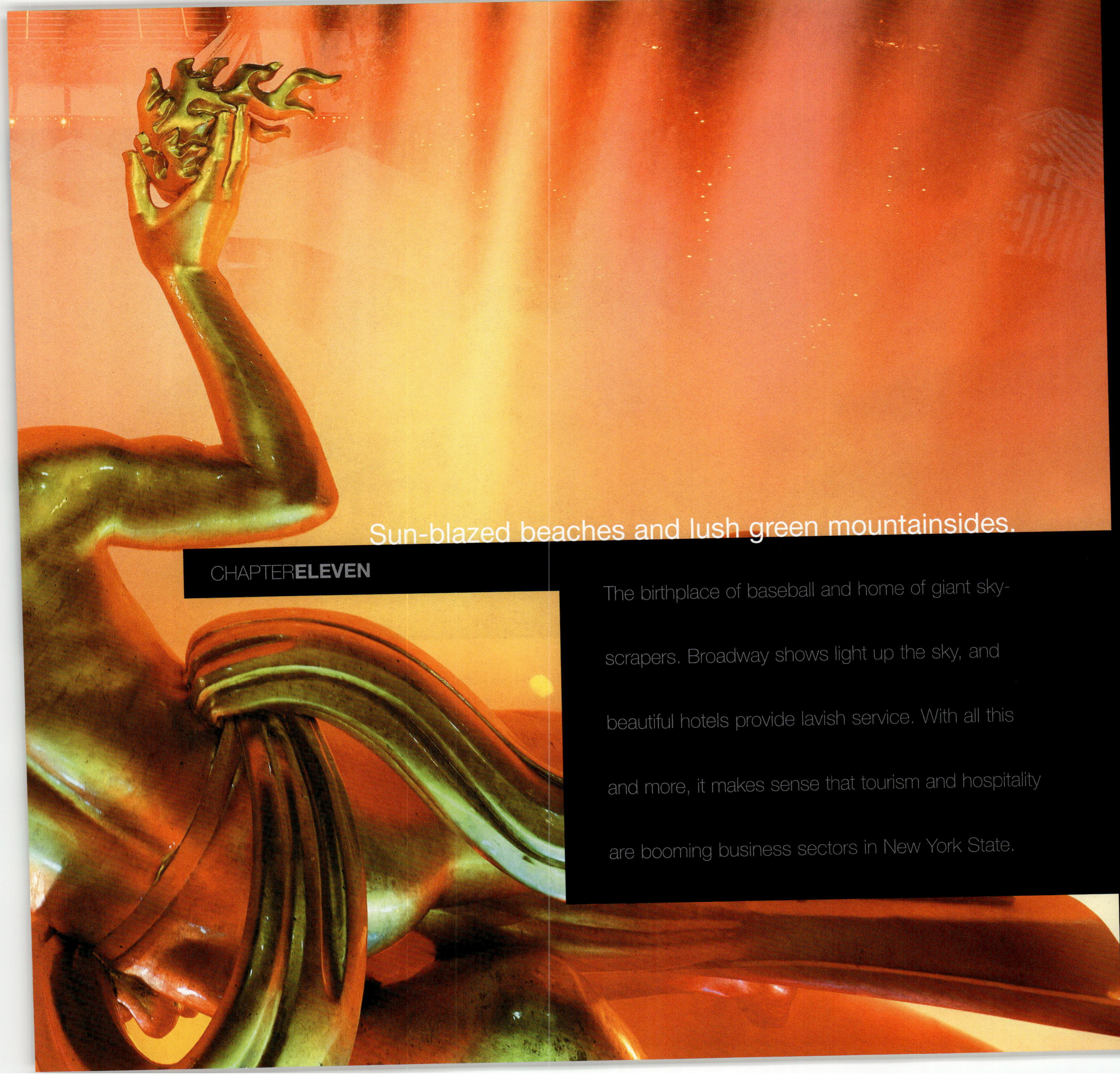

Sun-blazed beaches and lush green mountainsides.

CHAPTER**ELEVEN**

The birthplace of baseball and home of giant sky-scrapers. Broadway shows light up the sky, and beautiful hotels provide lavish service. With all this and more, it makes sense that tourism and hospitality are booming business sectors in New York State.

Hotels and lodging contributed almost $6 billion to the Gross State Product in 2001, while amusement and recreation brought in another $7.2 billion. Leisure and hospitality jobs employed 665,000 people in September 2003, an increase of 1.3 percent since the start of that year.

Like No Other Places on Earth

In her book on courtship, *Hands and Hearts*, Ellen K. Rothman tells how, in 1836, a young woman spoke to her fiancé of "the most wonderful and grand of the works of God," a spot, she explained, that she "had always longed to behold." She was talking about Niagara Falls, of course, which had been drawing tourists—and honeymooners—in increasing numbers since the 1820s. It is still awe inspiring. Over 10,000 years old, the great falls still pour an incredible 40 million gallons of water every minute over a 180-foot-high ledge that is two-thirds of a mile long. If tourists get soaked observing the spectacle, they can always dry off in the nearby Castellani Art Museum, which features modern and contemporary art.

Every part of the state has wonders on display. Rochester has the George Eastman House International Museum of Photography and Film, Ithaca has the Sciencenter, and Syracuse has its Milton J. Rubenstein Museum of Science & Technology.

Albany houses the state capitol, which as one writer put it, is "something of a Grand Guignol masterpiece." A 30-year project, it was the most expensive building in North America when it opened in 1897. Inside, the Great Stairway is 119 feet high (as tall as a 12-story building) and 70 to 77 feet wide.

Long Island is a big place—120 miles and four counties long—and includes hundreds of miles of fine white-sand

Above: Morning mist rises from Deer Pond in the Adirondack Mountains. Right: Albany's sleek skyline glows at twilight. Among the state capital's most famous attractions is The Egg (at center of photograph), a performing arts venue designed by Wallace K. Harrison and completed in 1978.

beaches, hidden dunes, secluded bluffs, and great restaurants. There are more than 150 public facilities operated by either federal, state, or local agencies, plus 21,000 acres of state parks alone. The area stretches from the fabled Hamptons to historic Montauk Point, out on the eastern tip of the island. The lighthouse at Montauk Point was commissioned by none other than George Washington.

Cooperstown is known to every sports fan as the home of the National Baseball Hall of Fame and Museum. The first election of inductees took place in 1936, and the judges appropriately chose five legends: Ty Cobb, Babe Ruth, Honus Wagner, Christy Mathewson, and Walter Johnson. Each year, 350,000 visitors stop by, then stay to take in other attractions in the surrounding area, such as the Glimmerglass Opera and the Farmers' Museum, a historic village and working farm, as well as the Fenimore Art Museum, whose collections cover fine art, folk art, and American Indian art.

The mountains of New York State provide ample opportunities for skiers, including those at historic Lake Placid, where modern skiing was introduced to America during the 1932 Olympics. The current site includes not only an Olympic museum but also the Verizon Sports Complex, with a combined track that can handle bobsled, luge, and skeleton racing. Whiteface Mountain in Wilmington has 73 trails and 10 lifts that take skiers up to 4,386 feet; the total vertical drop is 3,430 feet, the greatest in the eastern United States. While the total skiable area is 215 acres, The Slides section is reserved for expert-rated skiers only. Hunter Mountain Ski Area in Hunter was the first resort in the nation to have 100 percent snowmaking capacity and the first to

Manhattan is a never-ending party, extending an open invitation to tourists from throughout the world. Far left: No trip to New York would be complete without taking in the view from the 86th-floor observatory of the Empire State Building; approximately 3.5 million people do so each year. Center left and right: Whether alfresco or indoors, dining in New York presents unlimited options. Far right: Trump Tower at 725 Fifth Avenue offers five floors of high-end shopping in glitzy surroundings.

automate this system. It now has 1,100 snow guns capable of producing 40 tons of snow a minute; this means they can cover one acre of ground with a foot of snow every hour. There are 53 trails, 14 lifts, and 230 skiable acres.

While the state's natural wonders attract, the man-made canyons of New York City draw their share of visitors—40 million every year. The Big Apple boasts Radio City Music Hall, the Empire State Building, 38 Broadway theaters, and another 275 Off- and Off-Off-Broadway venues. There are 900 art galleries, 2,000 bars, 1,700 parks, and 12,184 taxis to take both locals and visitors everywhere.

A Home Away from Home

Taking care of visitors is a big business in New York State. The restaurant industry employs 450,000 people, up 1.1 percent since the start of 2003; New York City alone has 18,000 places to eat. Lodging is also an important sector in the state's economy, employing another 85,000 individuals.

There are good places to eat throughout the state, and history-making dishes as well. New York City features famous spots like Daniel, Le Cirque 2000, and the 21 Club. The Four Seasons was designed by Philip Cortelyou Johnson and Ludwig Mies van der Rohe and is the only Manhattan restaurant classified as an architectural landmark. For more casual dining, there is the signature Coney Island eatery, Nathan's, famous for hot dogs. Buffalo's most famous dish is buffalo wings.

Photo: © James Schwabel/Panoramic Images

New York State is not all bright lights, big city, though the midway at the Erie County Fair certainly lights up summer nights in Hamburg every August. One of the largest county fairs in the nation, the event lasts 11 days and has been celebrated since 1841, when Hamburg, south of Buffalo, was mainly agricultural.

This page, left: An estimated 14 to 16 million people visit Niagara Falls each year. A new convention and meeting center opened there in May 2004. This page, right: The National Baseball Hall of Fame and Museum, in Cooperstown, owns more than 35,000 three-dimensional artifacts and 130,000 baseball cards.

There are many stories of how this favorite came about, but experts like Calvin Trillin, renowned food critic, claim that the creation took shape at Teressa and Frank Bellissimo's Anchor Bar in the city, on Lake Erie.

The state also features excellent hotels. In New York City are the world-renowned Waldorf-Astoria and the Plaza. Saratoga Springs specializes in late-19th-century hotels that capture the glamour of that era, and there are even costume shops to fit visitors out for the horseracing season opener, when everyone turns out in turn-of-the-20th-century clothing. Buffalo is home to the magnificent Mansion on Delaware Avenue hotel—contemporary style in a restored 1860s building.

This page, right: Political conventions, rock concerts, sports events—it all happens at Madison Square Garden on Manhattan's Seventh Avenue. Visitors may take the center's All Access Tour, a behind-the-scenes look at the World's Most Famous Arena®, as the Garden bills itself. This page, left: A snowboarder enjoys the powder at one of New York's popular ski resorts.

There are also many great places to shop throughout the state. New York City alone has 30 department stores, with the parent operations of Macy's, Saks Fifth Avenue, Lord & Taylor, Bloomingdale's, and Bergdorf Goodman. Kaufmann's has stores in Buffalo and Rochester, while Albany, Binghamton, Clifton Park, and Nanuet feature Boscov's department stores.

Gathering Places

New York State has a number of places to hold large events, the most famous of which is Manhattan's Madison Square Garden. The original version was a drafty railroad shed used by P. T. Barnum in 1874, but the current facility opened in 1968, and in 1992 underwent a $200 million renovation. Seating in the Arena is 20,000, and the list of personalities who have appeared here range from Frank Sinatra to Elvis Presley, Madonna to Pope John Paul II. The MSG Network on cable carries the home games of various New York City teams, including the Rangers, the Knicks, and the Yankees.

New York City also benefits from the Jacob K. Javits Convention Center, on the West Side of Manhattan along the Hudson River. It covers 1.8 million square feet and has 814,400 square feet of exhibit space on four levels. At any one time, it can house 85,000 visitors, or one-quarter the entire population of St. Louis. There are 100 adjustable meeting rooms and an auditorium that can handle up to 2,500 people.

The rest of the state also provides first-rate accommodations for conventions and business meetings. The $18.8 million Conference Center Niagara Falls, opened in spring 2004, is a state-of-the-art 116,000-square-foot multipurpose venue that includes 2,000 hotel guest rooms. The Rochester Riverside Convention Center is 100,000 square feet, while the Empire State Plaza Convention Center has 80,000 square feet with six separate rooms that can accommodate from 150 to 450 guests. Just 27 miles southwest of Albany, the Rensselaerville Institute Conference Center is perfect for smaller parties. Originally a mill, the late 19th century structure is now an executive conference center offering 55 guest rooms on a secluded 100-acre estate.

New York State, with its wide variety of experiences, has an adventure for everyone, whether he or she is paying a visit, making a business trip, or setting up a convention. For the visitor with a family, for the road warrior, for the corporate planner, there is no better place to be.

Powering New York

Transportation and Energy

CHAPTER**TWELVE**

New York City and New York State both owe their greatness in large part to unique transportation networks and diverse and powerful sources of energy. • European explorers and colonists—first the Dutch and then the English—settled in

Both photos: © www.scottbarrow.com

New York City because it has one of the greatest harbors nature ever created. The secret is the Narrows, which separates Upper and Lower New York Harbors. This relatively small channel keeps the turbulent waters of the Atlantic from entering the Upper Harbor, whose waters remain calm, making for safe anchorage.

In 1825, another transportation route connected this port to the rest of the state and to a good part of America. That year, the Erie Canal opened, linking Buffalo to Albany. This provided new markets for upstate farmers and manufacturers who could now get their goods to a large port. For the nation, however, the significance was even greater. Prior to that time, the major water outlet for goods grown, caught, or produced in the country's interior was down the Mississippi River system to New Orleans. Now, all of these products could travel via the Great Lakes to Buffalo, take the canal to the Hudson River, then transit to New York, the East Coast marketplace, and even to Europe.

Current of Commerce

The Erie Canal is no longer used for shipping, but waterborne commerce in New York is still going strong. The Port of New York/New Jersey processes 70 million tons of seagoing goods each year, including 3.75 million TEUs (20-foot equivalent units) of containerized cargo. At the beginning of the 1990s, the port handled 318,000 imported cars, and by 2002 that figure had gone up to more than 550,000. By the end of 2002, the dollar value of general cargo imports and exports that went through the port was up 9.9 percent over the previous year's figures, and in the first half of 2003, container volume was up 14.6 percent.

Overseeing all this activity is one of the nation's most unusual governmental entities, the Port Authority of New York and New Jersey. By the early 20th century, local officials recognized that the port was a maze of conflicting companies with different interfaces, different rail systems, different schedules. Bottleneck after bottleneck stalled the flow of goods. To coordinate the activities of what was then the nation's largest shipping and receiving center for seaborne goods, two states created the Port of New York Authority in 1921. Based on the management structure of the Port of London, it was the first such port in the western world to be run in this way, receiving no tax revenues and financially self-supporting. It received its current name in 1972.

At the northern end of the state, New York connects to the Saint Lawrence Seaway, a system of canals and locks linking the Great Lakes to the North Atlantic that provides a much shorter route to Europe for waterborne goods from the interior of the United States. Ships traveling from Baltimore to Liverpool, for example, have to cover 3,936 miles, while the trip from Detroit via the seaway is only 3,673 miles. In 2002, the seaway handled more than 40 million tons of cargo.

Above: Freight containers sit at dockside, where they soon will be loaded for shipping. New York waterways have always played a vital role in the state's transportation infrastructure and economy. Opposite page: Large volumes of cargo travel on freighters like this one through the Port of New York/New Jersey.

Taking Flight

New York State is not just a major point of entry for goods arriving by sea; it is also a dominant player in air transportation. In fact, the New York–New Jersey region is not just the nation's largest air cargo market, it is the world's. In 2002, it handled 2.5 million tons (that is five billion pounds), while in the first four months of 2003 alone the figure was 850,000 tons, up by 8.2 percent from the same period in 2002. Almost 25 percent of all air cargo brought into the United States arrives at either John F. Kennedy International Airport or Newark Liberty International Airport, which house, between them, more than 1,000 cargo companies. Kennedy International alone is a massive site of 4,930 acres, with 30 miles of roadways. The airport employs 37,000 people and has an overall economic impact of $22 billion.

New York City also enjoys the services of LaGuardia Airport, a 680-acre facility with 72 gates. More than 9,000 people work in the various operations, and the airport generates $6.1 billion in overall economic activity.

But those are not the only air facilities in New York City. Most Americans have been stuck, at one time or another, getting to the airport, with time running short. For those working in Lower Manhattan, however, there is the Downtown Manhattan Heliport. This 84,000-square-foot facility is just north of the Battery and is accessible by both the East and West Side Highways, as well as by subway, bus, taxi, and even by foot from the Wall Street area. The Downtown Manhattan Heliport was the first heliport ever certified by the FAA for regular passenger service and the first to install a semi-automatic fire protection foam system. It handles helicopters up to 50,000 pounds, and while in 1960 it handled only 638 flights, by 2000 that figure had grown to almost 29,000.

Joining this network are airports throughout the state. Albany gained attention as an important flight destination in 1910 when Glenn Curtiss became the first aviator to fly between the state capital and New York City, picking up a $100,000 prize and giving the local flight industry a boost. A new airport opened in 1928, and fares for the same route Curtiss flew were as low as $14.70. The current facility, Albany International Airport, on 1,100 acres, features a new terminal inaugurated in 1998. Among its amenities are a first-class business center with computer and laptop workstations, conference rooms, and videoconferencing facilities. An 800-car addition to the parking structure opened in 2000. The airport is open on a 24/7 basis and handles 124 flights each day. Buffalo Niagara International Airport has 90 daily flights that include nonstop service to 18 cities. In 2002, 4.1 million passengers passed through its terminal. Orange County's Stewart International Airport, in New Windsor, serves the Hudson River Valley with 28 daily flights and counts 400,000 passengers a year.

Planes await permission for takeoff on a runway at John F. Kennedy International Airport. In 2003, the airport handled some 16 million enplanements; enplanements statewide were 34.7 million.

Photo: © GoodShoot/Agefotostock

Photo: © Patrick Batchelder

A familiar sight for New Yorkers, an N subway train departs on its rounds, serving Manhattan, Brooklyn, and Queens. The centennial of the New York Subway is being celebrated in 2004, but rapid transit actually began in 1868, when the West Side and Yonkers Patent Elevated Railway opened on Ninth Avenue.

CONTAINMENT SPRAY PUMPS
CONT SUMP

Both photos: © www.scottbarrow.com

Well Grounded

The longest toll superhighway system in the United States is not out in the West or up in Alaska. It is here in New York: the 641-mile Governor Thomas E. Dewey Thruway (the closest competition: the Oklahoma Turnpike, with only 536 miles). This giant network takes passengers and cargo from New York City to Buffalo, out to the Pennsylvania line, east to the Connecticut or Massachusetts Turnpikes, or southwest to the Garden State Parkway in New Jersey. Overall, 230 million vehicles cover more than eight billion miles a year as they whiz across New York State.

For many residents of New York City—and for many visitors—the most distinctive part of their day is a subway ride. The first subway opened on October 27, 1904, at City Hall, and the system is now one of the largest anywhere on the globe. Annual ridership on this system is 1.3 billion passengers, placing it fifth in the world, behind Moscow, Tokyo, Seoul, and Mexico City; that means, however, that New York City still beats Paris, Osaka, London, and Hong Kong.

New York City Transit is part of the larger Metropolitan Transportation Authority (MTA). Each of the MTA's divisions, from subways and trains to buses and bridges, is a giant. MTA Metro-North Railroad alone has 900 cars traveling 775 miles of track. The entire MTA network provides more than 7.5 million rides every single weekday.

Charged for Performance

Niagara Falls may be known as a spot for honeymooners, but its various generating stations provide one-quarter of all the power used in both New York State and Ontario. The volume of water pouring over Niagara's Horseshoe Falls is roughly 100,000 cubic feet per second, with peak flows of 225,000 cubic feet per second. Not surprisingly, the network of generators on both the U.S. and Canadian sides of the falls is the largest producer of hydroelectric power in North America.

New York's power grid includes important local firms. Con Edison's service region covers a vast 660 square miles in both New York City and Westchester County, an area with a total population of 8.3 million residents. Its power plants can generate 8.5 million kilowatts of electricity, and the company sells about 50 billion kilowatt hours each year. Getting electricity to customers requires 90,000 miles of underground cable—the largest system of electronic cable underground in the world—with another 35,000 miles of overhead wires. The company also has 6,600 miles of gas mains and supplies 200 dekatherms of natural gas every 12 months throughout its service area, and even sells steam for heating and cooling to 2,000 buildings, both residential and commercial, in Manhattan. The network supplying this—100 miles of steam pipes—is also the biggest in the world.

Throughout the state, there are companies of similar caliber. Rochester Gas and Electric Corporation (RG&E) provides electricity to 360,000 customers and gas to 300,000 in a nine-county area. It has 22,000 miles of transmission and distribution lines and can generate up to 900 megawatts. Its facilities include nuclear, fossil fuel, and hydroelectric generating plants. The Long Island Power Authority owns 14,000 miles of overhead and underground lines that bring power to more than 1.1 million customers and brought in 2002 revenues of $2.5 billion. Central Hudson Gas & Electric Corporation serves the Hudson River Valley and provides electric service to 280,000 customers and gas to 65,000.

New York State has retained the central position it first held when sailing ships entered its great port and barges carried goods along the Erie Canal. It is still the transportation hub of the nation, the major transmitter of goods, people, and power in this country.

Above: New York's efficient network of highways supports an astounding amount of traffic, facilitating the flow of goods throughout the state and beyond. Opposite page: An energy leader, New York is home to four nuclear reactors, including one of the country's two oldest reactors still in service.

Land of Plenty

Agriculture and Food Processing

CHAPTER**THIRTEEN**

Photo: Farmer in hay field, © www.scottbarrow.com

A study in contrasts, New York is renowned both for its cities and as one of the most important agricultural states in the nation. Roughly 25 percent of its land area—7.6 million acres—goes to 37,000 farms, which produced $3.1 billion worth of products in 2002. Its bounty ranges from dairy goods to field crops and vegetables, as well as a variety of processed products, including some of the nation's best wines.

Got Milk? Indeed.

Milk is New York's top agricultural product, and the state is the nation's third biggest producer. In 2002, its 678,000 cows produced 12.2 million pounds of milk, up 4 percent from the year before. Output per cow also increased to 18,019 pounds per annum, up 3 percent.

But that is only the tip of the ice cream sundae. New York had 122 plants producing dairy products in 2002, 11 percent of all such facilities in the United States. The Empire State is the largest producer of cottage cheese in the nation, both in the creamed and low-fat versions. Creamed cottage cheese production reached 60.5 million pounds in 2002, while dairy farmers produced 88.4 million pounds of the low-fat kind; this represents 24 percent of the nation's total output.

For other types of cheese, New York State ranked third in the country, producing a total of 717 million pounds, up 2 percent from the prior year's figure. In particular, the state made 12 percent of all the Italian cheese produced in this country—414 million pounds' worth—an increase of 2 percent from 2001.

Other commodities received attention in 2002 from New York State's dairy entrepreneurs. Butter production jumped by 8 percent that year to 28.3 million pounds. The state churned out 248.8 million pounds of yogurt in both plain and flavored versions and—for those seeking higher calorie counts—36.4 million pounds of ice cream.

In addition, New York State marketed 211 million pounds of meat in 2002. It ranks second nationwide in calves for slaughter, third in milk cows, and ninth in sheep and lambs.

Blooming Plants

When it comes to the plants and flowers that beautify homes and offices, New York State is a leader. It ranks sixth in the nation in commercial sales of floriculture products, with a value of $185 million in 2002. This was up by 7 percent from the previous year, which compared favorably to a 3 percent rise in the same period, nationwide. Bedding and garden plants comprised the largest sector in this activity, with sales of $104 million, a 7 percent increase. Sales of potted flowering plants brought in $47 million, up by 17 percent, while the value of cut flowers sold by New York State growers was $5.7 million, a figure 26 percent greater than the previous year's.

Crops of the Field, Fruits of the Vine

The Empire State is the fourth biggest in the country in reaping corn for silage and 21st in corn used for grain. Total cash value for this crop in 2002 was $65 million.

Apples are another winner for New York State, which ranks second in the

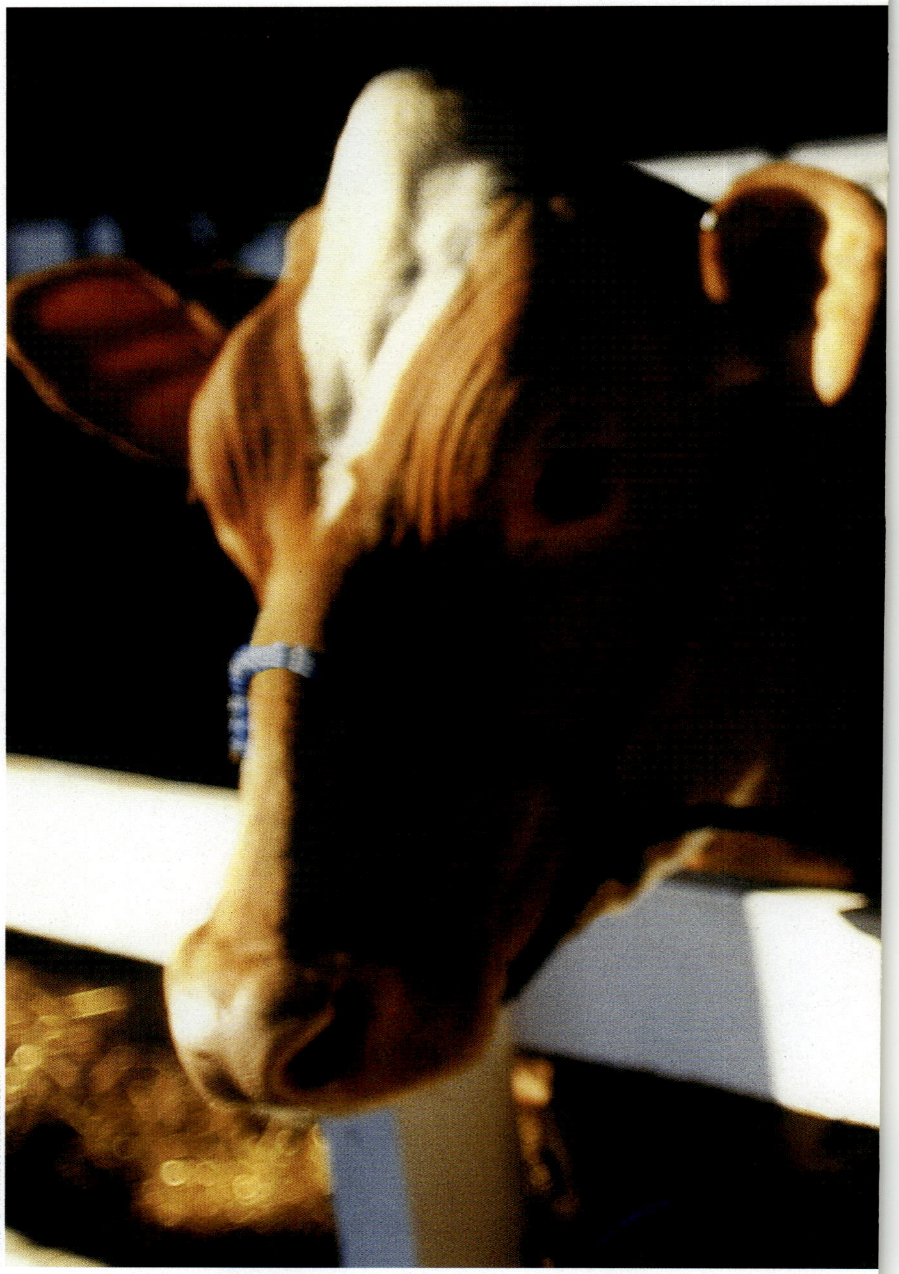

Photo: © www.scottbarrow.com

Fairs across New York celebrate the state's diverse agricultural economy, showing off animals like these dairy cows, which play such an important role in the industry. Milk is the state's leading agricultural product—in fact, it accounts for more than half of New York's total agricultural receipts each year. Wyoming County is the state's top milk producer.

Photo: © www.scottbarrow.com

New York's apple-growing history dates to the early 1700s, when missionaries and Colonists first began planting orchards. In 1730, the country's first commercial apple tree nursery was founded in Oyster Bay, Long Island. Today, McIntosh, Red Delicious, Empire, Rome, and Idared are the state's most popular apples.

The Empire State ranks third in the country (behind California and Washington) for wine and juice production, with about a third of grape crops used for making wine. New York boasts more than 125 wineries, which produce everything from merlots, cabernets, and chardonnays to blushes, ports, and special blends.

Photo: © www.scottbarrow.com

nation as a producer of the original health food, representing 12 percent of the country's total crop. Each year, 55,000 acres provide a harvest of more than a billion pounds of glowing apples, which returned $109 million to the state's farmers in 2002.

New York ranks number two among all states in production of cabbage and has healthy crops of other crucifers such as broccoli, cauliflower, brussels sprouts, turnips, and mustard greens. The fresh cabbage crop alone brought in $49 million in 2002.

The Empire State is also the sixth largest producer of onions, bringing forth bushels of the pungent yellow globes. More than 12,000 acres produced $34 million worth of onions in 2002.

Another New York staple is maple syrup. The state ranks second (behind Vermont) in the value of its maple syrup, producing 210,000 gallons of the golden nectar in 2003.

Grapes are another crop that often bears a "Grown in New York" stamp. The state ranks fourth in the nation in production of wine grapes, with 7,000 acres dedicated to this crop, returning $7.5 million each year. The state does even better when it comes to grapes for juices, jams, and jellies, ranking second in the country, producing 28 percent of the nation's output. This represents 25,000 acres, with a yearly return of $33 million.

Vintage New York

Wine is one of those delights that make a meal special. Walking through the canyons of Manhattan, a visitor may find it hard to believe that the first New York vines were planted near Wall Street, by Dutch settlers in the 1600s. Since then, wine making has become an important New York State economic sector, with more than 125 wineries. The state now makes wine in 32 of its 62 counties. As a result, vintners can be found almost everywhere; Long Island, for example, has 29 wineries. The most important areas, however, are the Finger Lakes, especially around Canandaigua, Seneca, and Cayuga Lakes; and near Lake Erie, in the southwestern part of the state. Chautauqua County, in this latter zone, is the second largest grape growing county outside of California, based on its 20,000 acres of vineyards. Overall wine production in the state is 150 million bottles a year, for a cash value of more than $300 million. Two thousand individuals work in wineries, with another 12,000 employed in vineyards, while almost 900,000 tourists visit the state's wine country each year.

The wine leader in New York is Canandaigua Wine Company, the second largest wine company in the world and producer of brands such as Almaden, Inglenook, Ste. Chapelle, Manischewitz, Paul Masson, and Cribari. The winemaker's parent firm, Canandaigua Brands, has acquired so many other lines—not just in wines but also in spirits and beer—that it changed its name in 2000 to Constellation

Brands, reflecting the flock of choices it offers. Constellation, headquartered in Fairport, handles 200-plus brand names and had 2003 sales of $3.6 billion.

Empire State beer producers include High Falls Brewing Company in Rochester, the fifth largest brewer in America. Best known for its Genesee line, High Falls produces a number of gourmet products as well, such as JW Dundee's Honey Brown Lager and Michael Shea's Irish Amber. These products are sold in 41 states and Canada.

To Market, To Market

With all this natural abundance, it stands to reason that food processing is a thriving business in the state. Rich Products Corporation in Buffalo not only makes soy-based whipped toppings and a nondairy coffee creamer, it also creates products ranging from bakery dough to seafood. In 2002, it enjoyed sales of $1.2 billion, up 4.8 percent from the previous year, and had 6,500 employees. The Dannon Company in Tarrytown makes the second biggest-selling yogurt brand in the United States, and had 2001 sales of $572 million. Seneca Foods of Marion cans and freezes vegetables for a number of brand names, including Libby's. Its 2003 sales reached $644 million, and the company employs 2,300. The Pro-Fac Cooperative in Rochester coordinates the work of its 548 member-owners, marketing and distributing produce, bringing in revenues of $104 million.

Research Support

One of the reasons agriculture has prospered in New York State is the research support it has received for more than a century. New York is one of only two states, along with Connecticut, to have an agricultural experimental station, funded by New York State and run by Cornell University's College of Agriculture and Life Sciences. Established in 1880, it now boasts 253 staff and 50 professors, with another 15 research associates as well as visiting scientists from around the globe. The facility has a 900-acre campus, and its four primary departments are entomology, which works to control insect pests; food science and technology, which discovers new ways of handling and processing foods after they are harvested; horticultural sciences, which specializes in developing new plant breeds; and plant pathology, which devises solutions to plant diseases. Among the advances created at this facility is the gene gun, which enables scientists to transplant genetic material down to the level of DNA into plant nuclei, thus producing new strains with features such as higher yield or resistance to bacteria and fungi.

New York State is an agricultural powerhouse, ripe for development not only because of the abundance of its soil but also the diversity of its crops. This enables it to withstand shifts in the market and to forge ahead, creating new products for a new century.

From left: A wide variety of foods, including canned vegetables and fruits, sauces, and specialty products, are produced by New York–based food processing companies; beer, juice, and soda are among the beverages made and bottled in the state; New York ranks fifth in the nation for green peas for processing.

Photos: Left to right, © Koopman/CORBIS; © Gary D. Landsman/CORBIS; © Brendan Regan/CORBIS

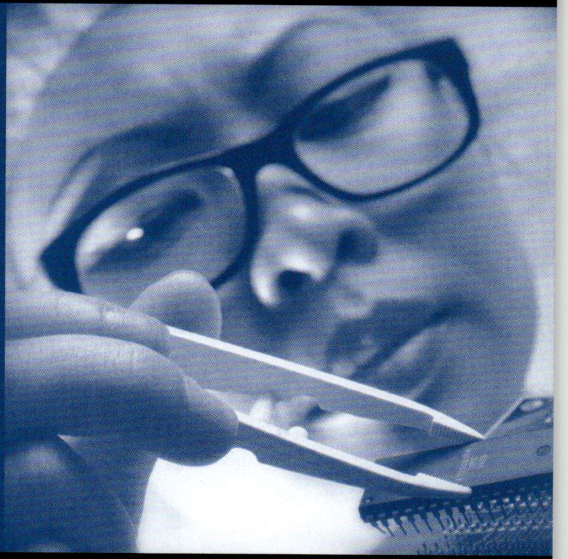

Emerging Technology

BAE Systems

Whether producing subsystems that manage critical flight functions on *Air Force One*, improving battlespace communications and threat response, or developing remote monitoring systems for public utilities, this company keeps New York State at the forefront of the aerospace and defense industry.

Hybrid electric drive systems developed and produced by BAE Systems in Johnson City, New York, power a new generation of clean, efficient buses for New York City.

From fighter jets to naval ships, guided weapons to global satellite imaging, and military communications networks to low-emission transit buses, BAE Systems is a major force in the aerospace and defense industry—and in the technology landscape of New York State.

Three units of Rockville, Maryland–based BAE Systems North America operate from the Empire State, employing 2,500 people on Long Island, in the Southern Tier, and in Central New York. Its products and capabilities can be found on most military and commercial aircraft and deliver the forefront of innovation and performance to American and allied military forces.

Johnson City, in the Southern Tier, is home to the company's Platform Solutions business. Military aircraft including the F/A-18 Hornet fighter, C-17 Globemaster III tactical transport aircraft, H-60 Black Hawk helicopter, and Air Force One presidential aircraft depend on electronic subsystems from BAE Systems that manage critical flight and engine control functions. And every day, commercial airline passengers count on the industry-leading reliability of the company's electronic engine controls. Every three seconds, a commercial plane equipped with BAE Systems engine controls takes off somewhere in the world.

At a time when the military services look to industry for solutions that both safeguard and maximize the effectiveness of combat troops, Platform Solutions is developing leading-edge technology to make the multiservice, multinational Joint Strike Fighter the most capable combat aircraft in history. And it is applying decades of experience in fielding high-performance electronics for piloted aircraft to a new generation of unmanned aircraft that will allow dangerous missions to be flown without putting pilots in harm's way.

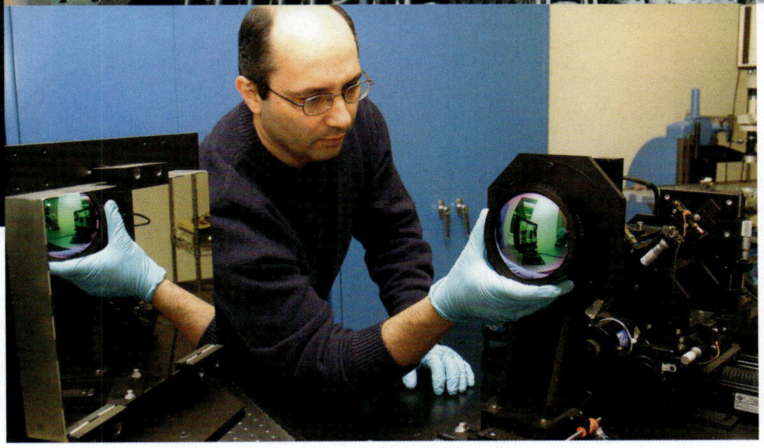

Platform Solutions is applying that same innovative spirit to military ground vehicles, both manned and unmanned, and to hybrid electric drive systems for transit buses that dramatically reduce emissions and improve fuel economy.

In Greenlawn, in the heart of Long Island, BAE Systems Communication, Navigation, Identification, and Reconnaissance (CNIR) provides technology solutions that enable the military services to detect and respond to enemy threats. As a world leader in electronic "friend or foe" systems, CNIR enables forces to distinguish friendly forces from enemy combatants with systems operating on numerous aircraft and ships. Among the significant components of these systems are award-winning antennas installed on aircraft, deployed on the battlefield, and worn by soldiers.

CNIR is an innovator in aerial reconnaissance and electro-optic systems, deploying leading-edge technology such as high-resolution imaging and night vision, and is a leader in airborne command and control and tactical reconnaissance and surveillance systems. It also is building on a long history of success in networked battlespace communications—technology that has proved itself time and again in the war on terrorism—preparing for a future where military superiority will be attained through sophisticated networks relaying real-time information among ground, naval, and air forces.

Technology developed in Greenlawn for military purposes also has found civilian uses. These include a remote monitoring system, developed for Consolidated Edison Company of New York, that provides central monitoring of underground electrical transformers, enabling crews to target trouble spots and more effectively avert power outages.

In Central New York, the BAE Systems Mission Solutions Northeast Engineering Development Center in Rome develops and supports software that is critical to viewing and managing satellite images and Earth mappings. The Rome facility's Image Product Library software provides accurate imagery, imagery intelligence, and geospatial information to the National Geospatial-Intelligence Agency for military and civilian uses.

Far left: BAE Systems delivers ruggedized, ultra-high-resolution display technology for applications on land, at sea, and in the air. Above: At the BAE Systems Johnson City plant, components for control electronics for military aircraft are assembled using high speed, automated production equipment. Left: A technician at the BAE Systems optics laboratory in Greenlawn, Long Island, tests an infrared lens assembly. The laboratory was opened in 2002.

Manufacturing & Distribution

L. & J. G. Stickley, Inc.

For more than a century, L. & J. G. Stickley, Inc., has defined an American aesthetic of timeless, handcrafted furniture and accessories—objects that are as much art and architecture as they are 'furniture rooted in the past, designed for the present, and destined for the future.'

Right: The fine furniture created for home and office by L. & J. G. Stickley, Inc., of Manlius, New York, includes a number of collections, from traditional to contemporary. Shown here is the Coates Arm Chair from the Williamsburg Reserve Collection.

To describe L. & J. G. Stickley, Inc., and its creations as legends is no exaggeration. The highly prized mission style of furniture continues to be synonymous the world over with the Stickley name. Stickley, however, produces more than a single style of home furnishings. Stickley encompasses a complete line of classic to traditional to future-forward home and office collections that are varied in their design periods and styles but unified by the standard renowned as "the Stickley Difference"—authentic designs and integrity of construction.

Stickley traces its heritage to 1900, when brothers Leopold and John George Stickley bought a furniture factory in Fayetteville, New York, and launched their first furniture line. Their Mission Oak Collection, a new aesthetic of sturdy construction and stark beauty, was a design rebellion against the ornate Victorian furniture of the time.

Alfred J. and Aminy I. Audi acquired the legendary manufacturer in 1974, and quickly reinvigorated the company's legacy. In 1985, the Audis moved manufacturing operations to Manlius, New York, and expanded into a 400,000-square-foot, state-of-the-art facility, employing more than 1,300 artisans. Alfred Audi serves as president of L. & J. G. Stickley, Inc., the manufacturing arm, and Aminy Audi serves as president of Stickley, Audi & Co., the retailing arm.

Past and Present Perfect

Stickley's heritage line includes its historic Mission Collection and the exquisite Williamsburg Reserve, Traditional, and French Collections. The Mission Collection, which has grown to more than 700 pieces, is a trove of reissued and new pieces. The Williamsburg Reserve Collection, with reproductions and adaptations of 18th-century and 19th-century American designs, is the result of an exclusive licensing agreement between Stickley and the Colonial Williamsburg Foundation in Virginia. The Traditional Collection, the most extensive of all the Stickley collections, features home and executive office furnishings that are designed for the present yet destined to become family heirlooms. The French Collection, with pieces reflecting 18th-century French style, is an example of Stickley's continuing diversification.

Stickley's contemporary lines include the Metropolitan Collection and the

21st Century Collection. The Metropolitan Collection—elegant and sophisticated, yet thoroughly modern —combines substance and style for today's lifestyles. Embracing the past and the future, the 21st Century Collection is a dramatic evolution of Stickley's mission style. To complement both the heritage and modern collections, Stickley also offers Stickley Fine Upholstery and Stickley Designer Rugs.

Future Growth and Success

Just as Stickley leads and succeeds in its home designs and products, the company leads in its business and employment practices. The company is dedicated to investing in its home state and the country. Toward this end, in 2002, Stickley acquired the John Widdicomb Company, established in 1858 in Grand Rapids, Michigan. Now operating as a division of Stickley, the John Widdicomb Collection is manufactured in Manlius and includes nearly 100 French, Italian, English, and Russian reproductions, as well as a broad range of early 20th-century Moderne pieces.

In 2004, Stickley also acquired the assets of Cibola Leather in Hickory, North Carolina, and changed the name of the company's products to Craftsman Leather by Stickley. The same year, Stickley and George Pataki, governor of New York, announced that Stickley would invest approximately $6 million to expand its Manlius production facility. The expansion includes the construction of a new high-bay warehouse and a reconfiguration of the factory finishing room and rough mill, and 30 new jobs will be created.

The investment makes Stickley eligible to apply for a capital grant from Empire State Development, a division of the state Department of Economic Development, whose mission is to promote business growth in the state.

"We believe in investing in New York State," says Aminy Audi. "And we are growing our business here. We are grateful to the governor for seeing the need to create incentives for companies to remain in this country and to be able to be competitive globally."

Above: The Stickley French Collection features the La Rochelle bedroom, with sleigh bed. Above left: The Hepplewhite Dining Table, Arm Chair, Side Chairs, and Breakfront are part of the Traditional Collection. Far left: In the Mission Collection is the Harvey Ellis Fall-Front Bookcase and Side Chair. Left: The Limbert Tabouret Table and Café Chair were designed by Charles Limbert, a contemporary of Gustav and Leopold Stickley, and are part of the Limbert Collection.

BorgWarner Morse TEC

This global leader in the design and manufacture of automotive chain systems and components has built its success upon cutting-edge technology, commitment to service and quality, and a strategic global presence balanced by a close working relationship with its customers.

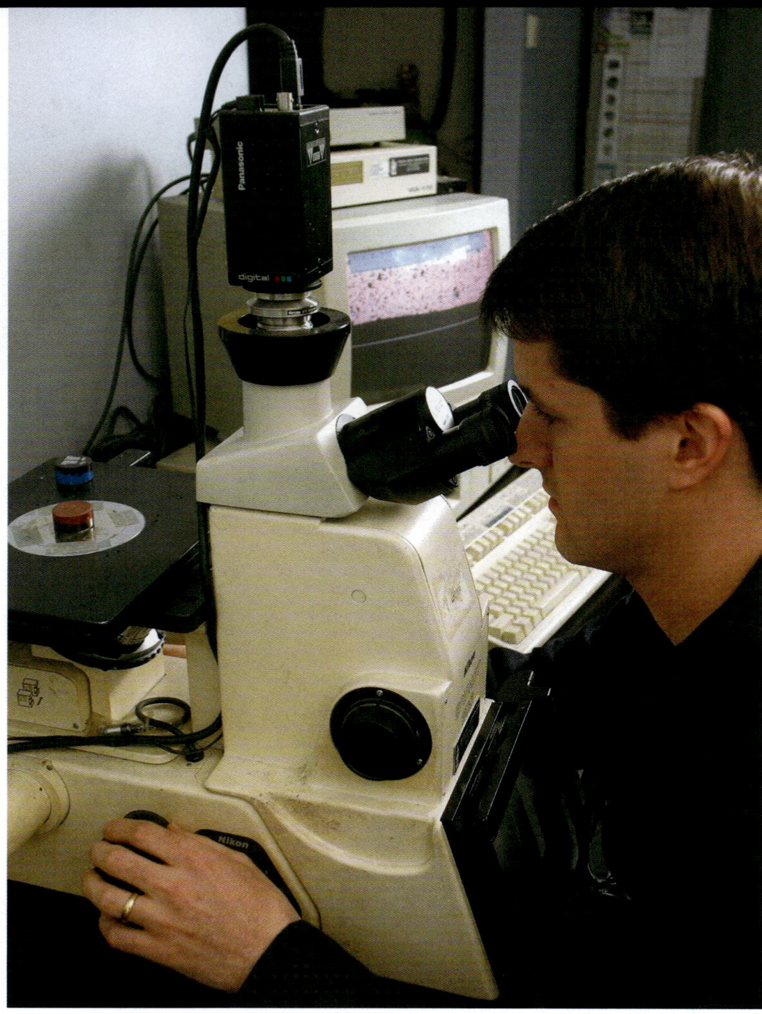

In automotive systems design as well as manufacture, attention to detail is critical. Here, a BorgWarner Morse TEC engineer examines the microstructure of a timing system component to ensure performance reliability.

In the rugged automotive supply market, leadership demands substance, substance in the form of a strategic global presence, advanced technology, a commitment to quality and continuous improvement, speed to market, and next-generation technology. Across the globe, as the auto industry seeks out suppliers with these attributes, the market demands BorgWarner Morse TEC. Among the world's most highly respected tier one suppliers, Morse TEC has set a global standard for engine, transmission, and transfer case chain systems. This position of product leadership has derived from Morse TEC's level of experience, its scope, and its ability to anticipate and meet the needs of its customers.

Established in 1880 in the small, central New York community of Trumansburg, Morse TEC joined BorgWarner in 1929. Today, Morse TEC is one of five major operating groups of BorgWarner Inc. Chicago-based BorgWarner is a product leader in highly engineered components and systems for vehicle power train applications worldwide and operates 43 manufacturing and technical facilities in 14 countries. Morse TEC operates 13 facilities in eight countries. From its headquarters in Ithaca, New York, home to 1,550 of its 3,000 employees worldwide, the company continues to grow with and for the automotive industry around the world.

Morse TEC understands that a close working relationship with its customers is essential. By providing the forward-looking services and capabilities expected from a product leader, Morse TEC ensures the development of timely, cost-effective solutions. From up-front component and system design to manufacturing facilities that assure global coverage, Morse TEC is in a class by itself.

With a history of investment in its manufacturing processes and product development, Morse TEC consistently creates new techniques and concepts. Leveraging these ideas worldwide creates a synergy that results in world-class products.

Morse TEC drives advanced technology from the simulated work of the laboratory to the real world of the road with exceptional talent and dedication. Integrating a strong research and development program with the latest equipment and technology, Morse TEC consistently maximizes the value that its products provide to its customers. Working as a design partner with its customers, Morse TEC uses design and modeling tools to create the best system for the operating environment.

Performance, price, quality, and on-time delivery are Morse TEC's priorities. Continuous improvement in these critical factors is the goal of the entire organization. Employees understand the importance of this goal to the customer, and this shared dedication is the foundation of Morse TEC.

Morse TEC understands that quality of life plays a critical role in each individual's ability to succeed. Since each employee's success is linked to the company's success, Morse TEC is committed to encouraging individual employee growth and the development of a sense of belonging and to providing opportunities for its employees to participate in meaningful ways. The company is further committed to recognizing the importance of the obligations, dreams, and desires that are elemental parts of life beyond the workplace. Being a part of the Central New York community assists Morse TEC in helping its employees satisfy their quest for that quality of life that is essential to their well-being. And in turn, those employees contribute their skills and their knowledge to bring success to Morse TEC.

Morse TEC is committed to the communities in which its people live and work. This strong sense of commitment is demonstrated regularly through both the company's philanthropic support of local nonprofit organizations and through encouragement of its employees' involvement in these same community organizations.

Morse TEC's success derives from its ability to stay ahead of the technology curve, never relinquishing its position as a pacesetter in the advancement of automotive technology. Morse TEC has grown with the automotive industry with a proven track record of accomplishment. Morse TEC has the knowledge, the technical dexterity and flexibility, the global presence, and the broad range of product capabilities to provide its customers with the industry's best chain systems and components, now and in the future.

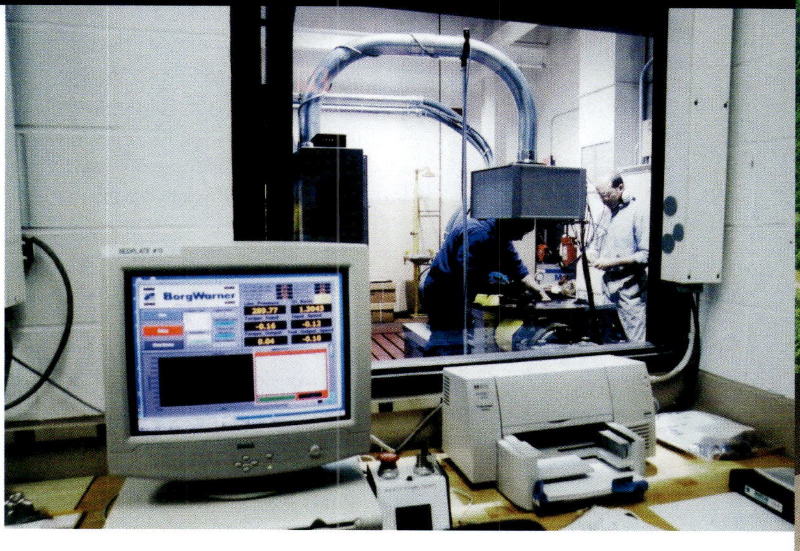

Above: The BorgWarner Morse TEC headquarters in Ithaca, New York, is a 163-acre site that includes a technical center for advanced product development and two manufacturing facilities. An additional manufacturing facility is located nearby. Above left: State-of-the-art engineering laboratories provide for the development of innovative product designs. Left: Manufacturing technology has provided Morse TEC with a competitive edge in the automotive marketplace. Here, a member of the manufacturing design team develops the latest tool designs.

Photos: Top left and bottom, © Dewey Neild; top right, © Aerial Photography

Mohawk Paper Mills, Inc.

This technologically advanced, environmentally sensitive manufacturer of fine printing stock is known for innovation, service, and the quality of its premium text and cover papers, including uncoated paper, digital and color copy papers, and a broad range of top quality recycled papers.

Tom O'Connor Jr. is president and CEO of Mohawk Paper Mills, Inc.

Founded in 1931 near Albany, New York, where the Hudson and Mohawk Rivers come together, Mohawk Paper Mills, Inc., is a leading North American manufacturer of fine printing paper. Well known to commercial printers for innovation, service, and quality, Mohawk operates two mills and three paper machines, with more than 100,000 tons of capacity, and has over 375 employees.

This highly competitive producer of low-cost premium papers for offset and digital printing offers a forward-looking product line of uncoated, coated, and digital printing papers. Mohawk's first entry into the commercial printing market is still one of America's best-known brands. Mohawk Superfine was introduced in 1946 and is widely considered a benchmark for premium uncoated papers. Building on the foundational quality of Superfine, Mohawk began developing its patented Inxwell® process in 1995. Mohawk Options and Navajo papers feature this exclusive surface treatment, which is designed to improve the ink holdout, printability, and opacity of premium uncoated printing papers. Then, in 1998, Mohawk began developing its extensive line of digital and color copy papers. Today, Mohawk supplies the basic ingredient—paper—for a myriad of documents ranging from annual reports, proposals, and company newsletters to wedding invitations and high-end illustrated books.

Despite a challenging economy and changing communications industry, Mohawk continues to thrive by combining service and logistics innovations with superior products. For example, the company opened its Specialty Converting Center in 2001. This best-in-class facility not only converts Mohawk papers for the highly technical digital market, but also serves a wide range of other clients, including paper mills, paper merchants, retailers, and original equipment manufacturers (OEMs). Then, in 2002, the company added warehouse locations to include Atlanta, Georgia; Reno, Nevada; and Albany, New York. As an independently owned company, Mohawk is able to react quickly to changing industry conditions and to continue critical investing in plants and equipment. As a result, Mohawk is not only a low-cost producer in its niche of premium text and cover papers, but also boasts a diverse customer base that includes printers, corporate customers, and digital equipment manufacturers in North America and overseas.

In addition to building a profitable and successful manufacturing enterprise, the company is also committed to pursuing environmental excellence in all its operations. Well known in the industry for its high environmental standards and sustainable practices, Mohawk strives to minimize environmental impacts through biosphere protection measures, sustainable use of natural resources and energy, waste reduction and recycling initiatives, energy conservation, and ongoing programs focused on environmental risk reduction. The company offers a broad range of recycled papers certified by Green Seal (an independent, nonprofit organization that identifies and promotes environmentally friendly products) and the Forest Stewardship Council (FSC), a nonprofit group that encourages responsible management of forests. And finally, in 2003, Mohawk became the first major manufacturing company in New York State—and the first paper mill in the nation to derive a significant amount of its energy from renewable wind power.

Above: Mohawk's pickup backstands are capable of unwinding rolls of paper of up to 60 inches in diameter. Left: At the Mohawk Specialty Converting Center, the Jennerjahn rewinder converts both small format and wide format rolls. Far left: Packaged reams of finished paper trundle off the line at Mohawk Paper Mills.

New Technologies

Mohawk, known for its innovative products and practices (such as its exclusive Inxwell process, to take just one example), also manufactures the leading brand of premium papers for high-end color digital printers and color copiers—the fastest growing market segments in the print industry. Mohawk Digital papers are designed to work across different platforms on all digital and offset equipment. Mohawk Digital papers possess characteristics that set them apart for offset printing—outstanding formation, brightness, and smoothness—and make them an excellent choice for digital printing.

Mohawk Color Copy is a highly successful new product line that features Mohawk's proprietary new Digital Imaging Surface™, a unique technology from Mohawk that creates an even, uniform, smooth paper for superior color copies with extraordinary toner adhesion. Winner of *Electronic Publishing* magazine's "Best New Product Award" in 2003, Mohawk Color Copy has created a new category of highly differentiated premium papers for the professional color copier market.

Mohawk Paper Mills today is a blend of the best of the old economy and the new economy, and is seen as a market leader by its customers in the United States and internationally. Above all, Mohawk Paper Mills strives to remain a technologically advanced, environmentally sensitive company committed to providing its customers with the highest quality papers and service at competitive prices.

New Venture Gear, Inc.

New Venture Gear produces transaxles, drivetrains, and four-wheel-drive transfer cases for some of the world's most famous automobiles at its New Process Gear manufacturing division in East Syracuse, New York, with the mission of making Central New York the 'four-wheel-drive capital of the world.'

The New Venture Gear, Inc., division New Process Gear is the world's largest designer and manufacturer of four-wheel-drive transfer cases. Its mission of making Central New York the "four-wheel-drive capital of the world" was founded in the New Process family of companies dating back to the late 1800s.

In 1888, the New Process Rawhide Company was formed in Auburn, New York, as a manufacturer of rawhide boats. The company's ingenuity started to show before long. It was discovered that New Process Rawhide's patented process for making strong and hard rawhide could be converted to manufacture rawhide gears. These gears were initially used in trolleys, and ultimately this led to the manufacturing of steel gears for the automotive industry. As the 20th century approached, the company was no longer manufacturing rawhide gears, and in 1912 it was renamed the New Process Gear Corporation (NPG). NPG has had some dynamic leaders, including Walter P. Chrysler, the founder of Chrysler Corporation, and Anthony A. Henninger, who later became the mayor of Syracuse, to name just two.

The U.S. manufacturing arm of Troy, Michigan–based New Venture Gear, Inc., is New Process Gear, headquartered in East Syracuse, New York.

A premier manufacturer of drivetrain components, NPG produces transfer cases, front-wheel-drive manual transaxles, and automatic transmission overdrives. With its great diversity and expertise, in 1990 NPG became part of the first joint venture between two of the Big Three automobile producers in the United States—Chrysler and General Motors. NPG combined with the General Motors Muncie, Indiana, Hydramatic plant and New Venture Gear was formed, with headquarters in Troy, Michigan, and manufacturing plants in Indiana and New York.

In the late 1990s, New Venture Gear became a multinational corporation, opening its third manufacturing facility, in Roitzsch, Germany. New Venture Gear has a broad customer base, including DaimlerChrysler, General Motors, Ford Motor Company, BMW, Volkswagen, and Porsche, with exports to companies across the world.

The NPG New York manufacturing plant was moved from Auburn to Syracuse and then to its present location (shown above) in East Syracuse. Built in 1960, this facility was expanded with several additions over the years as the demand for its products increased. The NPG complex is now approximately 1.7 million square feet and employs approximately 3,000 workers. When its Engineering and Product Development Laboratories were added in 1995, NPG became a full-service automotive supplier. "We can provide design, prototypes, manufacturing, and assembly for a wide variety of drivetrain systems all under one roof," says Michael Baur, vice president and division manager of the New Process Gear division of New Venture Gear. "This is a great asset to our community, our company, and our customers." New Process Gear is not standing still. It is with an eye to the future that it is developing a new generation of all-wheel-drive and traction-control products for use worldwide.

Advertising & Public Relations

DDB Worldwide Communications Group Inc

This highly respected, award-winning global agency network of self-avowed 'enemies of the ordinary' is responsible for creating some of the most memorable, amusing, and innovative advertisements for such well-known clients as Budweiser, McDonald's, and Volkswagen.

At DDB Worldwide Communications Group Inc, creativity is regarded as the most powerful force in the business. With 206 offices in 96 countries, DDB pairs the resources of one of the world's largest advertising agency networks with the creative culture of a boutique firm. While enjoying global network support, DDB New York has the freedom it needs to realize its distinct vision for its New York clients. DDB New York clients include many of America's leading brands and companies, such as CIGNA, Exxon Mobil Corporation, Johnson & Johnson, Merck, NYC2012, the New York Lottery, and Philips North America. DDB New York created 80 percent global awareness and over 30 percent name awareness of the merger of Exxon and Mobil one week after the campaign launched. When it was charged with launching Amsterdam-based ING into the United States, DDB New York created a campaign that brought unaided awareness of the brand from 0 percent to 31 percent within two years.

The DDB global network provides clients with traditional advertising, direct marketing, sales promotion, strategic consulting, and through Tribal DDB Worldwide, digital marketing. The agencies—all of them "enemies of the ordinary"—create and support brand campaigns for such giants as Anheuser-Busch, Bayer, Dell, Hershey Foods Corporation, Johnson & Johnson, McDonald's Corporation, Merck, Royal Philips Corporation, and Volkswagen AG.

Ned Doyle and Maxwell Dane established the agency in 1949 with legendary copywriter Bill Bernbach. Doyle Dane Bernbach was founded on the principle that it is not enough to touch the mind of the consumer—to sell, one must touch the heart as well. This continues to resonate with clients today.

In 1986, the agency merged with Needham Harper Worldwide to form DDB Needham Worldwide. In 1999, the agency simplified its name to DDB Worldwide in recognition of its heritage and the global importance of the DDB brand.

For its creativity and effectiveness, DDB has earned the respect of its peers. It has won more Grand Prix awards during the 50-year history of the International Advertising Festival in Cannes than any other agency network. Its creations have been hailed as classics, including the 1959 Volkswagen campaign, which was voted in 1999 by *Advertising Age* as the number one campaign of all time. In the 20 years from 1983 to 2003, DDB agencies in 22 countries won the "Agency of the Year" title. DDB was named Network Agency of the Year at the Clio Awards in 2001, 2002, 2003, and 2004. Also in 2004, *Advertising Age* named DDB its Global Agency Network of the Year and *Adweek* magazine named DDB its Global Agency of the Year.

And how does DDB do what it does? As Bernbach put it, "It's not just what you say that stirs people. It's the way that you say it."

Media & Publishing

Thirteen/WNET New York

This pioneering broadcaster produces and presents programming via the Public Broadcasting Service (PBS) for millions of viewers in the New York metropolitan area and across the United States from its new state-of-the-art digital and broadcast facility in midtown Manhattan.

Thirteen/WNET New York's productions and broadcasts reach people of all ages, interests, and walks of life.

Photos: From left, top row, © Sesame Workshop, © Jamie Bloomquist, © Alistair Muir/Joan Marcus;

On September 16, 1962, Edward R. Murrow ushered New York City's first noncommercial television station onto the airwaves with a caveat: "This instrument can teach, it can illuminate, yes, and it can even inspire," the distinguished journalist said, "but it can do so only to the extent that humans are determined to use it to those ends. Otherwise, it will be merely lights and wires in a box."

The journey preceding this debut of Thirteen/WNET New York was a long and arduous one, undertaken by a grassroots citizens group that got the attention of Federal Communications Commission (FCC) chairman Newton Minnow. With the encouragement of then-president John F. Kennedy, Minnow, who had famously dubbed television a "vast wasteland," helped convince Washington that the largest metropolitan area in the nation deserved to have a television station that would be used for the public good.

Today, Thirteen is a major producer for the Public Broadcasting Service (PBS), operating out of a new, state-of-the-art digital production and broadcast facility in midtown Manhattan. The box with "lights and wires" is now filled with microchips and semiconductors, and the spectrum has been divided into a proliferation of channels. But one thing that has not changed is Thirteen's commitment to its educational mission and the vital community it serves.

As the flagship public broadcaster for the New York metropolitan area—which includes New York, New Jersey, and Connecticut—Thirteen reaches millions of viewers with public television programs produced around the nation and its own local productions that explore the region's rich culture and astonishing diversity. As a producer and presenter for PBS, Thirteen engages audiences nationwide with such acclaimed series as *Nature*, *Great Performances*, *American Masters*, *Religion & Ethics NewsWeekly*, *Wide Angle*, and

Cyberchase, as well as the work of another distinguished broadcast journalist, Bill Moyers.

Thirteen has made definitive contributions to the history of television, pioneering entirely new genres. One example is *An American Family* (1973), arguably television's first reality series, which anthropologist Margaret Mead called ". . . a new way in which people can learn to look at life, by seeing the real life of others interpreted by the camera." *The NewsHour*, with Robert MacNeil and Jim Lehrer, began at Thirteen as television's first hour-long national news program. *Charlie Rose* set the standard for informed, insightful conversation with the day's newsmakers. Thirteen's landmark documentaries in the sciences and humanities, including *Heritage: Civilization and the Jews*, *American Visions*, and *New York: A Documentary Film*, have transformed the television landscape into a place of enlightenment and adventure.

Thirteen is taking advantage of advances in technology to enhance its educational mission. It has been a leader in the production of high quality digital programming and in the creation of innovative Web sites and CD-ROMs, computer software, and other products.

As broadcast and digital media converge, Thirteen is effectively positioned for a future in which television will be an interactive experience, rich with information and immediacy. Thirteen has merged with its sister station, WLIW21 New York Public Television, located on Long Island, and also has inaugurated a suite of exciting new digital and video-on-demand channels.

Thirteen has enjoyed a long tradition of going beyond the screen directly into the community with outreach activities that have made a viable difference in people's lives. Teacher training and health awareness campaigns are just two examples. Thirteen further demonstrated its commitment to the community after the September 11, 2001, terrorist attacks, which took the life of Thirteen transmitter engineer Gerard "Rod" Coppola, who was at his post atop Tower One of the World Trade Center that day. In the wake of the tragedy, Thirteen opened its doors to the Red Cross and the Mayor's Office of Emergency Management, which set up operations at Thirteen's midtown Manhattan facility. In the ensuing days and months, Thirteen also provided New Yorkers and the nation with information, analyses, and perspective by presenting special programs and online materials.

More than 40 years after its first broadcast, Thirteen continues to live up to the challenge inherent in the wise words of Edward R. Murrow, proving that the powerful, ubiquitous medium of television can be a positive force in people's lives—teaching, illuminating, and, yes, even inspiring.

Above left: The Thirteen/WNET New York production and broadcast center is located in midtown Manhattan, in the heart of the community it serves. Above: From a state-of-the-art master control room at the center, programming is beamed to millions of viewers.

Both photos: © Joe Sinnott

WNBC

The pioneering station that produced the first national commercial television program is today a powerful network television broadcaster and leader in local news programming for the New York metropolitan area.

Above: WNBC began setting the pace with its news coverage in the early days of television. Shown here, WNBT cameras capture a story in the streets of New York in 1948.

July 1, 1941, marked an event that would change American social culture forever: the debut of national commercial television. At 1:29 P.M., WNBC became the nation's first station to sign on the air, as WNBT, setting a precedent of company firsts that would continue throughout the decades and into the 21st century.

That day, along with its first national telecast—a Brooklyn Dodgers vs. Philadelphia Phillies baseball game live from Ebbets Field—WNBC brought viewers the first television commercials. As a Bulova clock marked time in a corner of the station's test pattern and Irene Hubbard's dishpan hands found relief in Ivory soapsuds, a tradition was born.

It was natural that the station would set the pace in its groundbreaking industry. Its parent company, RCA, a leading name in radio of the era, had begun in 1928 to pour profits from its lucrative networks into television research. By January 1930, W2XBS—RCA's pioneer television laboratory and experimental station—transmitted the company's first television program from the Fifth Avenue studios of NBC Radio to an audience at a theater about 20 blocks away. At the end of the summer, NBC assumed control of W2XBS operations.

Energized by W2XBS's success, NBC installed a transmitter atop the Empire State Building and began experimental telecasts in 1931. Its technicians would refine the process for another eight years until the defining moment arrived on April 30, 1939: With a telecast of then-president Franklin D. Roosevelt opening the New York World's Fair, W2XBS began transmitting the U.S. television industry's first regularly scheduled local programming.

December 1941 saw regular programming interrupted for a special news bulletin—the attack on Pearl Harbor—which was the forerunner of WNBC's renowned special news coverage. Wartime also brought the use of television technology for purposes such as distance learning. NBC installed television sets in New York City Police Department Precinct Station Houses and conducted televised instruction for air-raid and fire wardens.

Today, WNBC has emerged as a powerful network television broadcaster and leader in local news programming. The 11 P.M. news team, featuring co-anchors Chuck Scarborough and Sue Simmons, sports anchor Len Berman, and meteorologist Janice Huff, embodies the verve and vitality of the city that never sleeps. Scarborough and Simmons, together nearly 25 years, are among the top anchor teams in the business. The cover of the *New York Daily News* for August 10, 2003, featured the pair with the headline "The Best."

WNBC is the nation's leading revenue-producing station, and its decision makers have a clear understanding of how it got there. The station vigorously supports its base,

Far left: One of the most recognizable anchor teams in the business, Chuck Scarborough and Sue Simmons have worked together at Channel 4 in New York for nearly 25 years. Left: The annual Rockefeller Center Tree Lighting Ceremony is just one of the many community events aired on the station.

the diverse and energetic communities of New York. WNBC is the media sponsor of countless signature New York events, including the Tribeca Film Festival, the New York International Latino Film Festival, and the Central Park Conservancy's celebration of Central Park's 150th anniversary. It is the media sponsor of the MTA's New York Subway Centennial and the Apollo Theater's 70th birthday. And, as the media partner of the American Museum of Natural History, WNBC spreads the word of this preeminent scientific institution to the community.

The station is also the media sponsor for numerous volunteer and fund-raising efforts, including the Gay Men's Health Crisis (GMHC) AIDS Walk New York, the Revlon Run/Walk for Women, the National Multiple Sclerosis Society MS Walk, the American Diabetes Association Tour de Cure, the Susan G. Komen Breast Cancer Foundation's Komen Race for the Cure, and The New York Cares Coat Drive.

WNBC is also the official broadcast station for many of the Big Apple's highest profile events, from the annual lighting of the Christmas tree at Rockefeller Center to the New York City Marathon. Along with this roster of support, the station continually produces and airs public service announcements and honors New York diversity with special on-air tributes that air at various times throughout the year.

First to deliver national commercial television to the public, WNBC now channels the drive and enthusiasm of its visionaries toward a new challenge: shaping the industry's future.

Financial Services

OppenheimerFunds, Inc.

Headquartered in New York City—the financial capital of the world—OppenheimerFunds, Inc., manages assets in excess of $160 billion, making it a formidable force as an investment adviser for mutual funds, pension and retirement plans, and privately managed accounts.

Joined hands have always symbolized security and teamwork. Four hands together, forming the "fireman's carry," represent working collectively to create greater strength and support than any individual could provide. The OppenheimerFunds logo builds on the legacy of this image, standing as an enduring icon of the firm's belief in the power of partnership.

Since 1960, millions of investors have entrusted their dollars, their hopes, and their dreams to OppenheimerFunds, Inc. (OFI), the investment adviser for the Oppenheimer family of mutual funds. Headquartered in New York City since its founding, OFI has grown into one of the largest and most respected asset-management companies in the United States.

Today, OFI manages assets exceeding $160 billion, including assets in more than seven million mutual fund shareholder accounts across 65 mutual funds. As of January 2004, OFI was the eighth largest investment adviser to mutual funds in the country, as ranked by industry consultant Strategic Insights, Inc.

With a strong commitment to serving the needs of investors and their financial advisers, the company has grown and diversified its products and services. The product line of OFI and its affiliates now includes mutual funds, hedge fund of funds, qualified retirement plans for individuals and corporations, privately managed accounts, and investment management for pension plans, foundations, and other institutions.

While markets rise and fall, OFI firmly believes the rewards of investing result from a steadfast commitment to basic principles that define "The Right Way to Invest:" excellent long-term performance; having a goal, a plan to achieve it, and the commitment to stick to the plan; diversification; and benefiting from the advice of an investment professional.

"People entrust us with their retirement money, their kids' college funds, and other savings," says John V. Murphy, chairman, president, and CEO. "These are their most important assets and we take our responsibility for shepherding them and delivering value very seriously."

OppenheimerFunds pursues investment excellence using a unique approach to portfolio management. Ten specialized teams manage the Oppenheimer funds, with portfolio managers having access to the analytical resources and expertise of the other portfolio managers, analysts, and traders on the team. However, these portfolio managers retain responsibility for making final investment decisions for their funds based on their knowledge and experience. This approach has proven itself over time with a number of OppenheimerFunds portfolio managers being ranked among the top 100 mutual fund managers by *Barron's* magazine in each of the past five years.

The company's origins can be traced back to Oppenheimer & Company, a brokerage firm founded in the early 1950s. The Oppenheimer Fund was launched in 1959. A year later, Oppenheimer & Company created a separate subsidiary to manage its fund business: Oppenheimer Management Corporation, now called OppenheimerFunds, Inc. Through a series of transactions, OFI was separated from Oppenheimer & Company and now has no corporate ties to either Oppenheimer & Company or Oppenheimer Capital. The company is majority-owned by Massachusetts Mutual Life Insurance Company (MassMutual) with an ownership stake retained by the company's management team.

The company was directly affected by the terrorist attacks on September 11, 2001, losing its then headquarters in Two World Trade Center. Fortunately, all the firm's employees survived the attacks and the company was able to conduct business when the New York Stock Exchange reopened just days later. After two years in temporary offices, OFI renewed its commitment to Lower Manhattan by establishing its headquarters in the World Financial Center.

Joined by George Pataki, governor of New York, and Michael Bloomberg, mayor of New York City, in announcing the decision, OFI's Murphy said, "We are proud to be part of this historic revitalization and are thrilled to return to our roots in the financial district. It's where we began 50 years ago, it's where we grew into a thriving asset-management company, and it will always be the financial capital of the world."

The company employs nearly 550 people in lower Manhattan as well as more than 100 others in New York State in the offices of its Rochester Division and its subsidiary, Tremont Capital Management, in Rye. The company has more than 2,100 employees in total.

OFI is an active participant in the local community, with long-standing relationships with local chapters of Teach for America, Special Olympics, the American Cancer Society, and the March of Dimes. Also, in conjunction with the Governor's Committee on Scholastic Achievement, the company has provided an extensive mentoring program to students of Seward Park High School on Manhattan's Lower East Side for nine years. To commemorate the events of September 11th, the company has underwritten the cost of a meal delivery each September since 2002, and provided volunteers to deliver meals to the homebound elderly of Lower Manhattan through Citymeals-on-Wheels.

OppenheimerFunds CEO John Murphy (center) announced the firm's return to lower Manhattan in October 2003. A former resident of the World Trade Center, OppenheimerFunds relocated to the World Financial Center. On hand to celebrate the auspicious occasion were (left to right) Michael Bloomberg, mayor of New York City; George Pataki, governor of New York State; Timothy Carey, president and CEO, Battery Park City Authority; and Andrew Alper, president, New York City Economic Development Corporation.

J.P. Morgan Chase & Co.

This leading global firm, with operations in more than 50 countries, provides full banking and investment services for individuals, investors and institutions, corporate clients, and communities.

Corporate headquarters for J.P. Morgan Chase & Co. are located in New York City.

J.P. Morgan Chase & Co. (NYSE: JPM) is a leading global financial services firm with operations in more than 50 countries. In January 2004, J.P. Morgan Chase & Co. and Bank One Corporation announced that they agreed to merge in a strategic business combination that would establish the second-largest banking franchise in the United States, based on core deposits.

The combined company will have assets of more than $1 trillion, a strong capital base, 2,300 branches in 17 states, and top-tier positions in retail banking and lending, credit cards, investment banking, asset management, private banking, treasury and securities services, middle-market, and private equity. The merger of the holding companies is expected to be completed by midyear 2004.

Prior to the Pending Merger

JPMorgan Chase is a leader in investment banking, financial services for consumers and businesses, financial transaction processing, investment management, private banking, and private equity. A component of the Dow Jones Industrial Average, JPMorgan Chase is headquartered in New York City and serves more than 30 million consumer customers nationwide and many of the world's most prominent corporate, institutional, and government clients.

JPMorgan Chase delivers value to its shareholders by delivering for its clients. Clients come to JPMorgan Chase with financial problems that have broad implications, not only for their entire organizations but for the financial markets themselves. Problems like these require innovative solutions—meeting unprecedented levels of consumer demand for financing, and helping companies grow. The solution is more than effective, it is transformational: turning growing companies into global leaders and endowing leading companies with eminent influence.

Delivering outstanding results requires partnership—with clients and with colleagues. A truly effective firm possesses expertise across all functions, and integrates those functions seamlessly. JPMorgan Chase has this winning combination: deep, varied expertise, residing in multiple areas of the firm, fused for the benefit of its clients. When colleagues partner across business units—harnessing combined ideas, experience, knowledge, and resources—the results are powerful. Exponential benefits accrue to clients, who get comprehensive and innovative solutions; to employees, who continually broaden their knowledge and stimulate their creativity; and to the firm, which fortifies its leadership across markets, solidifying its position as the full-service financial firm of choice.

The firm has found that market leadership and customer satisfaction go hand in hand. That is why positioning JPMorgan Chase for growth is an essential part of its strategy—its own and its clients'. The firm builds on the strengths of the JPMorgan Chase franchise to expand its leadership, both in market share and in client satisfaction. The pending Bank One merger will help JPMorgan Chase achieve these goals: complementing its strengths, giving it the scale to be a market-leading financial firm, and giving it a broader platform from which to serve its clients. JPMorgan Chase continues to pursue growth in countless ways: acquiring complementary businesses,

The JPMorgan Chase Sports & Arts Festival, organized by the Sports & Arts in Schools Foundation, which supports the New York City Department of Education, provides enrichment for approximately 15,000 inner-city students between six and 14 years of age during the President's Week midwinter school break in February. The festival is a mixture of 40 sports and arts activities hosted at city parks, museums, and the Chelsea Piers complex, among other locations. JPMorgan Chase has been the lead sponsor of the event since 1998.

capitalizing on current positions, even helping to expand global markets.

Making Communities Thrive

JPMorgan Chase vigorously supports the development and prosperity of the communities it serves. Committing time, money, and creativity, the firm and its employees make a difference at crucial development stages for cultural and human-services organizations, countries and societies, and individuals.

In 2003, JPMorgan Chase contributed more than $90 million to thousands of not-for-profit organizations around the world and provided more than $1 billion in community development lending and investing beyond its traditional small-business and home finance activities. These efforts support human services and education providers, sponsor artistic and cultural endeavors, make homeownership possible for minorities, and spur sustainable economic development—all necessary ingredients to help communities flourish.

Information about the firm is available on the Internet at www.jpmorganchase.com.

Atlantic Bank of New York

Serving New York for over 75 years, Atlantic Bank, with over $3 billion in assets and a global reach, provides full financial services for individuals and small to midsize companies, continuing the special attentiveness its customers have come to expect while also implementing its overall growth strategy.

Atlantic Bank held a ribbon-cutting ceremony for the opening of its branch at the corner of Park Avenue and 54th Street, in Manhattan.

Atlantic Bank of New York, a full-service commercial financial institution based in the New York metropolitan area, is branching out. Having opened three branch offices in midtown Manhattan—including one at 54th Street and Park Avenue acquired from Allied Irish Banks, P.L.C.—Atlantic Bank has positioned itself as a major player in this fiercely competitive financial market. With more than $3 billion in assets, Atlantic Bank ranks as one of the top 20 commercial banks in the New York metropolitan area and among the top 5 percent of all commercial banks in the United States.

Atlantic Bank's journey began in 1926, when it was opened to serve the shipping industry working out of lower Manhattan. As customers moved beyond Manhattan to areas such as Brooklyn and Queens, Atlantic Bank followed, establishing new branches and expanding its range of services. Today, Atlantic Bank provides a comprehensive range of financial services to retail customers as well as small and midsize businesses. A bank with global reach, Atlantic Bank is a subsidiary of the NBG Group (NYSE: NBG), which has approximately $55 billion in assets and operates in 17 countries worldwide.

Under the leadership of its president and CEO, Thomas M. O'Brien, Atlantic Bank has charted a new course for growth and expansion, while continuing to focus on its core business. In a major step toward achieving this objective, Atlantic Bank acquired Yonkers Financial Corporation and its branch network in 2002, increasing the bank's assets by nearly 25 percent and doubling the number of branches. By the end of 2003, Atlantic Bank was operating more than 22 branches in locations both in and around New York City, including Manhattan, Brooklyn, Queens, Long Island, and Westchester and Dutchess Counties, as well as a branch in downtown Boston. The bank plans to open additional branches during the next few years, eyeing locations in Manhattan, Westchester County, and the Bronx.

The bank also offers commercial financial services on a nationwide basis through wholly owned subsidiary Standard Funding Corp. Adding significant value to the bank's overall services for its business clients, Standard Funding provides companies with financing solutions for their commercial insurance premium costs.

Having enhanced its operations and bolstered its small business and corporate banking services, Atlantic Bank is vigorously pursuing its strategy for long-term growth and continued profitability. A key component is serving as a financial partner to middle-market companies, commercial real estate investors and developers, corporations, and emerging small businesses. By tailoring its services to the individual needs of its customers, and by offering the kind of personal attention that larger institutions can rarely match, Atlantic Bank has become a trusted ally for its growing roster of clients. Atlantic Bank's experience encompasses a wide

range of industries, including professional and business services, manufacturing and construction, entertainment, media, and technology.

Commercial real estate financing has long been a traditional mainstay of Atlantic Bank's business lines. Accustomed to transactions ranging from $1 million to $15 million, Atlantic Bank provides financing for office buildings, retail stores and shopping centers, industrial buildings, warehouse and distribution centers, multiple-family residential properties, and mixed-use properties. With their thorough understanding of the commercial real estate market, Atlantic Bank's experienced professionals provide creative solutions for complex transactions.

Atlantic Bank also offers an excellent range of electronic banking services that focus on providing convenient banking options for both business and consumer clients. These services include an extensive ATM network; state-of-the-art 24-Hour Telephone Banking; and OnLine Banking, the bank's premier Internet banking and bill payment service. The bank's Web site (www.abny.com) has become a customer resource as well, offering such amenities as a large menu of financial calculators that are useful for answering such questions as "How can I save a million dollars?" or for figuring out rates on loans, retirement accounts, and leases.

Atlantic Bank has also built a growing presence among nonprofit institutions, which account for a significant share of New York City's employment base. Such clients include a broad range of focuses, from health care, educational, and cultural organizations to social services associations and private clubs. Through its investment options and cash management solutions, Atlantic Bank helps these clients to maximize their financial position responsibly without sacrificing safety and control.

Atlantic Bank is proud of its community service and involvement with charitable organizations. In 2004, the bank continued its longtime support of Habitat for Humanity's Westchester County chapter, contributing both financial resources and volunteers for its various projects. Atlantic Bank also joined with customers and staff to raise money for the annual March of Dimes WalkAmerica fund-raising campaign. Additionally, Atlantic Bank volunteers participate in the Federal Reserve Bank of New York and the New York City Department of Employment's Banking on Youth program, teaching teenagers the fundamentals of banking, budgeting, and personal money management.

Commitment to the community is a reflection of Atlantic Bank's personal approach to banking. By continuing to offer personal attention and services tailored to the specific needs of its clients, Atlantic Bank is on the right track for continued growth and success.

For additional information, phone 800-535-2269; or visit the bank's Web site at www.abny.com.

Above: Thomas M. O'Brien is Atlantic Bank's president and CEO. Left: A new branch, at 56th Street and Third Avenue in Manhattan, was added in 2003 as part of Atlantic Bank's overall expansion strategy.

Photo, top right: © Catherine Gibbons

Community Bank, N.A.

This bank focuses on the financial needs of people in small towns and villages across upstate New York and in Pennsylvania, offering a complete line of individual and business banking and financial services—both traditional and electronic—with a commitment to enhanced customer assistance and local-branch decision making.

Shown here, from left, are Sanford A. Belden, Community Bank System, Inc., president and CEO, and James A. Gabriel, chairman of the board.

What's in a name? A good deal, when the name is Community Bank, N.A., an independent bank with a growing presence in upstate New York and northeastern Pennsylvania. For Community Bank, being responsive to the local community is not only policy, it is a matter of pride.

Community Bank, N.A., is the wholly owned national banking subsidiary of Community Bank System, Inc. (CBSI), which has been in the area since 1866, when it was the St. Lawrence National Bank; CBSI was incorporated as a registered bank holding company in 1983. Today, it is the second largest commercial banking franchise headquartered in upstate New York, employing approximately 1,400 people.

From its base in the Syracuse, New York, suburb of DeWitt, Community Bank provides a full range of individual and business banking services and financial services at 132 customer facilities serving 27 counties.

Community Bank is making a name for itself with its focus on fast, responsive service at the branch level. In an era of consolidation, centralization, and Internet banking, Community Bank remains true to its small town and village roots. It maintains a continued commitment to serving its communities by empowering branch employees, rather than distant managers, as key decision makers. In practical terms, this means customers can obtain home loans or business financing faster and find many other services tailored to their needs. Combined with a reputation for accuracy and high credit standards, the personal touch found at Community Bank has quickly gained trust for the bank—and market share. In 2003, deposits grew to nearly 8.8 percent above 2002 levels.

To make its decentralized business model work, Community Bank has adopted a "strength in numbers" strategy. Since 1994, 109 branches have been added to the system through 11 separate acquisitions. In May 2001, the purchase of First Liberty Bank and Trust's 13 branches gave Community Bank its first foothold in Pennsylvania. In 2003, 12 branches were added to the First Liberty division when CBSI acquired Grange National BancCorp, in Pennsylvania. In 2004, the acquisition of First Heritage Bank, also in Pennsylvania, added a strong commercial loan portfolio to the mix. As of mid-2004, assets rose to $4.2 billion with the First Heritage acquisition, up from $3.9 billion in 2003.

Financial services are another growth area for Community Bank. The advantages are threefold: revenue sources are diversified, reliance on net interest income is reduced, and the menu of customer services is increased. Here again, acquisitions have played a significant role.

In 1996, Benefit Plans Administrative Services, Inc., of Utica became a subsidiary of CBSI. Three years later, Community Investment Services, Inc., in New York (known as First Liberty Investment Services in Pennsylvania) was created as an in-house replacement for relationships with third-party broker dealers. The investment firm of Elias Asset Management Inc., based in Williamsville, was acquired in 2000. Elias Asset has some $700 million under management. Its president, chief investment officer, and founder, David J. Elias, is an investment advisor with two books to his credit who frequently provides expert comment in financial publications and on national television. Syracuse-based Harbridge Consulting Group of Syracuse, formerly pension and health benefits consultant for PricewaterhouseCoopers, was added in 2003, approximately doubling the number of Community Bank's clients for such services.

By year-end 2003, noninterest income, from financial services and other sources, had risen to more than 20 percent of total operating income—up from 18 percent in 2002. The long-term goal is to reach 40 percent in five to 10 years.

While resisting some of the riskier technology trends that drove banking in the 1990s, Community Bank has by no means been averse to harnessing high-technology solutions that make sense—for example, to enhance customer interactions with bank personnel without allowing ATMs to become a substitute for personal service. Technology has also made it possible to link the bank's many locations efficiently, as well as to offer products and services such as Internet banking, electronic statements, and

a state-of-the-art Web site. Also, Community Bank's implementation of automated loan-processing tools has improved decision-making speed and reduced operating costs.

Community Bank may be growing up, but it has no intention of leaving home.

For more information, visit the bank's Web site at www.communitybankna.com.

Above: Community Bank's Washington Street office in Watertown, New York, is an example of the bank's Main Street style of banking, with managers making decisions right at the local branch.

Value Line, Inc.

This dynamic company, one of the largest independent investment advisory services in the country, publishes *The Value Line Investment Survey*—considered the bible of Wall Street—providing potential investors with a unique ranking system for assessing price performance, risk, and short-term price change.

Value Line, Inc., CEO Jean Bernhard Buttner, whose father, Arnold Bernhard, founded the company in 1931, has continually upgraded and expanded the product line over two decades, resulting in a more than 34-fold increase in shareholder equity as of fiscal year-end 2004.

As America's stock market struggled during the Great Depression, Wall Street advisor Arnold Bernhard developed an approach to making investment decisions that was not in existence at the time. His unique standard of value would signal when stocks were overvalued and when they were undervalued—and would not give way to emotionalism. His faith in that idea cost him his job. So in 1931, Bernhard started publishing *Value Line,* a service that would irrevocably change the way investors think.

By transforming the investment process, *Value Line* has become one of the nation's largest independent investment advisory services—a dynamic company that publishes crucial financial information and manages mutual funds and other financial assets.

Wall Street Bible

Value Line's flagship publication, *The Value Line Investment Survey,* is considered the bible of Wall Street. Every week some 130,000 subscribers, and an estimated half-million readers, turn to its pages for financial information and guidance.

More than a forum for descriptive information, *The Value Line Investment Survey* guides investors to stocks most apt to be top performers by means of its exclusive ranking systems.

These systems work. For three decades, *Value Line*'s stock rankings have been borne out by subsequent relative price performance. Since 1965, stocks that have been ranked number one and two for Timeliness™ as a group have outperformed stocks in groups three, four, and five combined. In addition, the publication's most highly ranked stocks have won kudos from *The Hulbert Financial Digest,* a leading rating service for evaluating investment-letter recommendations.

New Leadership, New Products

Having built a multimillion-dollar company, Bernhard was succeeded in 1988 by his daughter, Jean Bernhard Buttner. She has consistently assessed, upgraded, and expanded the company's product line to make it even easier for people to make informed investment decisions.

Since Buttner has run the company, *Value Line* has expanded its coverage of securities from only 1,700 stocks to more than 8,000 stocks, 13,000 mutual funds, 80,000 options, and more. Retained earnings have grown an average of 68 percent per year. When Buttner first joined *Value Line* in 1983, shareholder equity was $5.9 million. More than two decades later, as of April 30, 2004, shareholder equity exceeded $208.5 million; and incredibly, even while paying out large dividends (50 percent of earnings in 2003), shareholder equity had grown by more than 34-fold.

Despite the demands of serving as CEO of a leading financial company, Buttner is active in many nonbusiness roles. She is dedicated to supporting excellence in education and assisting women to realize their potential. As a proponent of educational achievement, Buttner has served on 10 school boards. She has been a trustee or director of Radcliffe, Skidmore, Williams, Emma Willard, Choate Rosemary Hall, the College Preparatory School, and the Berkeley Montessori School. She also has served as president of the Piedmont public school board of education and been a member of the Harvard Business School Visitation Committee, as well as the Stanford Business School Advisory Committee. She is a recipient of the Emma Lazarus Award, the Rosemary Hall Alumnae Award, the Emma Willard Life Achievement Award, and Harvard's prestigious Alumni Achievement Award.

Buttner has been named one of New York's 75 most influential business women by *Crain's*, one of the Top 60 women business owners in America by *Savvy* magazine, and one of 50 top businesswomen by *Working Woman* magazine.

Four major strengths—nearly 75 years of the highest of ethical standards, a powerful brand name, proven quantitative investment techniques, and an expert staff—will help *Value Line* continue to fulfill its longtime mission: to help individual and institutional investors find top quality, independent, unbiased research.

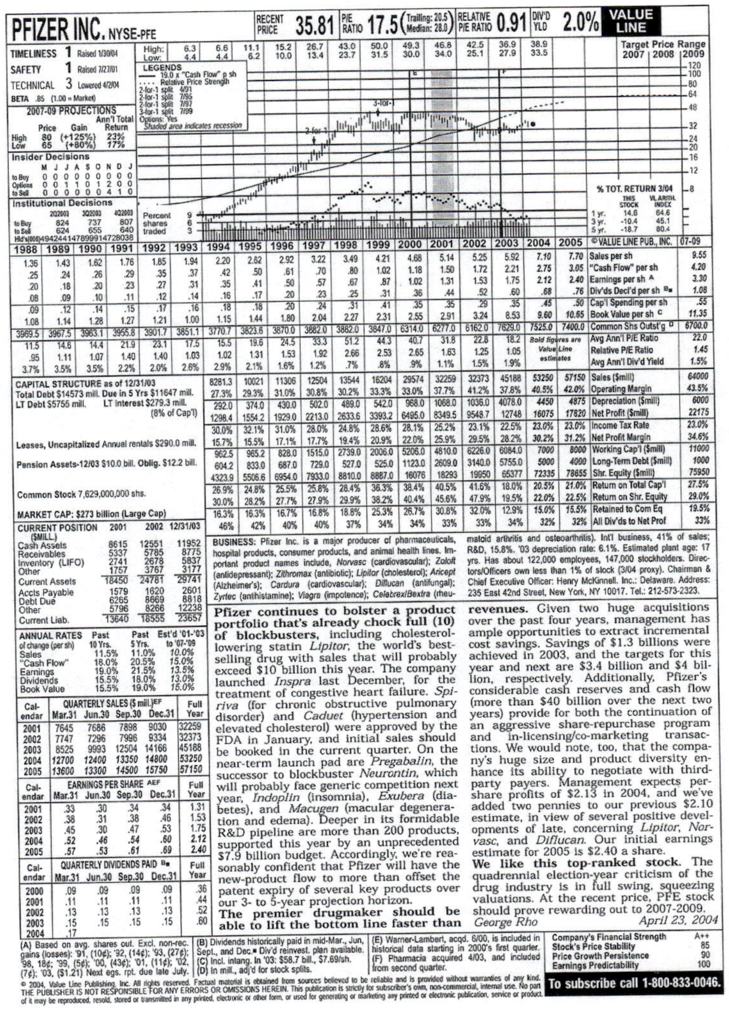

PFIZER INC. NYSE-PFE — RECENT PRICE 35.81 — P/E RATIO 17.5 (Trailing: 20.5; Median: 28.0) — RELATIVE P/E RATIO 0.91 — DIV'D YLD 2.0% — VALUE LINE

BUSINESS: Pfizer Inc. is a major producer of pharmaceuticals, hospital products, consumer products, and animal health lines. Important product names include, *Norvasc* (cardiovascular); *Zoloft* (antidepressant); *Zithromax* (antibiotic); *Lipitor* (cholesterol); *Aricept* (Alzheimer's); *Cardura* (cardiovascular); *Diflucan* (antifungal); *Zyrtec* (antihistamine); *Viagra* (impotence); *Celebrex/Bextra* (rheumatoid arthritis and osteoarthritis). Int'l business, 41% of sales; R&D, 15.8%. '03 depreciation rate: 6.1%. Estimated plant age: 17 yrs. Has about 122,000 employees, 147,000 stockholders. Directors/Officers own less than 1% of stock (3/04 proxy). Chairman & Chief Executive Officer: Henry McKinnell. Inc.: Delaware. Address: 235 East 42nd Street, New York, NY 10017. Tel.: 212-573-2323.

Pfizer continues to bolster a product portfolio that's already chock full (10) of blockbusters, including cholesterol-lowering statin *Lipitor*, the world's best-selling drug with sales that will probably exceed $10 billion this year. The company launched *Inspra* last December, for the treatment of congestive heart failure. *Spiriva* (for chronic obstructive pulmonary disorder) and *Caduet* (hypertension and elevated cholesterol) were approved by the FDA in January, and initial sales should be booked in the current quarter. On the near-term launch pad are *Pregabalin*, the successor to blockbuster *Neurontin*, which will probably face generic competition next year, *Indoplin* (insomnia), *Exubera* (diabetes), and *Macugen* (macular degeneration and edema). Deeper in its formidable R&D pipeline are more than 200 products, supported this year by an unprecedented $7.9 billion budget. Accordingly, we're reasonably confident that Pfizer will have the new-product flow to more than offset the patent expiry of several key products over our 3- to 5-year projection horizon.

The premier drugmaker should be able to lift the bottom line faster than revenues. Given two huge acquisitions over the past four years, management has ample opportunities to extract incremental cost savings. Savings of $1.3 billions were achieved in 2003, and the targets for this year and next are $3.4 billion and $4 billion, respectively. Additionally, Pfizer's considerable cash reserves and cash flow (more than $40 billion over the next two years) provide for both the continuation of an aggressive share-repurchase program and in-licensing/co-marketing transactions. We would note, too, that the company's huge size and product diversity enhance its ability to negotiate with third-party payers. Management expects per-share profits of $2.13 in 2004, and we've added two pennies to our previous $2.10 estimate, in view of several positive developments of late, concerning *Lipitor*, *Norvasc*, and *Diflucan*. Our initial earnings estimate for 2005 is $2.40 a share.

We like this top-ranked stock. The quadrennial election-year criticism of the drug industry is in full swing, squeezing valuations. At the recent price, PFE stock should prove rewarding out to 2007-2009.

George Rho — *April 23, 2004*

(B) Dividends historically paid in mid-Mar., Jun, Sept., and Dec. ■ Div'd reinvest. plan available. (C) Incl. intang. In '03: $58.7 bill., $7.69/sh. (D) In mill., adj'd for stock splits. (E) Warner-Lambert, acqd. 6/00, is included in historical data starting in 2000's first quarter. (F) Pharmacia acquired 4/03, and included from second quarter.

Company's Financial Strength	A++
Stock's Price Stability	85
Price Growth Persistence	90
Earnings Predictability	100

To subscribe call 1-800-833-0046.

A single page from *The Value Line Investment Survey* presents all the information an investor needs to make a preliminary evaluation of a stock.

SEFCU

The largest credit union in the Capital Region offers its members a full range of financial services, including Internet and telephone banking; real estate, vehicle, and personal loans; fixed and variable rate deposit products; wealth management services; and insurance products, available through its wholly owned subsidiary.

This artist's rendering depicts SEFCU's new headquarters as of 2004, in Albany, New York.

SEFCU (formerly State Employees Federal Credit Union) was established in 1934 when a group of New York State employees was granted a charter under the Federal Credit Union Act of 1934, to create Albany's first credit union. Today, SEFCU manages more than $1.2 billion in assets for its 122,000 members. While the majority of its membership is concentrated in New York, SEFCU has active members in all 50 states and 13 foreign countries. The credit union has grown from a savings institution with less than $10,000 on deposit to a complete financial services operation striving to meet its members' every financial services need.

In addition to SEFCU's steady growth, mergers with other credit unions have made SEFCU an amalgam of credit unions from Syracuse, Binghamton, and Albany, reflecting the region's diversity of population and employers. SEFCU's experience and capabilities have positioned the credit union to meet the financial needs of not only state employees, but also thousands of individuals and businesses from all walks of life.

Because SEFCU is member-owned, it dedicates its efforts toward providing a comprehensive range of financial products to help its members achieve their economic goals. In addition to traditional savings accounts, checking accounts, debit and credit cards, and direct deposit and payroll deduction options, SEFCU offers term savings certificates; no-risk market index certificates; and a full complement of loan products, including consumer, education, real estate, and home equity loans, as well as specialty mortgages for low-income borrowers. SEFCU also provides members with a wide range of business banking products and services.

SEFCU was one of the first financial institutions in the Capital Region to offer Internet banking. Its members have access to banking options such as online bill payment, wireless access to accounts, and electronic statements. Via SEFCU Online, the credit union's Internet banking service, members can view, print, or save images of cleared checks; download account histories to Quicken or Money spreadsheets; and communicate securely with SEFCU Online specialists. Members may also maintain accounts and pay bills online—whether they are at home, at work, or on the road—through SEFCU iPay.

The credit union's wealth management services include retirement plan rollovers, investment and retirement planning, and stock and mutual fund investment options. Through its wholly owned subsidiary, SEFCU members can also take advantage of various kinds of insurance, including life, automobile, and long-term care.

SEFCU members can conveniently access many of these services at one of the branch offices in the credit union's extensive network throughout the Capital Region, as well as in the Binghamton and Syracuse areas. In addition, members have surcharge-free access to the Allpoint™ ATM network, available at 25,000 machines nationwide.

The SEFCU State Street branch office in Albany, New York, is one of an extensive network of SEFCU branches throughout the Capital Region and in the Binghamton and Syracuse areas.

SEFCU and its employees actively support community events and charitable functions. In 1991, employees created the SEFCU Employees' Charities Committee to support fund-raising activities that benefit children in need. Now renamed the SEFCU Foundation, the group has provided more than $600,000 in financial support to children and families in the Albany, Binghamton, and Syracuse areas through various annual fund-raisers. Among the foundation's activities are Bowl for Kids' Sake, to benefit Big Brothers Big Sisters of the Capital Region; the Labor Day 5k Race, on behalf of various organizations for children; the Monopoly Tournament, to benefit The Center for the Disabled; and the Holiday Sharing Program, which brings holiday gifts to children living in difficult circumstances. The SEFCU Foundation also has sales of special products throughout the year to help gather donations for various children's organizations.

SEFCU is more committed than ever to enhancing its offerings to the communities it serves. Michael J. Castellana, president of SEFCU, is proud of the credit union's outstanding record of service to the membership and the community.

"As we celebrate 70 years of service to members throughout New York State, SEFCU is proud to offer 21st-century products and services tailored to the emerging financial needs of both individuals and businesses," Castellana says. "I am excited about our position in the financial services industry and in our communities, because we are able to combine the founding cooperative principle of superior member service with the speed and convenience of advanced technology that gives our members the best banking experience possible."

CFCU Community Credit Union

With seven locations, sound management practices, a strict code of ethics, and $380 million in assets, this not-for-profit financial institution is well situated to offer its members the highest quality of credit and savings plans—but it is the personalized service that sets it apart.

Above left: CFCU Community Credit Union's main building is located in Ithaca, New York. Above right: Banking at CFCU Community Credit Union is "a people thing."

Of the people, by the people, and for the people—democracy in a nutshell. It is also a good description of what a credit union is all about. People helping people and neighbors helping neighbors—CFCU Community Credit Union in a nutshell. In other words, it is "a people thing."

CFCU Community Credit Union opened its doors in 1953 and has roots deep in the Finger Lakes Region of upstate New York. Back then, it was known as Cornell Federal Credit Union, and it served the employees of Cornell University. In 1997, it adopted a state charter and became Cornell FingerLakes Credit Union. Then in 2003, it converted to a community charter for Tompkins and Cortland Counties and officially became CFCU Community Credit Union. This means that anyone who lives, works, or attends school in the two counties may become a member.

And membership certainly has its advantages. It means being part of a dynamic, democratically controlled, not-for-profit financial cooperative. The mission of CFCU Community Credit Union is to provide the highest level of personal financial services in a friendly, professional manner; to encourage thrift, savings, and the wise use of credit; to increase the knowledge and ability of members to manage and control their financial well-being; and to provide sound financial management in order to maintain earnings for CFCU Community Credit Union's continued growth.

With seven locations, more than 55,000 members, and in excess of $380 million in assets, CFCU Community Credit Union is one of the largest and most successful credit unions in New York State. Its ongoing success can be traced to a number of factors, including sound management practices, adherence to a strict code of ethics, and excellent rates and great products, year after year. But what sets CFCU Community Credit Union apart from other financial institutions is its ability to deliver highly personalized, quality service. At CFCU, it really is "a people thing."

Photo: David Muir/Masterfile www.masterfile.com

Citigroup Inc.

The world's largest financial services firm, with 200 million accounts and 275,000 employees—nearly 25,400 of them in New York City—provides a full range of financial products and services, supports financial education, and awards grants through its businesses and the Citigroup Foundation.

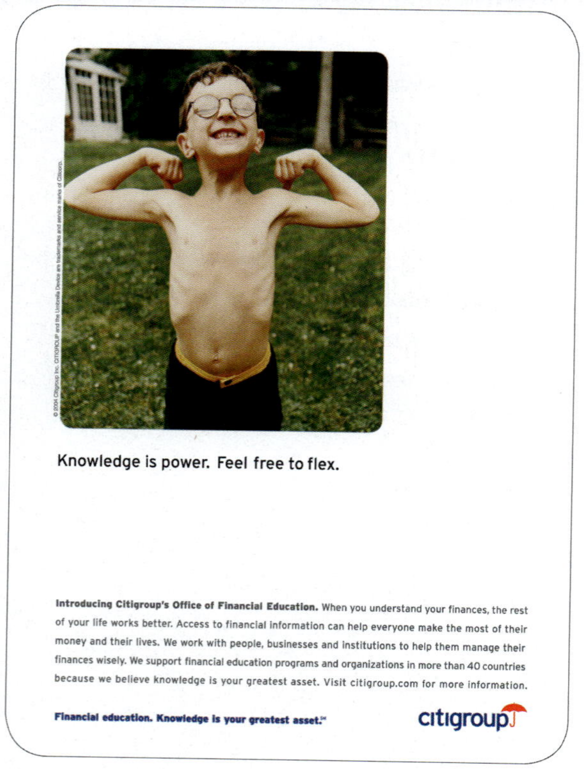

This advertisement appeared in 2004 in publications around the world, announcing Citigroup's and the Citigroup Foundation's unprecedented 10-year, $200 million global commitment to financial education.

Citigroup Inc.—the first modern diversified financial services company of its kind in the United States—was formed on October 8, 1998; but its history reaches back to September 14, 1812, when City Bank of New York opened for business to serve a group of New York merchants.

Today, Citigroup is the preeminent global financial services company, with 275,000 employees serving 200 million customer accounts that cover every part of the global economic spectrum.

While Citigroup does business in more than 100 countries, it is proud to call New York home. It is also proud of its work to provide access to capital and to strengthen New York communities from Long Island to Buffalo.

With 32,500 employees in the state, nearly 25,400 of whom are located in New York City, Citigroup is one of New York's largest employers. Frequently cited by publications such as *Fortune, Working Mother, LATINA* Style, and *DiversityInc* as an employer of choice, Citigroup has a strong commitment to diversity and opportunity.

Citigroup also has an excellent record of giving back to New York's communities through charitable contributions and employee volunteerism. In fact, of $88.8 million in grants made by Citigroup's businesses and the Citigroup Foundation in 2003, more than 660 grants totaling more than $11 million were awarded to nonprofit organizations that are based in and serve New York.

Also during 2003, Citigroup made nearly $2 billion in Home Mortgage Disclosure Act loans to low- and moderate-income (LMI) families or to borrowers purchasing properties in LMI census tracts throughout New York State. In addition, the company made $1.2 billion in small-business loans and provided more than $300 million in community development loans and investments in New York.

And when Citigroup announced its 10-year, $200 million global commitment to financial education in April 2004, it did so from the Harlem YMCA Jackie Robinson Youth Center, where Citigroup has supported a variety of community programs since 1999.

For nearly 200 years, Citigroup has worked to provide access to capital and investment products in thousands of cities and neighborhoods around the world. New York, its headquarters city, is most prominent among them.

For more information about Citigroup, its businesses, or the Citigroup Foundation, please visit www.citigroup.com.

Photo: © Bartomeu Amengual/agefotostock

Insurance Services

HIP® Health Plan of New York

This financially secure, growing, and innovative health care provider works diligently toward improving the health care system itself as well as bettering the lives of its 1.2 million members in the five boroughs and Nassau, Suffolk, and Westchester Counties.

HIP® HEALTH PLAN OF NEW YORK

Right: Anthony L. Watson serves as chairman and CEO of HIP Health Plan of New York.

"At HIP® Health Plan of New York," says Anthony L. Watson, HIP's chairman and CEO, "we take deep pride in providing access to quality, affordable health care. Our mission is to improve not only the lives of our members, but to help improve the health care system overall. The growing numbers of New Yorkers who call HIP their health plan know that maintaining good health is about informed choice. They know that the dialogue that takes place between doctor and patient is what drives health care decisions. They know that the way in which health care decisions are reached is as important as the quality, affordability, and convenience of the care itself. And they trust us to be their partners in health care—one reason we're the largest HMO in the metropolitan area."

Adds Daniel T. McGowan, president and COO, "We are proud of our New York heritage, as well as our success as an innovative force in health care. We believe that HIP has one of the finest management teams to be found anywhere in health care, a key reason why we are a financially secure and growing company. HIP has recently expanded to include Vytra Health Plans, a 200,000-member health plan that currently operates on Long Island. And, in a continuing commitment to New York City, we will move to new headquarters in the summer of 2004 as part of revitalizing historic downtown Manhattan."

In New York City, which many consider the capital of the world, HIP is a long-established and distinguished part of the health care community. It draws its members from Fortune 500 companies and small businesses alike. In addition, its members include federal, state, and city employees, including police officers, firefighters, and other civil servants. They come from Brooklyn, the Bronx, Manhattan, Queens, and Staten Island. They live in Nassau, Suffolk, and Westchester Counties. In all, they number 1.2 million, and their numbers keep growing.

In its service area, HIP is everywhere a health care company needs to be. It has never been easier to find

HIP participating doctors. They are down the block, around the corner—maybe right next door. Indeed, HIP has more than 21,000 doctors in nearly 32,000 service locations. What is more, HIP is the only health care company in the New York metropolitan area with three separate delivery systems, providing its members with an unparalleled level of quality, affordable health care options.

Among those options are more than 50 conveniently located health care centers. In Queens, on Long Island, in Brooklyn, and on Staten Island, the centers are operated by outstanding medical groups of multispecialty physicians: Queens–Long Island Medical Group, Central Brooklyn Medical Group, and Staten Island's Medical Group. In Manhattan, HIP centers are operated by physician groups in concert with Beth Israel Medical Center and St. Luke's–Roosevelt Hospital Center (Continuum Health Partners, Inc.) and Lenox Hill Hospital. In the Bronx and Westchester County, the centers are operated by physician groups together with Montefiore Medical Center and St. Barnabas Hospital. As if that were not enough, HIP's largest network is a rapidly growing system of physicians in independent practice.

All of this and more have pushed HIP's reputation well beyond the New York metropolitan area. In a recent survey, *InformationWeek* ranked HIP number one among all insurance companies in the nation for its innovative use of information technology. *BusinessWeek* named HIP to its corporate Web Smart 50 for online streamlining that links doctors, patients, and health care administrators. And is there another health care company with an interactive Web site that has been translated into Spanish, Chinese, and Korean?

HIP's mission since its founding is to continually improve everything it does for its members. That is why it is an award-winning company, providing more health care services than ever before, making them more accessible and convenient than ever before. Now that's HIP.

Left: Daniel T. McGowan is HIP's president and COO. Above left: Striving to exceed the industry's fast pace, HIP builds its success on constant evolution, making innovative moves such as forming a strategic alliance with Vytra Health Plans.

Greater New York Insurance Companies

Licensed in 44 states and the District of Columbia, this mutual group of property/casualty insurance companies writes multiperil, excess/umbrella, workers' compensation, and other types of commercial policies in addition to its original business of providing liability coverage of multiunit residential properties.

Greater New York Insurance Companies (GNY) chairman and chief executive officer, Warren W. Heck, and president, Dominick Vicari, conduct the Annual Meeting of Policyholders at company headquarters in New York City.

The Greater New York Insurance Companies (GNY) has been an important member of the insurance industry in New York since it was formed in 1914 to serve the coverage needs of tenement owners on the city's East Side. The company has subsequently evolved into one of the largest and most successful insurers of multiperil business in the state. Moreover, today's GNY—which comprises the Greater New York Mutual Insurance Company, the Insurance Company of Greater New York, the Strathmore Insurance Company, and Brite Insurance Agency, Inc.—ranges far beyond the East Side. Still headquartered in New York City, GNY does business in New York State and the northeastern United States.

Over the years, GNY also has significantly expanded its core products. In addition to liability coverage of multiresidential buildings, GNY also offers such products as multiperil insurance, which provides protection from many potential hazards; excess/umbrella policies, which protect assets by providing higher limits and broader coverage beyond primary liability limits; and commercial automobile insurance. In addition, GNY provides customized business owner's policies (BOPs) to its major accounts and competitive dividend plans for workers' compensation risks.

While GNY remains a prominent niche insurer of multiunit residential properties, its products also are available to owners of light industrial buildings, offices, restaurants, retail establishments, nursing homes, hospitals, and hotels, among others.

What has not changed over the years is GNY's focus on service, its consistent profitability, and a claims

strategy that embraces the prompt payment of legitimate claims while giving questionable claims a long, hard look.

"A company cannot afford to pay liability claims that have no merit," says Warren W. Heck, chairman and chief executive officer of GNY, in explaining how the firm remains financially strong.

As for the company's future, Heck, who began his career with GNY in 1962 as an underwriter, is optimistic about the firm's continued growth and success. He points out that GNY is well positioned to meet the challenges of the future in the insurance business because, unlike publicly held companies, which are held captive to the quarterly profit pressures of their shareholders, GNY is a mutual operation and thus can plan for the long term.

GNY is one of only two survivors of six mutual insurance firms formed in New York City around the turn of the 20th century to address the commercial liability coverage needs of specific trade groups. Its history is woven into the fabric of New York City's own history during the last century.

GNY was born when a group of some 150 lower East Side tenement house owners, most of them immigrants who worked hard as tradesmen to earn the money to purchase the apartment houses, joined together in 1907 to form the Greater New York Taxpayers Association to protect their interests.

One of the association's primary concerns was the lack of affordable public liability policies from old-line insurance companies. With increasingly large numbers of immigrants crowding into the lower East Side, the tenement-house owners saw a proportional increase of litigation against them and their properties. Traditional insurance companies, unable to cope with the growing number of claims, gradually withdrew from the neighborhood. Soon, the association members were having to fend for themselves.

In 1914, the members of the association created the Protective and Defense Committee to provide substitute insurance coverage to owners who registered their buildings with the committee. For a fee of $25 per year (later increased to $50 per year), the committee investigated all liability claims against a registered building, defended any lawsuit filed against it, and paid any judgment up to $5,000 resulting from an adverse court verdict.

The committee operated as a quasi insurance company until 1927, when the state's insurance superintendent required that the association organize as a full-fledged insurance firm under the jurisdiction of the Insurance Department. The committee incorporated as a mutual insurance company, calling itself the Greater New York Taxpayers Mutual Insurance Association. It adopted its current name in 1954.

Within five years of its incorporation, the company began to do business through insurance brokers. Until 1952, the only policies the company wrote covered liability claims against landlords and tenants. That year, GNY added workers' compensation policies.

In the early 1960s, GNY became a multiline property/casualty insurer, adding automobile, fire, multiperil, inland marine, fidelity, surety, burglary, disability benefits, and boiler and machinery coverage. In 1967, GNY formed the Insurance Company of Greater New York, a wholly owned stock company, and created

Vicari and Heck are seen as "the guiding lights" of the Greater New York Insurance Companies.

Greater New York Insurance Companies

Right: Talented young junior underwriters, such as (from left) Benjamin Hawkins, Sarah Chang, and Kathia Acosta, are considered to be "the eyes and ears" of GNY.

Strathmore Insurance Company, another wholly owned stock company, in 2000. Brite Insurance Agency was formed in 1998.

GNY is licensed to do business in 44 states and the District of Columbia. In 2002, it was the fourth largest writer of commercial multiperil insurance in New York State, the 11th largest writer of that business in New Jersey, and the 16th largest multiperil writer in Connecticut. The company has had branch offices in Connecticut since 1962 and in New Jersey since 1964, and recently opened a branch office in Massachusetts.

With assets of $659 million, direct written premiums in excess of $279 million, and a surplus in excess of $231 million along with strong operating results, especially within the last five years, GNY's financial position is excellent. Proof of its strong financial position can be seen in the ratings bestowed on the company by the nation's top business-rating services. The A. M. Best Company, Inc., leading provider of ratings for the insurance industry, gives GNY's group of companies an A+, and Standard & Poor's, leading provider of numerous independent ratings, gives the firm an A.

"Both rating agencies have classified the capital strength and operations of our companies as superior," Heck says. "Our balance sheet, which on a relative basis is one of the strongest in the industry, reflects asset strength, superior liquidity, conservative leverage, and full loss reserves."

The Ward Group, a management consulting firm specializing in watchdogging the insurance industry, offers further proof of GNY's strong financial standing. Out of 2,700 property/casualty insurance companies in the United States, the Ward Group put GNY in the 2003 Ward's 50 Benchmark Group of top-performing property-casualty insurance companies for the five-year period of 1998 through 2002.

Besides GNY's prudent handling of claims and its status as a mutual company, Heck attributes the financial success of the company to its strict adherence to basic fundamental principles. These principles include investing only in the safest and least volatile of securities, maintaining a conservative ratio of net written premiums to surplus, and writing only quality business at adequate rates.

"By espousing these principles," Heck says, "we believe that we best protect the interests of our policyholders."

Another important reason for much of the company's growth and financial success, Heck points out, is the capabilities of GNY's officers. The company has a dedicated and highly trained staff of 350 employees; a strong, talented, and experienced network of 250 independent brokers; an outstanding board of directors; and a prime asset in Dominick Vicari, the company's president, who is in charge of the company's day-to-day operations.

"Without their hard work, expertise, and dedication, we would not be able to achieve such superior results," Heck says.

Looking back, Heck characterizes GNY's nearly century-long journey as "long and arduous," but one that has proved enormously rewarding. He notes that the company will continue to be a prime mover in the insurance business by remaining committed to its mission "to provide quality property and casualty insurance products at affordable rates to small and large businesses throughout the northeast and the Atlantic region."

Above: At GNY are, from left, Ray Lee, vice president of loss control; John Moylan, vice president of underwriting; and Samantha Rovin and Kristin Philipps, junior underwriters. Above left: With Heck and Vicari are Elizabeth Heck, controller, and Max Solomon, board director and retired executive vice president.

Oxford Health Plans, Inc.

With more than 60,000 providers in 80,000 locations, and more than 300 hospitals in its network, this managed care company can provide employer groups and members with the choice and flexibility they need in choosing benefit options that are right for them.

Oxford Health Plans' e-solutions team leader Sue McLaughlin (seated) talks with Peggy Lazzari (standing), New York United Hospital Medical Center's supervisor of admitting, about the services Oxford makes available to clients via the Internet.

When it comes to managing their health care needs, many employers and individuals in New York State place their trust in Oxford Health Plans, Inc. They recognize that Oxford never stops working on ways to help its members stay healthy.

Oxford is a 1.5 million–member health care company headquartered in Trumbull, Connecticut, with offices in New York, New Hampshire, New Jersey, and Florida. Its services include traditional health maintenance organization (HMO) plans, point-of-service (POS) plans, preferred provider organization (PPO) plans, exclusive provider organization (EPO) plans, and consumer-directed health plans, as well as Medicare Advantage (Medicare "Part C" plans, which are Medicare programs run by private businesses). The company had nearly $5.5 billion in revenue in 2003, with some $4.7 billion deriving from POS, PPO, HMO, and similar plans; $0.6 million coming from Medicare; and the rest earned through investments and administrative services.

Oxford's founding mission—to deliver a better, more satisfying health care experience—remains the company's hallmark. Its product portfolio, value-added health and wellness programs, and network of providers offer choice, flexibility, and value to employers and individuals. Oxford works diligently to provide superior service to all of its constituents, including brokers, employers, providers, and members. While doing so, Oxford also ensures that its prices are in line with medical costs, keeping premium costs as low as possible.

Recognizing that individuals have individual needs, Oxford strives to design benefit and health and wellness programs to fit individual situations. By creating a broad portfolio of products, Oxford helps its customers balance their desires to provide high quality benefits at a price point that fits their budgets. To reach this goal, Oxford meets regularly with physicians and employers to discuss and resolve issues quickly and to develop programs and initiatives.

Oxford works collaboratively with the physician community to enhance care, with a particular focus on the needs of members with elevated health conditions. For example, Oxford has joined forces with the Heart Failure Center at the Columbia-Presbyterian Medical Center in Manhattan to launch the Best Practices Network for the prevention, care, and management of congestive heart failure. This initiative is part of Oxford's Best Practices Program℠, whose goal is to help motivate members to take the best possible care of themselves. Oxford launched the Diabetes Best Practices Network in 2003.

Oxford ensures that its customer service team has the technology, training, education, and incentives to support its members while constantly seeking new ways to improve customer service.

Oxford offers its members access to more than 200 different types of providers, representing all major specialties, from orthopedic surgery to gastroenterology. Its network offers more than 60,000 primary care physicians and specialists at more than 300 hospitals. Oxford has expanded into dental and vision coverage as well.

Oxford promotes healthy lifestyles for its members through a variety of exercise and health promotion programs. The Healthy Bonus® program, for instance, offers discounts on health and wellness equipment, gym memberships and equipment, Weight Watchers® memberships, spa visits, and more. Members can also access Oxford's network of alternative medicine practitioners for information on additional ways of staying well.

Oxford's benefits are designed to complement patients' needs. A case in point is its highly successful oncology program, which recognizes that patients in the advanced stages of cancer need more than just excellent clinical care: they need to be around friends and family. Oxford's support extends beyond the patient, assisting caregivers in ways not covered by ordinary health insurance.

Among the numerous awards received by Oxford is an accreditation of "Excellent" for its HMO and POS plans from the National Committee for Quality Assurance (NCQA) in 2002.

Oxford constantly develops and offers new products as it strives to provide customers with access to high quality health care, service, and information. Dedicated to creating health plans that offer choice and flexibility at attractive prices, Oxford continues to grow, to change, and to demand more of itself in the pursuit of the ideal health plan.

Above: Richard Fleder, president of Thesco Benefits, LLC, and broker for Oxford Health Plans, analyzes health plan options for employers. Top left: Writer/producer Kevin Dawkins of Dawkins Productions participates in Oxford's Best Practices Program℠. Lower left: Oxford service associate Jerry Remington helps customers get questions answered quickly.

Health Plus, PHSP Inc.

This not-for-profit managed care provider works with uninsured and underinsured New Yorkers to make certain they have access to cost-effective, good quality medical care; participates in parenting workshops and child immunization drives; and sponsors sports, reading, arts, and other community events.

Dedicated to building healthy communities, Health Plus, PHSP Inc., is a not-for-profit managed care organization that offers health care programs to New York City residents who would otherwise be uninsured.

"Our mission at Health Plus is to work to ensure that every child and adult in New York City has access to free or affordable health care," says Tom Early, executive director. "Together with our providers and community partners, we strive to keep our members healthy, happy, and strong."

Health Plus, a community-based organization, fulfills this mission, in part, by providing three programs:

- Child Health Plus—the state's health plan that offers free or low-cost coverage for children under the age of 19 who are uninsured and not eligible for Medicaid, depending on family size and household income;
- Family Health Plus—a state program that provides adults ages 19 through 64 who are ineligible for Medicaid with free health care benefits, depending on income;

Right: Tom Early, executive director of Health Plus, PHSP Inc., teaches children at P.S. 169 Sunset Park Elementary School in Brooklyn as "Principal for the Day," part of a New York City initiative that brings students in touch with positive role models from the worlds of business and the arts. This is just one of the thousands of events in which the company participates annually as part of its ongoing commitment to supporting the communities and people it serves.

- Health Care Plus—a state-sponsored medical plan that provides people who receive Medicaid with extra benefits at no added cost.

Health Plus also serves its nearly 250,000 members by offering access to quality health care through a solid provider network. This network includes affiliations with more than 2,900 primary care providers and 9,000 specialists. In addition, it offers access to 11 multi-lingual community-based offices, which are open seven days a week; 320 health care centers; more than 1,900 private offices; and 60 hospitals.

Health Plus, one of the fastest growing managed care organizations in New York City, was established in 1984 when Lutheran Medical Center (LMC),

a 476-bed community hospital in southwest Brooklyn, created a Medicaid managed care plan to help improve what was then a costly and unwieldy Medicaid system. By applying managed care principles, LMC intended to provide cost-effective, good quality, coordinated medical care to the Medicaid recipients enrolled in its plan, which it first called Health Care Plus.

Health Care Plus continued to grow during the next six years, reaching an enrollment of 4,000 members.

Participation in a state-sponsored pilot demonstration project called the Southwest Brooklyn Mandatory Medicaid Enrollment Demonstration Project in 1991 led to an enrollment of 13,798 members.

The plan added to its offerings when it began marketing the state-funded Child Health Plus plan in 1992 and expanded its reach to work with other medical centers. After receiving licensure in 1995, LMC transferred its existing contracts to the new Health Plus, which continued to expand its service area over the next five years to include all five boroughs of New York. In 2002, Health Plus added its newest plan, Family Health Plus.

Health Plus continues to seek ways to help its members lead healthier lives and to help them meet their health care needs. It encourages them to take advantage of its many programs, including child immunization drives, child health and wellness workshops and presentations, parenting education classes, health education programs, classes on chronic disease and case management, and a pilot program to help combat obesity in children.

An important project initiated by Health Plus in 1999 is the Keeping Kids in School Asthma Education Program to help increase asthma awareness and teach management of the disease. Since its inception, more than 10,000 children and adults have taken part in the program.

Deeply committed to the communities it serves, Health Plus sponsors immigration forums, health fairs, arts events, museum admissions for children, summer reading events, sports events, and educational competitions. The company's strong sense of community carries over into all its programs and services. This has been recognized in numerous ways. In 2003, the New York State Department of Health's "A Consumer's Guide to Medicaid Managed Care in New York City" rated Health Plus number one in quality for the fourth year in a row.

The annual Health Plus member satisfaction survey showed that more than 91 percent of members rated the quality of medical care received as "excellent." In addition, low rates of voluntary disenrollment suggest a high level of member satisfaction.

Health Plus continues to be proactive in making sure its members take advantage of their benefits, get preventive care, and adopt healthier lifestyles. Health Plus looks forward with bright hopes and specific goals to increasing its involvement in the communities it serves, continuing to grow its membership, expanding its network of care givers, enhancing the quality of its services and programs, and making health care accessible throughout New York City and beyond.

Left: For the 2004 opening of the new, community-based Health Plus office in Washington Heights, the ceremonial ribbon is cut by Manhattan borough president the Honorable C. Virginia Fields, attended by 75th Assembly District representative Ruben Diaz Jr. (center), the Reverend Millie Rios (second from left); and Health Plus staff members. With 11 offices serving all five boroughs of New York City, the company plans to continue expanding, bringing its services to Long Island and beyond.

Empire BlueCross BlueShield

Empire BlueCross BlueShield's commitment to innovation and customer advocacy has led to more than six decades of providing access to high quality, affordable health care for the people of New York City and New York State, with a dedication to members that distinguishes this award-winning organization from the competition.

Right: Empire BlueCross BlueShield builds local relationships in the New York region and has gained national recognition. Nearly one in three Americans carries a BlueCross and BlueShield card.[1]

Since 1935, Empire has built a tradition of service excellence in the New York region. Its time-tested relationships with an extensive network of doctors and hospitals in New York are coupled with national brand recognition and respect for the BlueCross and BlueShield plans, benefiting the health and welfare of all of its members. This means that no matter where members live or work, the most recognized card in the health care industry can take care of their needs.

Benefits go much further than simply health coverage. Empire's emphasis on high quality health care at an affordable cost, its range of product choices, outstanding service to its customers, and an overall commitment to excellence provide businesses with the flexibility and confidence necessary to make decisions quickly and with financial assurance.

Innovative Programs Result in Lower Costs

Whether it is the personalized online resource center available 24 hours a day, seven days a week or the innovative, new 360° Health[SM] program, Empire consistently finds ways to simplify the complexities inherent in the health insurance industry. Through these innovations, Empire is able to improve service while delivering lower overall costs to its customers.

The award-winning Web site (www.empireblue.com) offers employers the opportunity to administer the company's health insurance online, while members can securely manage their claims, as well as find a wealth of valuable and personalized information regarding their health and health plan benefits.

Empire's unique, new 360° Health program is a comprehensive suite of programs and services that provide members with personalized health care support to help them improve, manage, and maintain their health. From preventive care to case management and care coordination services, 360° Health helps Empire members achieve optimal health outcomes through innovation, experience, technology, and service.

Empire is committed to finding solutions for the challenges that are present in the health insurance industry and will continue to be a leader in this sector.

Dedication to Service Excellence

Empire is recognized for its high standard of customer advocacy and for making access to the health care system easier for its members. And with so many doctors and hospitals in Empire's network, Empire's members gain the satisfaction that is evident in their customer loyalty. The 91 percent customer-satisfaction rating[2] demonstrates that Empire is doing things the way members want them to be done.

Empire serves more than 4.8 million members nationwide and more than 32,000 employer accounts. Empire's PPO and EPO members have access to more than 668,000 provider locations and 8,500 hospitals nationwide through the Blue Card® PPO program, administered by the Blue Cross and Blue Shield Association. Empire's HMO, Direct HMO, and POS networks, sited in 28 New York State eastern and southeastern counties and 10 contiguous counties in New Jersey and Connecticut, provide access to more than 65,000 practitioner locations.

For more information about Empire BlueCross BlueShield, please visit the Web site www.empireblue.com.

Above: New York and its residents are well served by Empire BlueCross BlueShield's leading health care networks and commitment to customer service.

[1] Blue Cross and Blue Shield Association enrollment count as of December 31, 2003, divided by U.S. Census Bureau population count.
[2] Cumulative results of Empire BlueCross BlueShield daily call-satisfaction surveys for all product lines from January 5 to April 16, 2004.
Services provided by Empire HealthChoice HMO, Inc., and/or Empire HealthChoice Assurance, Inc., licensees of the Blue Cross and Blue Shield Association, an association of independent Blue Cross and Blue Shield Plans.

MetLife, Inc.

Founded and headquartered in New York City since 1868, the MetLife companies provide insurance and other financial services for institutions and individuals, with a commitment to building financial freedom for everyone.

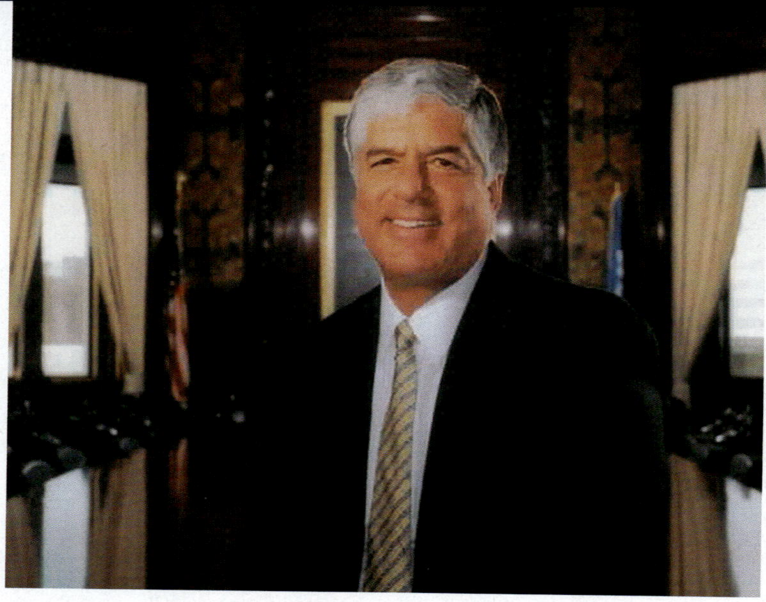

Robert H. Benmosche is chairman and chief executive officer of MetLife, Inc.

When people hear the name "MetLife," they might find themselves thinking of Snoopy. Though Snoopy and the rest of the PEANUTS® comic strip characters have been associated with the company for close to 20 years, MetLife has been around much longer, offering insurance and other financial services products for more than 135 years. Founded and still headquartered in New York City, MetLife has a long heritage of providing its customers with high quality financial products and services backed by strong financials and a commitment to the highest of business standards.

A Proud History

MetLife's commitment to meeting the needs of working Americans began in 1868, when the company was chartered to sell "ordinary" insurance to the middle class. The name "Metropolitan Life" was chosen because a predecessor company had been most successful in New York City—"the Metropolitan district."

One of MetLife's strong characteristics has been its commitment to producing programs that promote and strengthen the welfare of Americans. In fact, the company has created many programs that have become models for American public health intervention. Over the years, MetLife also has played a central role in more than just the lives of its customers. In the 1930s, for example, the company underwrote many large-scale commercial real estate projects, including the Empire State Building and Rockefeller Center.

In 2000, MetLife reached another milestone when the company completed an initial public offering, and MetLife stock became the most widely held in North America.

A Diverse Financial Services Provider

Today, MetLife has a customer base that is as diverse as the products and services it provides. In addition to being the largest life insurer in the United States, MetLife counts 88 of the Fortune 100 as group customers, as it provides insurance for 37 million employees and family members through their plan sponsors.

The MetLife companies also serve individuals in approximately 13 million households in the United States and an additional eight million individuals internationally. These customers rely on MetLife for a wide variety of financial solutions, including life, automobile, homeowners, disability, dental, and long-term care insurance; annuities; and individual banking products through MetLife Bank.

In addition to its diverse financial solutions, MetLife offers a bold and universal vision: to build financial freedom for everyone. To fulfill this purpose, MetLife focuses on building partnerships with its customers in order to help them become more confident about their financial security.

Looking to the future, MetLife has plans to build upon its long history of providing unique solutions for its customers by launching new and innovative products, expanding its role as a leader, and continuing to provide high quality financial solutions that are backed by a trusted, well-recognized brand name and strong financial performance.

Photo: © Digital Vision/age fotostock

Business-to-Business Services

Grand Central Partnership

With the mission to 'clean, protect, beautify, build, and promote' the 68-block Grand Central neighborhood in the heart of Manhattan, this model organization has successfully transformed an important and popular district into a good-looking, vibrant place to visit or live, work, dine, shop, and enjoy entertainment.

The neighborhood surrounding Grand Central Terminal in New York City's midtown Manhattan is truly a vibrant place.

By day, thousands of workers, visitors, and residents pour into the 68-block community to work in its corporate offices, shop in its numerous flagship stores, absorb the sights of its architectural landmarks, or visit its many prominent cultural institutions.

By night, New Yorkers and visitors by the thousands dine in the neighborhood's diverse restaurants, relax in its stylish cocktail lounges, enjoy early breakfast in its fine hotels, or take in one of the first-rate concerts and special events held throughout the year.

This was not always so. In the 1970s and early 1980s, like many urban central business districts around the nation, the area was in the throes of physical decline and economic deterioration. It was not the dynamic place that flourishes today.

Midtown Manhattan property owners and residents became appalled by the neighborhood's downward slide, punctuated by the flight of several Fortune 500 companies, and in 1985 they sprang into action, creating the nonprofit Grand Central Business Partnership to address the critical issues confronting the midtown Manhattan community.

As a result of those grassroots efforts, in 1988 the Grand Central Business Improvement District was established, which today is one of the largest business improvement districts in the United States. It consists of 76 million square feet of commercial space in an area bounded roughly by Fifth Avenue and Second Avenue, from 35th Street to 54th Street, in the heart of Manhattan. The revitalization plan included an ambitious streetscape improvement program, innovatively funded by capital improvement bond proceeds; a privately managed sanitation, maintenance, and public safety operation; a social services component; a business-assistance initiative; and a broad-based tourism and visitor services program.

Funded principally through special assessments collected from the district's commercial property owners and managed by a board of directors and officers elected by the district's volunteer management association, the Grand Central Partnership managed to transform the neighborhood into one of New York's most lively hubs—a bustling center of commercial activity by day and a destination for fun and culture by night.

The district contains more than 23,000 businesses, including nearly 800 retail stores. It is home to some of the world's major corporations, financial institutions, and law firms, such as Metropolitan Life, Altria Group, Pfizer, J.P. Morgan Chase, Bear Stearns, and Citigroup. It is also headquarters for three professional sports leagues: Major League Baseball, the National Football League, and Major League Soccer. It offers hundreds of restaurants, serving meals from simple to gourmet; popular lounges; and 30 hotels, two of which—the Grand Hyatt New York and the Roosevelt—host some of New York City's largest meetings and conventions. And, along with the landmark Grand Central Terminal anchoring the heart of the neighborhood, the district encompasses such world-famous landmarks as the

All photos: © Danny Bright

Chrysler Building, the Citigroup Center, the Seagram Building, Lever House, and St. Bartholomew's Church.

The Grand Central Partnership today is in the vanguard of the movement to provide supplemental services in urban centers, having changed the face of once-blighted midtown Manhattan with innovative, cutting-edge solutions. Through the vigilant efforts of the Grand Central Partnership's own sanitation team, the neighborhood's streets and sidewalks, once marred by litter and graffiti, are clean. The area has become vastly more safe thanks to the Grand Central Partnership's uniformed public safety officers, who provide a highly visible auxiliary security presence from early morning until late at night. By 2003, major crime in the district had been reduced by an impressive 67 percent over the previous decade. And through the organization's efforts, an uplifting sight of urban landscaping and horticulture pervades the district, with hundreds of trees, as well as shrubs and flowers in sidewalk planters and elevated baskets; street furniture; festive decorations; and more than a few miniparks, secluded courtyards, and plazas.

As part of the master plan for the Grand Central neighborhood, the Grand Central Partnership has initiated two major improvement projects along thoroughfares that feed into Grand Central Terminal. Completed in 2003, the transformation of East 41st Street between Park Avenue and Fifth Avenue into Library Way created a dramatic promenade featuring 100 bronze plaques with quotations from prominent figures in the world of literature and poetry, making it a suitable entryway to The New York Public Library's Humanities and Social Sciences Library. Earlier, the organization created U.N. Way, on East 43rd Street between Lexington Avenue and Tudor Place, as a fitting grand gateway to the headquarters of the world's preeminent organization for promoting international peace. It also established, in front of Grand Central Terminal on Park Avenue, Pershing Square Plaza—an urban oasis where pedestrians can pause to sit, consume a bag lunch, or simply absorb the sun's rays in fair weather.

The Grand Central Partnership has proved itself to be one of New York City's prime movers. The organization serves as a model for other business improvement districts, providing leadership and assistance to entities around the world that are hoping to emulate the group's extraordinary success.

Opposite page: The midtown Manhattan business improvement district served by the Grand Central Partnership (GCP) is home to many of the city's world-famous architectural and cultural landmarks, with the beaux arts–style Grand Central Terminal, on East 42nd Street, anchoring the neighborhood. This page, left: GCP programs range from business assistance, social services, and tourism to public safety and streetscape improvement. Its year-round horticultural program is responsible for cultivating and maintaining hundreds of trees, as well as shrubs and flowers in sidewalk planters and elevated baskets, throughout the neighborhood. Far left: The GCP's Public Safety division staffs a full-time taxi-dispatching stand outside Grand Central Terminal on East 42nd Street to help ease congestion in one of midtown Manhattan's busiest corridors.

Support Services Alliance, Inc.

This small business membership organization provides affordable group health insurance, employee benefits administration, payroll administration, and government advocacy, as well as other services, for small businesses and the self-employed.

Support Services Alliance, Inc., team members demonstrate the strength and stability that come from working together.

Support Services Alliance, Inc. (SSA), based in Oneida, New York, provides benefits and assistance to more than 14,000 small businesses and people who are self-employed in upstate New York. The company's membership includes manufacturers, retailers, wholesalers, professionals, and service providers. Combined, SSA's member companies employ more than 100,000 New Yorkers. SSA members are able to purchase a variety of services and programs at prices and terms usually reserved for large companies.

With corporate offices in Oneida, New York, and an operations center in Schoharie, New York, SSA employs a staff of 60. SSA staff members use their expertise, experience, and contacts to assist businesses with 50 or fewer employees. SSA offers more than 20 programs and services, some of which are created and implemented by SSA and some contracted through providers selected and monitored by SSA.

SSA's programs and services are many. They include advocacy in the state legislature; group insurance programs, including health, dental, vision, and life; payroll and benefits administration; a monthly news magazine; and a toll-free Member HelpLine.

In addition to its direct membership, SSA is affiliated with 67 associations, for a collective membership of 50,000. These associations include many chambers of commerce and trade associations.

SSA was started in New York City in 1977. Founder Herb Heaton, an author and CPA, believed small businesses were the economic backbone of America and could strengthen their economic position by forming a purchasing alliance. His idea worked, and he operated the company successfully for eight years.

In 1985, a group of businessmen, including Charles Wright of Schoharie and Keith Johnson of Oneida, purchased SSA, which then had 1,000 employees of small businesses enrolled in its group health insurance plan. After Wright and Johnson purchased SSA, the company was relocated to Schoharie.

Big Solutions for Small Business

Inc. magazine named SSA one of the country's 500 fastest growing enterprises

in 1993 and 1994. By 1995, SSA employed a staff of more than 50 and had enrolled more than 20,000 small-business employees in its group health plans. In 1997, the company opened the Center for Small Business in Oneida, which eventually became the organization's corporate office. The Lifetime Healthcare Companies—a not-for-profit company—bought SSA in 2001.

In 2004, SSA joined the New York Main Street Coalition, whose purpose is to consolidate the influence of representatives of small business on legislators and other state officials. The move allows SSA to have a greater presence in Albany. As an advocate for small business, SSA is committed to working on behalf of its members and for the issues that impact them the most. SSA has dedicated itself to being a primary voice for small businesses in upstate New York and a leader in making New York a more vibrant and attractive place to work, live, and own a business.

"There are a host of issues facing lawmakers that could affect small business," says Steven C. Cole, SSA president and chief operating officer. "SSA's advocacy initiative provides a voice for small businesses to register their concerns directly."

With health care costs rising beyond the reach of many working Americans, SSA continues to offer affordable solutions. A health savings account (HSA), for instance, combines a tax-free savings account with a high-deductible health plan. Money put into an HSA is tax-free when spent on medical care, and any balance remains in the account and can accumulate year to year. Additionally, SSA offers a wide variety of group health insurance plans to meet the needs of all small-business owners across the state, giving them more flexibility in choosing the plan that is right for them. SSA allows small businesses to offer the same health insurance benefits to their employees as large companies are able to provide.

"SSA provides service and pricing for small businesses that even larger corporations cannot get," Cole says. "Mr. Heaton's dream is now a reality."

Above left: SSA staff members gather at headquarters in Oneida, New York.
Above: Shown clockwise from top left are Steven C. Cole, SSA president and COO; Herb Heaton, SSA founder; Lori Warner, SSA director of underwriting; representatives of one of SSA's members, the Bernier Carr Group architecture, engineering, and construction firm; and Sally McLean, SSA member relations representative.

The Fashion Center Business Improvement District

The nonprofit Fashion Center Business Improvement District promotes and assists businesses in Manhattan's famed Fashion District, providing public safety and sanitation, district promotions and events, business development initiatives, information services, and streetscape improvements.

At the crossroads of high fashion and high art, the Fashion Center Business Improvement District enhances the economy and quality of life in and around New York City's famed Fashion District.

The Fashion Center Business Improvement District (BID), a New York State nonprofit corporation, was founded in 1993 as a cooperative initiative of property owners, local businesses, and the City of New York. This organization's mission is to enhance the economic vitality of the area, promote and assist local businesses, and improve the quality of life for all who visit, work, and live in New York City's famed Fashion District.

A historic look at the Fashion District reveals an evolving neighborhood that epitomizes everything New York City stands for and provides an overview of the global economy at work. Built in the 1930s as the center for apparel design and manufacturing in the United States, the Fashion District has been home to many of fashion's most recognizable names: Oscar de la Renta, Bill Blass, Calvin Klein, and Donna Karan, to name just a few. The midtown Manhattan district's Fashion Walk of Fame on Seventh Avenue immortalizes the greats that built the industry and the city into a world fashion capital.

Today, how the world does business has changed, and so has the Fashion District. Still home to many of America's greatest designers and more than 1,000 showrooms, the neighborhood has evolved from a manufacturing hub to a creative epicenter with a burgeoning arts community, off-Broadway theaters, and related organizations and services. With numerous photographers, fine and graphic artists, architects, and other members of the "creative economy," the district provides an authentic New York gateway to the Hudson Yards development project. Also, the Fashion District, with its location in the heart of Manhattan, offers unparalleled transportation options and walking proximity to many of the city's best shopping and sights.

Programs provided by the Fashion Center BID include public safety and sanitation, district promotions and events, business development initiatives, fashion industry information services, and streetscape improvements. In addition to tracking economic, real estate, and employment trends, the Fashion Center Business Improvement District serves as ombudsman and liaison to city government officials on issues affecting the area and its constituent companies.

Contact the Fashion Center at 249 West 39th Street, New York, NY 10018; phone: 212-764-9600; Web site: www.fashioncenter.com.

Above: The unique, octagonal Fashion Center Information Kiosk, located at the heart of the business district, serves as a central information source for fashion professionals around the world. Above right: Centrally located in midtown Manhattan, the Fashion District boasts some of the highest pedestrian activity in the city, with economic spending power of more than $700 million annually.

Alliance for Downtown New York, Inc.

This organization works to enhance the quality of life in lower Manhattan, providing a wide array of services—such as security and maintenance, transportation, marketing and special events, economic development, streetscape, and visitor services—to create a vibrant community for living, working, and visiting.

It is the mission of the Alliance for Downtown New York, Inc., to transform lower Manhattan into a vibrant setting that supports a healthy, prosperous business and residential community and is a welcoming destination for visitors.

Founded in 1995, this nonprofit corporation, which manages the Business Improvement District (BID) area south of Chambers Street, has made extensive improvements to the downtown community with a myriad of neighborhood and business services, economic development and design programs, and marketing initiatives. The district extends from City Hall to the Battery, from the East River across to West Street.

Every day, Downtown Alliance maintenance staff members haul away garbage, sweep sidewalks, and remove graffiti. They have pitched in to beautify parks, plant flowers, and renovate public plazas. Working closely with the New York Police Department, dozens of Downtown Alliance public safety officers patrol the area daily, producing one of the city's lowest crime rates. The organization also has launched the Downtown Connection, a free shuttle bus service for the neighborhood, operating seven days a week.

The Downtown Alliance scored a major success with the Stone Street restoration, which it coordinated. The 19th-century look of this historic but neglected thoroughfare was recreated, transforming it into an attractive and lively destination for dining and nightlife. And the organization's award-winning Streetscape Program has given a sophisticated new look to lower Broadway.

The Downtown Alliance promotes businesses in the neighborhood through advertising campaigns, publications, and special events. Wildly popular promotional events such as Dine Around Downtown, Love Downtown, Music at Castle Clinton concert series, and Downtown for Dinner showcase local destinations. Free walking tours and information kiosks help visitors discover the neighborhood's historic and architectural treasures.

The Downtown Alliance spearheaded the Downtown NYC River to River Festival, now an annual event. The festival brings millions of people to lower Manhattan all summer long to enjoy world-class performers in music, dance, theater, and more, held at major historic and picturesque venues.

Right: Among its many projects, the Alliance for Downtown New York, Inc., coordinated the restoration of historic Stone Street, in lower Manhattan. As seen here, the street is bustling after office hours.

An innovation by the Downtown Alliance to speed the recovery of the neighborhood was to work in partnership with Seedco, an effort that secured pledges of more than $24 million in aid for local businesses. Intensive marketing and recruiting efforts have successfully boosted the area's rate of commercial occupancy.

And now, thanks to another Downtown Alliance innovation—the Lower Manhattan Wireless Network—the district has become technologically one of the best-connected neighborhoods in the nation. This cutting-edge program created wireless hotspots—providing free, high-speed Internet access for mobile devices—in seven major public spaces in the area.

The Downtown Alliance stands firmly behind this historic, dynamic, and resilient New York City neighborhood, continuing its ongoing mission to ensure that the area will remain a center of culture and the financial capital of the world for decades to come.

Photo: © Aspen Stock/age fotostock

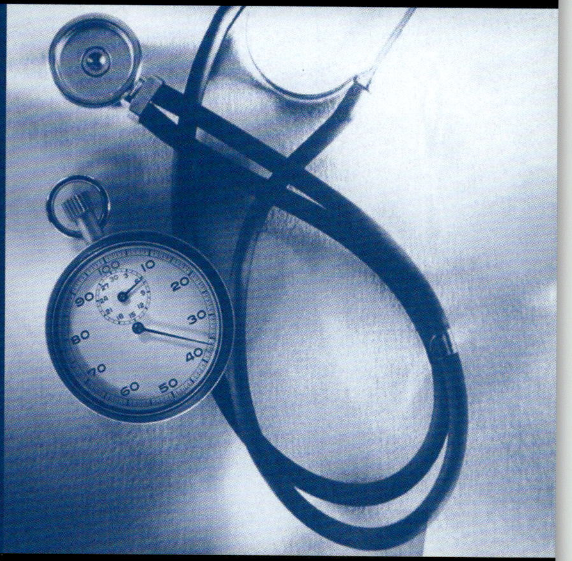

Health Care, Medical Services, & Medical Centers

St. Joseph's Hospital Health Center

Founded by the Third Franciscan Order and still operated by the Sisters of St. Francis, this top-rated health center includes a school of nursing, a psychiatric emergency program, and two outpatient surgery centers, and provides general medical and surgical care, dental services, and pediatrics.

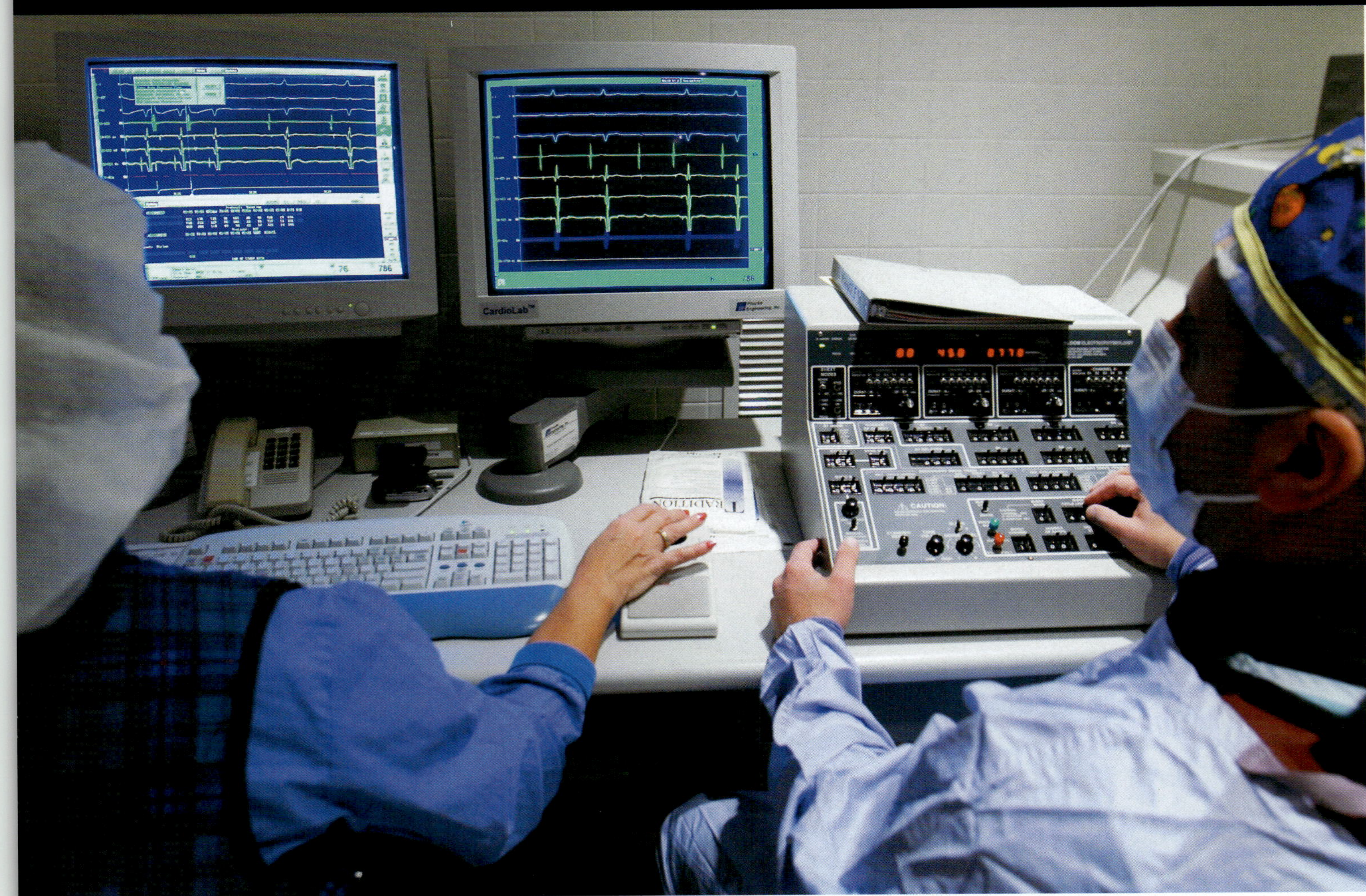

St. Joseph's Hospital Health Center is known for the high quality of its cardiac services. Its cardiovascular laboratory serves more than 5,000 patients annually and that number is growing.

St. Joseph's Hospital Health Center is a 431-bed, comprehensive medical care institution dedicated to providing quality health care to the residents of 16 counties in central New York State. St. Joseph's and its ambulatory programs, mental health services, home care, and Franciscan Health Support are accredited by the Joint Commission on Accreditation of Healthcare Organizations.

Syracuse's first hospital has stood as a community landmark atop Prospect Hill in Syracuse since 1869, when five sisters of the Third Franciscan Order transformed a dance hall and bar into a 15-bed hospital. Its growth has paralleled that of the city. The institution, which is still operated by the Sisters of St. Francis, has evolved into a health care system that, in addition to the hospital, includes a school of nursing, a psychiatric emergency program, and two outpatient surgery centers.

As well as providing general medical and surgical care, St. Joseph's offers several specialty services, including hemodialysis, maternity and pediatric services, a separate birth center, emergency care, intensive care, dental services, suicide prevention, and certified home health care. St. Joseph's also operates several satellite facilities, including family and maternal child clinics, a dental clinic, a psychiatric services center, the Wellness Place, a regional dialysis center, neighborhood dialysis centers, and a cardiopulmonary rehabilitation center.

St. Joseph's has been designated by New York State as a special care neonatal unit, apnea center, cardiac diagnostic center, cardiac surgical center, and community mental health center. The hospital's busy emergency department records more than 52,000 visits a year; inpatient visits average 23,000 a year, and outpatient visits throughout the health care network number 400,000 a year.

St. Joseph's, with an annual operating budget of $311 million, is staffed by more than 800 physicians and dentists representing a broad spectrum of specialties. It employs more than 3,600 other health care professionals and support personnel, and more than 1,000 devoted volunteers and members of the hospital's auxiliary help support patient care programs.

In 2002, St. Joseph's received a Magnet Recognition for Excellence in Nursing Service from the American Nurses Credentialing Center in Washington, D.C. Magnet recognition is the nation's highest honor for nursing services. The same year, Solucient—a health care database provider—named St. Joseph's in a national benchmarking study as one of the country's 100 top hospitals. St. Joseph's also has won the National Research Corporation's Consumer Choice Award for four consecutive years, and when surveyed by Press Ganey Associates, Inc., a health care consulting firm, 90 percent of St. Joseph's patients said they would recommend St. Joseph's to others.

St. Joseph's is well known for the high quality of its cardiac services. In 1958, St. Joseph's performed the area's first open-heart surgery, and the hospital's commitment to providing exceptional cardiac services is evident in its patient outcomes and dedication to providing the community with a network of diagnostic, treatment, and rehabilitation services.

The New York State Department of Health ranked St. Joseph's surgeons number one in the state for coronary artery bypass graft surgery in 1997, 1998, and 1999, the most recent years for which data are available. St. Joseph's cardiac surgeons also perform minimally invasive bypass and valve surgery, when appropriate for the patient.

Not everyone who has cardiac disease needs cardiac surgery. St. Joseph's state-of-the-art cardiovascular laboratory has the highest volume for a facility of its type in central New York, serving more than 5,000 patients annually. The interventional cardiologists on staff have participated in national studies of promising new technologies such as the drug-eluting stent, a device for use in angioplasty procedures to open clogged coronary arteries, enabling St. Joseph's to offer patients the very latest in proven techniques to fight coronary artery disease.

St. Joseph's cardiovascular laboratory was renovated and expanded in spring 2004 to serve a growing number of patients needing diagnostic and/or interventional procedures such as angioplasty and stent. The expanded laboratory features four cardiac catheterization suites and uses the latest digital imaging equipment, allowing cardiologists to view down to one 100th of an inch.

St. Joseph's Hospital Health Center was founded by the Sisters of the Third Franciscan Order in 1869. Today, the institution is an award-winning hospital with revenues of $311 million.

St. Joseph's has an exciting future as it continues to meet the demands of a growing community and keep pace with financial and technological challenges. A capital campaign, "A Tradition in Excellence," is expected to raise $8 million for St. Joseph's Hospital Health Center—funds that will help the hospital purchase brand-new, high-tech equipment to keep it on the cutting edge of health care in the 21st century.

For more information, contact the health center at 301 Prospect Avenue, Syracuse, NY 13203; phone: 1-888-STJOES1; Web site: www.sjhsyr.org.

North Shore–Long Island Jewish (LIJ) Health System

Determined to set new standards in the diagnosis, treatment, and research of diseases affecting people of all ages, this 17-hospital system includes three world-class tertiary hospitals, a nationally recognized children's hospital and research institute, and a 731-bed facility rated among the best hospitals in America.

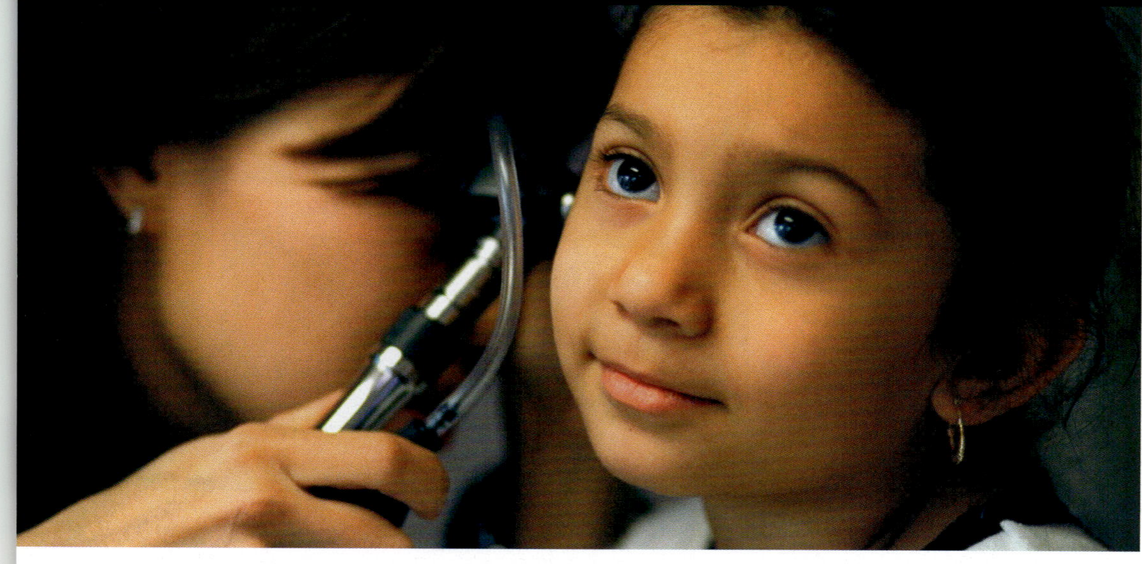

The North Shore–Long Island Jewish (LIJ) Health System strives to provide high quality, compassionate care to patients young and old, regardless of their ability to pay.

Much like the neighborhoods of Long Island, Queens, and Staten Island, the North Shore–Long Island Jewish (LIJ) Health System draws its strength from its diversity. From the cutting-edge technologies being explored at the North Shore–LIJ Research Institute to the caring touch of the health professionals at its community hospitals, the health system strives to provide an unparalleled spectrum of services for the region.

The North Shore–LIJ Health System's 17 hospitals, four long-term care facilities, three trauma centers, seven home health agencies, and dozens of outpatient centers offer the latest in medical care without sacrificing compassionate concern. The health system's facilities house more than 5,670 beds and are staffed by more than 7,000 physicians, 7,000 nurses, and a workforce of about 33,700. The system is the largest employer on Long Island and the seventh largest in New York City.

The unique relationship among these facilities allows patients to take advantage of the specialized expertise of thousands of medical professionals. What distinguishes the North Shore–LIJ Health System? Some of its many accomplishments include:

- **North Shore University Hospital** in Manhasset was rated the nation's number one metropolitan hospital in a study by the nonprofit consumer information resource firm Consumers' Checkbook, published by *AARP Modern Maturity* (now *AARP The Magazine*).
- **North Shore University Hospital** in Manhasset and **Long Island Jewish Medical Center** in New Hyde Park have two of the best ratings for cardiac care in New York State.
- **Schneider Children's Hospital** in New Hyde Park is regarded as one of the best children's hospitals in the state.
- **The North Shore–LIJ Neurosciences Institute** in Great Neck is a destination of hope for patients from around the world who suffer from debilitating brain malformations and neurological conditions.
- **The North Shore–LIJ Research Institute** is world-renowned for its studies of such illnesses as cancer; Parkinson's, Alzheimer's, and Huntington's diseases; rheumatoid arthritis; sepsis; AIDS; schizophrenia; depression; and obesity.
- **The Zucker Hillside Hospital** in Glen Oaks is recognized nationally for its pioneering work in the diagnosis, treatment, and research of mental illness.

An Employer of Choice

As a health care provider, the overriding mission of the North Shore–LIJ Health System is to provide its patients with a safe, reliable, caring, and trustworthy environment. Recognizing the direct link between patient satisfaction and employee satisfaction, North Shore–LIJ has invested heavily in building a "learning organization" that offers workers at all levels the opportunity for personal and professional growth. Two years ago, the health system teamed with the General Electric Company and the Harvard School of Public Health to create a "corporate university" called the Center of Learning and Innovation—the largest such organization in the U.S. health care industry.

"An investment in our employees leads to better patient care, helping us to achieve our goal of becoming both an employer and provider of

Right: North Shore–LIJ Health System hospitals have some of the top surgeons in the New York area. Below: The nursing staff of North Shore–LIJ is recognized for its excellence.

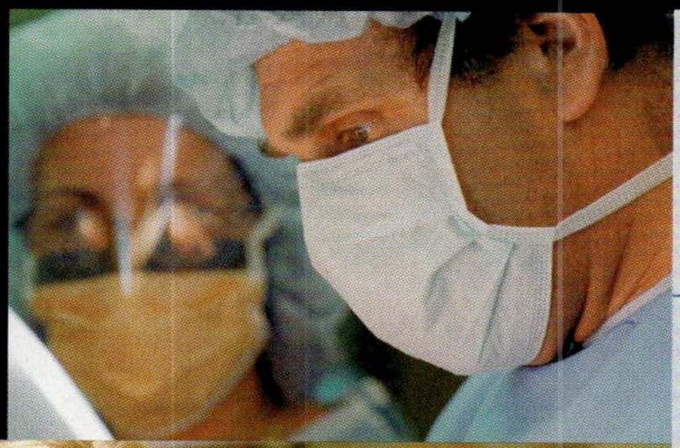

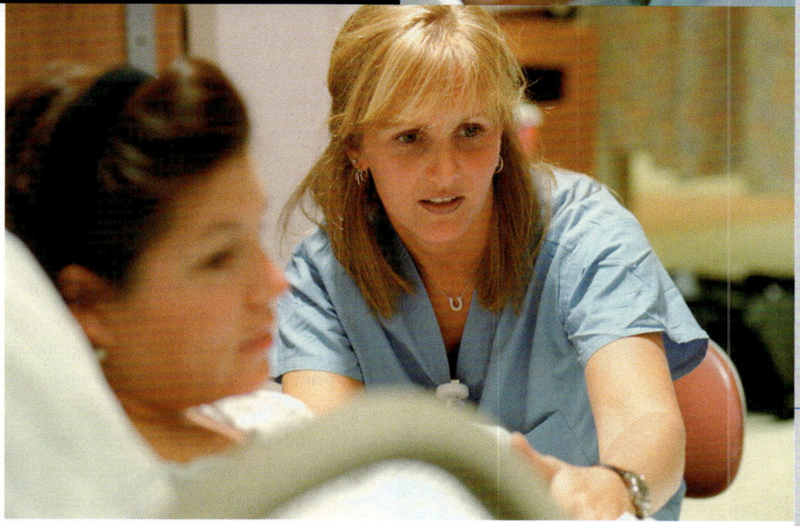

choice in the health care industry," says Michael Dowling, president and CEO of the North Shore–LIJ Health System.

A Commitment to Nursing

Nurses are at the heart and soul of the North Shore–LIJ Health System. It is no coincidence that while the nationwide nursing vacancy rate is approaching 15 percent, less than 6 percent of nursing jobs are unfilled at the health system's hospitals. Results speak for themselves. Long Island Jewish Medical Center and North Shore University Hospital in Manhasset were the first two hospitals in New York to earn the prestigious honor of Magnet Recognition for Excellence in Nursing Service. Magnet recognition, the nursing profession equivalent of an Olympic gold medal, is recognized as a valuable recruiting advantage in attracting top nursing talent.

For additional information on the North Shore–LIJ Health System, visit the Web site www.northshorelij.com; to find a physician affiliated with North Shore–LIJ, phone 888-321-DOCS (888-321-3627).

Facilities

At North Shore–LIJ Health System facilities, staff members come in contact with more than three million patients every year. They are committed to excellence in patient care, medical training, and community service at all of the facilities.

Hospitals

- Central Suffolk Hospital (affiliate), Riverhead 631-548-6000
- Eastern Long Island Hospital (affiliate), Greenport 631-477-1000
- Franklin Hospital Medical Center, Valley Stream 516-256-6000
- Huntington Hospital 631-351-2000
- Long Island Jewish Medical Center, New Hyde Park 718-470-7000
- North Shore University Hospital in Manhasset 516-562-0100
- North Shore University Hospital at Forest Hills 718-830-4000
- North Shore University Hospital at Glen Cove 516-674-7300
- North Shore University Hospital at Plainview 516-719-3000
- North Shore University Hospital at Syosset 516-496-6400
- Peninsula Hospital Center (affiliate), Far Rockaway 718-734-2000
- Schneider Children's Hospital, New Hyde Park 718-470-3000
- Southampton Hospital (affiliate) 631-726-8200
- Southside Hospital, Bay Shore 631-968-3000
- Staten Island University Hospital, North and South Divisions 718-226-9000 (North) and 718-226-2000 (South)
- The Zucker Hillside Hospital, Glen Oaks 718-470-8000

Long-Term Care Facilities

- Center for Extended Care and Rehabilitation, Manhasset 516-562-8000
- Orzac Center for Extended Care and Rehabilitation at Franklin Hospital Medical Center, Valley Stream 516-256-6700
- Central Suffolk Skilled Nursing Facility (affiliate), Riverhead, 631-548-6078
- Peninsula Center for Extended Care and Rehabilitation (affiliate), Far Rockaway 718-734-2750
- Glenhaven Health Care Organization (affiliate) Glen Cove, 516-676-1100

Centers of Innovation

- Core Laboratory in Lake Success, 516-719-1000
- Center for Learning and Innovation in Lake Success 516-719-6150
- Research Institute in Manhasset, 516-562-1002
- Center for Emergency Medical Services in Syosset 516-719-5000

Centers for Progressive Care

- Center for Autism, Bethpage 516-802-8600
- Center for Weight Management, New Hyde Park 718-470-4045
- Home Care Network, Westbury 516-876-7788
- Hospice Care Network, Westbury 516-832-2520
- Sports Therapy and Rehabilitation Services (STARS), East Meadow/Roslyn 516-393-8900
- Transitions of Long Island, Manhasset 516-719-3700
- Adults and Children with Learning Disabilities, Bethpage 516-822-0028

United Health Services

This regional system of health care providers offers services ranging from brain and spinal cord surgery to medical rehabilitation, while providing immediate care and lifetime knowledge to patients with chronic, life-changing illnesses such as diabetes, AIDS, and chemical dependency.

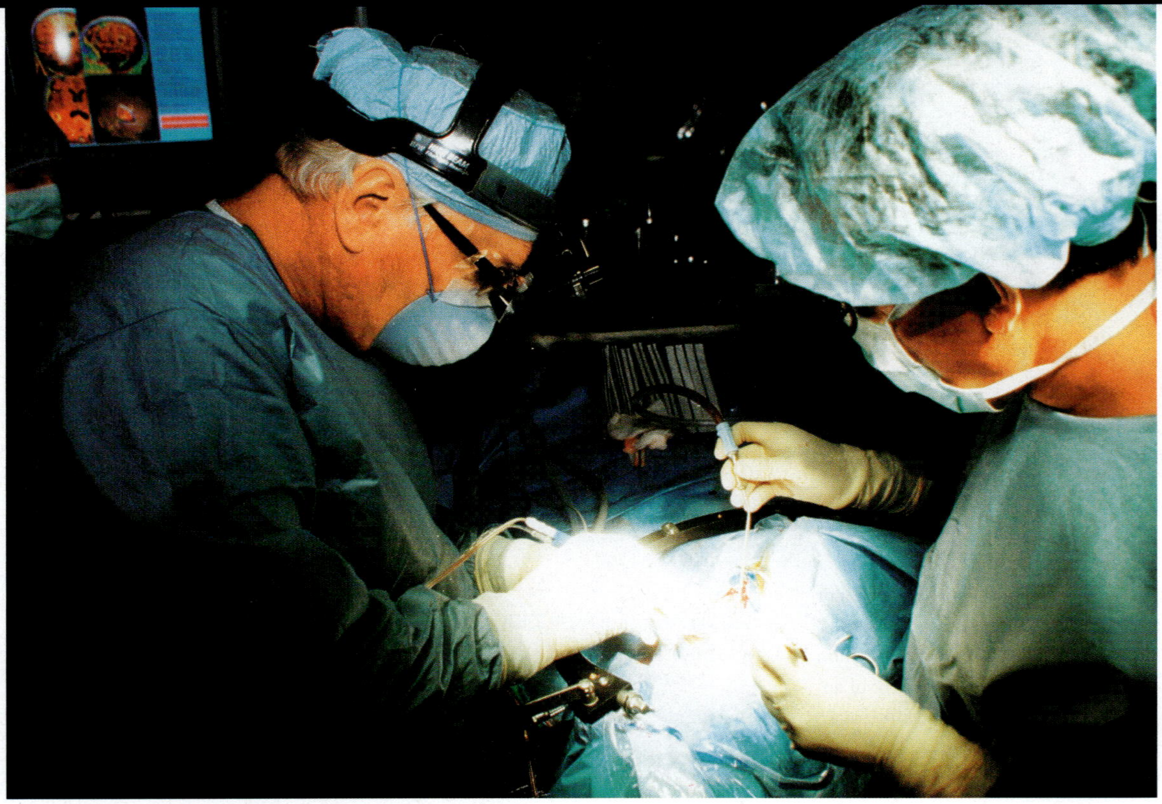

Right: Surgeons here are performing brain surgery at Wilson Memorial Regional Medical Center, one of several United Health Services affiliates in the Southern Tier.

When people in Greater Binghamton think of hospital and physician care, home care, and long-term care, they often think of United Health Services, a locally owned, not-for-profit health care system serving the cities, towns, and rural areas of New York's Southern Tier. Formed in 1981 through the consolidation of three community hospitals, United Health Services has set a goal to become the best regional health care system in the country.

United Health Services member and affiliate organizations have joined together to form a progressive partnership, a family of providers devoted to offering convenient, comprehensive, and compassionate care to people at every stage of life. As individuals and as a network, United Health Services staffers strive for excellence, working to meet real needs and deliver effective and efficient care.

The system operates United Health Services Hospitals, a 516-bed, tertiary care organization made up of Wilson Memorial Regional Medical Center in Johnson City, Binghamton General Hospital in Binghamton, and a group of primary care centers in surrounding communities. United Health Services Hospitals is a regional referral center for a number of medical and surgical specialties, including trauma care, heart surgery, brain and spinal cord surgery, cancer care, high-risk obstetrics, neonatal intensive care, reconstructive surgery, renal dialysis, and medical rehabilitation. In addition, the hospitals are dedicated to providing immediate care and lifetime knowledge to people with chronic, life-changing illnesses such as diabetes, asthma, mental illness, chemical dependency, and AIDS. With a 450-member medical staff, internships, and a medical residency program, United Health Services Hospitals is a major teaching affiliate of the Binghamton Clinical Campus of the State University of New York Upstate Medical University.

Other members of the health system are Chenango Memorial Hospital, a 139-bed community hospital serving the Norwich–Chenango County area; Delaware Valley Hospital, a 33-bed rural hospital in the Walton–Delaware County region; Ideal Senior Living Center, a national award-winning geriatric campus that includes a 150-bed skilled nursing facility, in Endicott; and Professional Home Care and Twin Tier Home Health, two home health agencies serving Broome County and surrounding areas. The system is affiliated with United Medical Associates, P.C., a locally owned multispeciality medical group with more than 140 practitioners skilled in some 25 separate medical and surgical specialties; and with the United Health Services Foundation, which seeks private donations to help support the equipment and facility needs of nonprofit system members.

The region's largest private employer and largest health care provider, United Health Services has led the way in developing and expanding new services to meet the community's changing needs. Starting in the 1980s, United Health Services has invested millions of dollars to enhance its facilities and technology to better serve patients in the Southern Tier, creating or expanding such facilities as the Decker Center for Advanced Medical Treatment, the Minimally Invasive Surgical Suite, the Gastroenterology Laboratory, the Neonatal Intensive Care Unit, and the Renal Care Center. The system has made physical improvements at its campuses and added new services, such as advanced diagnostics, laparoscopic surgery, computer-assisted medication administration, automated record-checking, and online scheduling of appointments at primary care offices.

The system has a significant economic impact on its community, approaching nearly $1 billion per year. It provides more than $21 million annually in uncompensated care, charitable endeavors, and free programs to help community residents stay well and improve their health.

Through the ongoing "Campaign for Excellence," United Health Services employees seek ways to improve personal service and consumer satisfaction in every area of inpatient and outpatient care, and use performance improvement techniques to continually find better ways to provide care.

The physicians, employees, and leadership of United Health Services believe that advances in care and service depend on the organization's ability to use the latest medical technology in concert with the skills of involved, caring health professionals. The organization continues to draw on the strength of its member and affiliate organizations, all of which work together to make a positive difference in the lives of patients and the health of the community.

Above: Located in Johnson City, Wilson Memorial Regional Medical Center is part of United Health Services Hospitals, an organization operated by United Health Services that also includes Binghamton General Hospital in Binghamton and a group of nearby primary care centers. Above left: Twin Tier Home Health nurses, like this nurse, at left, provide highly specialized, compassionate care.

Seton Health System, Inc.

With its long-standing reputation for excellence, innovation, and accountability, this award-winning health care system offers primary, acute, and continuing care at more than 20 facilities in the Capital District, while also maintaining numerous good works in the community.

The Seton Health Childbirth Center at St. Mary's Hospital provides state-of-the-art technology and large, spacious birthing suites. Additionally, programs such as Seton Health's *The Mommy Project* help young mothers prepare for birth and motherhood.

Seton Health System, Inc., is a comprehensive, integrated health care system anchored by St. Mary's Hospital in Troy, New York. A member of Ascension Health, the nation's largest not-for-profit, faith-based health care system, Seton Health provides health care services from sites in Rensselaer, Saratoga, and Albany Counties.

Dedicated to holistic care of body, mind, and spirit, Seton Health is rooted in a tradition of caring and service that began in New York's Capital District more than a century ago. In 1849, a Troy pastor requested the assistance of the Daughters of Charity religious community in caring for fever-stricken immigrants, many of whom were orphaned children. After the arrival of the Daughters, the citizens of Troy united to raise funds to build a place to care for those in need. This hospital, the first in Troy, is now St. Mary's.

In 1995, St. Mary's merged with Leonard Hospital in north Troy to create Seton Health.

Recognized as one of the finest community hospitals in the region, St. Mary's Hospital continues to pioneer some of the most advanced health care services. A state-of-the-art intensive care unit was opened in 1999 and ranked in 2000 by Solucient as one of the nation's top 100 intensive care units. In 2003, a new medical imaging wing was completed and a sleep lab opened, providing comprehensive diagnosis and treatment of sleep disorders. Also in 2003, Seton Health launched the region's only anticoagulation clinic to assist patients in the management of blood thinners. Other specialized units include an emergency department; cardiac care, oncology/hospice, orthopedic, diabetic, and pediatric units; and the Seton Health Childbirth Center. The Childbirth Center, opened in 1999, is the only facility in the region to offer single-room maternity care exclusively. Seton Health also offers a full range of outpatient services.

Seton Health offers a continuum of care, from primary through acute to continuing care, from more than 20 sites throughout the region. With 11 physician offices, Seton Health is among the area's largest primary care providers and is also a major Capital District employer, with over 1,700 associates. The system operates a variety of community-based programs including primary care and obstetrics and gynecology practices, a dental practice, cardiac and pulmonary rehabilitation programs, physical rehabilitation,

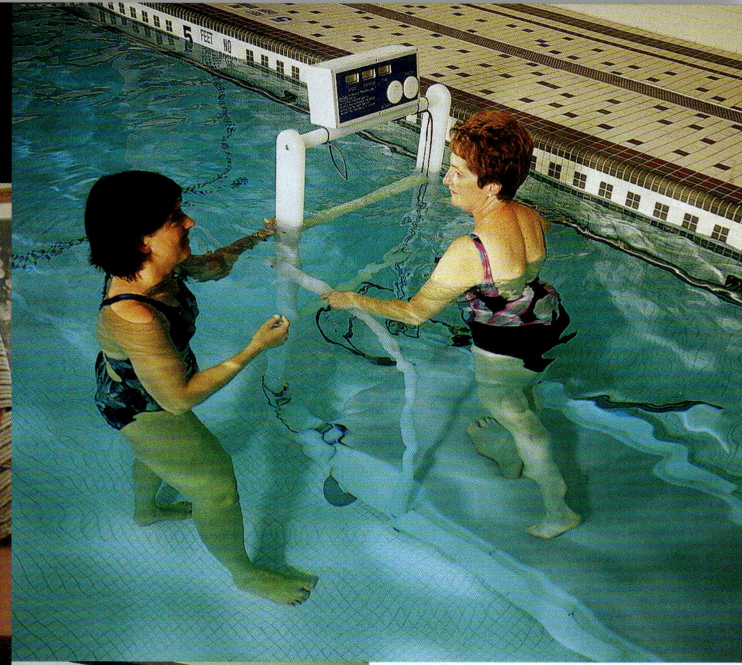

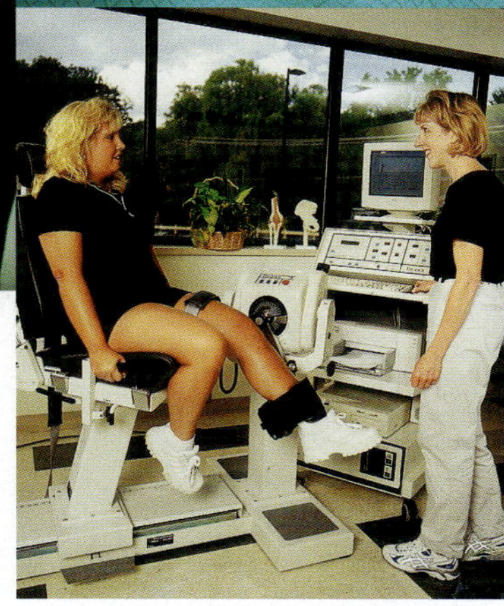

Above and left: Seton Health's physical, cardiac, and pulmonary rehabilitation services in Rensselaer and Saratoga Counties use high-tech equipment, such as an underwater treadmill and Biodex machine, to help patients integrate back into productive lifestyles. Far left: Schuyler Ridge Residential Health Care Center and Adult Day Care Program offers an alternative to traditional nursing homes by providing medical care in an environment that nurtures the social and spiritual growth of its residents.

a long-term care facility, certified and licensed home care agencies, an incontinence treatment center, and an urgent care facility.

Seton Health subscribes to the Ascension Health "Call To Action": Health care that works, health care that is safe, and health care that leaves no one behind. In working to fulfill this mission, Seton Health has provided $43 million in community benefits and uncompensated charity care to Capital Region residents since 1995.

Seton Health's mission is rooted in seeing persons, not just patients; in seeing communities, not just population numbers. Along these lines, the entire organization is committed to promoting healthful living throughout the community.

The Mommy Project, designed to help young women prepare for birth and motherhood, debuted in the fall of 2002 to address the issues of the large number of unprepared teenage mothers-to-be receiving care at the Childbirth Center.

The Butt Stops Here is an award-winning smoking cessation program developed and administered by Seton Health. Of all the similar programs funded by the New York State Department of Health, Seton Health's program has the highest rate of participation and completion. It also boasts the highest quit rate: 48 percent of participants are smoke-free at the end of the program, and approximately 33 percent are not smoking at the six-month and one-year marks.

Seton Health was instrumental in providing maintenance support and start-up funds for the Roarke Center, a food cooperative and community service agency in downtown Troy. Seton Health continues to serve the center by setting up health fairs, donating food and gifts, and offering classes and support groups.

Through the Rensselaer County Youth Employment Program, Seton Health offers disadvantaged teens hands-on experience in a variety of health care career fields.

By sponsoring free health screenings, support groups, and community health and education programs, Seton Health strives to improve the health of those in the communities it serves.

The Seton Health Foundation, the charitable arm of Seton Health/St. Mary's Hospital, raises funds to help ensure the continuation of high quality programs and state-of-the-art patient care as well as meeting the special needs of the poor and underserved.

With plans under way for construction of a new emergency department, Seton Health continues to respond to the community's changing health care needs, driven by a commitment to excellence, innovation, and accountability.

Capital*Care* Medical Group, LLC

In addition to adult and pediatric care, immunizations, and laboratory services, this physician-owned medical group offers services in endocrinology, diabetes education, preventive medicine, and nutritional counseling.

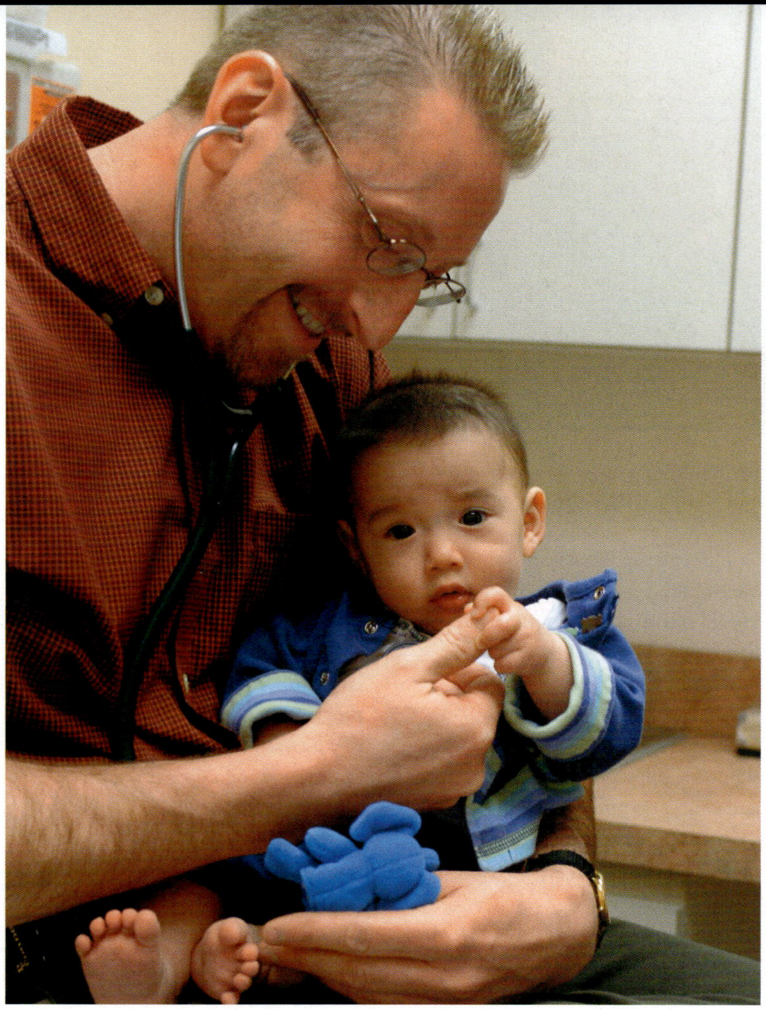

A young patient is examined by a Capital*Care* pediatrician.

Founded in 1997, Capital*Care* Medical Group is one of the largest independently operated primary care physician groups in upstate New York. The group, which is physician-owned and -directed, serves more than 130,000 patients from 19 offices in Albany, Saratoga, and Schenectady Counties. Capital*Care* has chosen to maintain its medical offices in many local communities, while achieving economies of scale by moving essential business functions to one central office. Its pediatric, family practice, and internal medicine services include preventive examinations, acute care, immunizations, and health education.

Advocating Wellness

According to the Centers for Disease Control and Prevention, chronic illness claims the lives of more than 1.7 million Americans each year and accounts for more than 75 percent of the nation's health care costs. The prevention and management of these diseases through medical checkups, nutritional programs, patient education, and the use of state-of-the-art technology are Capital*Care*'s primary focus.

Endocrine disorders, including diabetes, osteoporosis, and thyroid disease, are among the most prevalent chronic diseases. Capital*Care* also provides comprehensive services by endocrinologists specializing in these conditions, as well as thyroid nodules and cancer, and sexual dysfunction. Postmenopausal women, who are at high risk for osteoporosis, can undergo noninvasive DXA (dual emission X-ray absorptiometry) scanning, today the gold standard in measuring bone density. If loss of bone density is detected early, effective medical treatment can reduce the risk of debilitating fractures.

In addition, Capital*Care* offers a comprehensive diabetes education program: Diabetes Matters . . . Steps Toward a Healthy Lifestyle. The program is recognized by the American Diabetes Association, which estimates that diabetes affects more than 18 million Americans and their families. Patients in the program learn to monitor their blood sugar levels and how to balance food, medication, and exercise to help manage diabetes and prevent its complications, which include heart and kidney disease, poor circulation, and blindness. A certified insulin pump trainer works with those patients who are using continuous insulin delivery systems. Equally important, all participants are taught

Photos, both pages: © Timothy Raab–Northern Photo

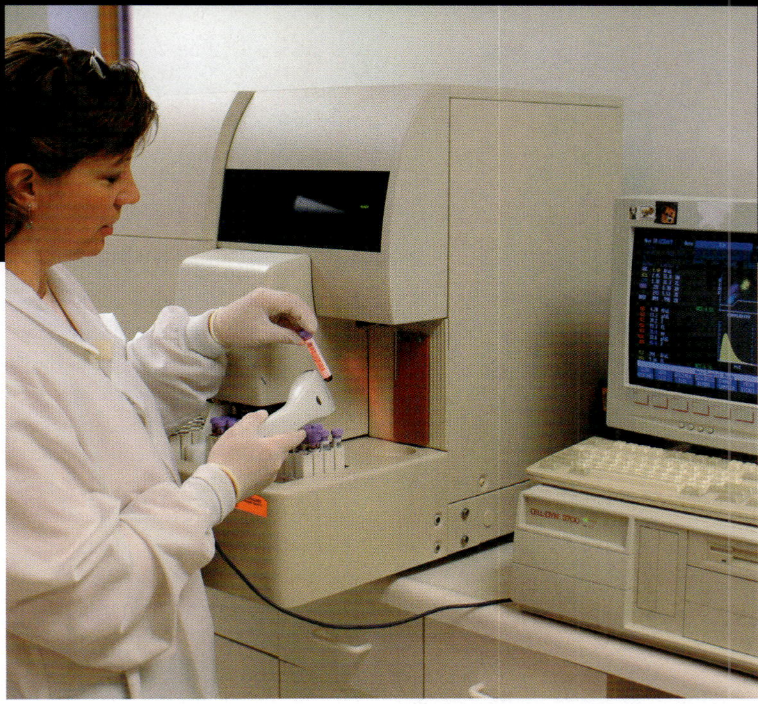

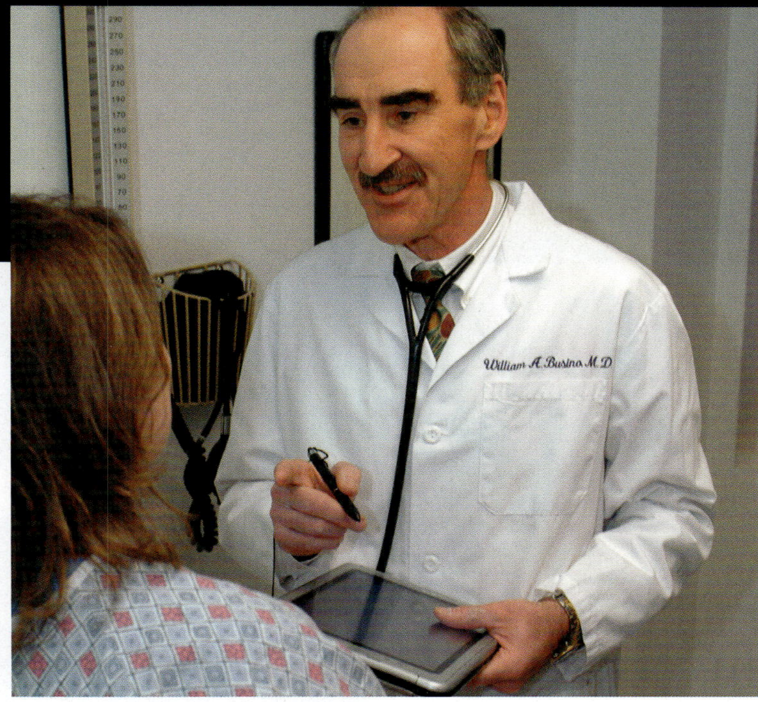

Far left: A technologist at the Capital*Care* centralized, state-of-the-art laboratory scans a specimen before processing. Left: A Capital*Care* internist uses a wireless PC tablet in the examining room.

coping strategies for stress reduction and living with diabetes.

The program also offers specialized instruction for women who develop diabetes during pregnancy, and sessions for children with diabetes. Directed by a nurse practitioner, the program staff also includes registered dietitians and certified diabetes educators.

Capital*Care* physicians recognize the importance of good nutrition and regular physical activity in preventing cardiovascular diseases. As the major causes of death in the United States, cardiovascular disorders can be directly linked to unhealthy lifestyles. To help minimize the impact of these illnesses, Capital*Care* offers a nutritional counseling program that addresses the needs of patients in all age groups. It includes individual patient assessments as well as dietary and behavior modification.

Committed to Excellence

Quality and efficiency are the hallmarks of Capital*Care*, which repeatedly has been named a Better Performing Practice by the Medical Group Management Association, one of the nation's leading organizations for medical group practice administration. Capital*Care* physicians, relieved of most administrative functions by the central business office, have more time to focus on patient care.

Using wireless PC tablets at the point of service, they can retrieve complete information on a real-time basis from anywhere—including their homes, hospitals, and other remote locations. The same state-of-the-art technology allows them to complete charts, obtain accurate test results from the full-service centralized laboratory, and write prescriptions, while also reducing the risk of medical errors. All Capital*Care* locations share the same information systems and are interconnected with broadband data lines.

As a member of the Healthcare Quality Roundtable—an organization of medical leaders in the Capital District—Capital*Care* participates with other physician groups, hospitals, insurers, employers, and academic institutions to provide better quality care throughout the region. The group also supports the Institute for the Advancement of Health Care Management at the State University of New York at Albany, which sponsors programs to assist health care organizations in applying effective management techniques. Clearly, Capital*Care's* commitment to quality, preventive medicine, and disease management places it on the leading edge of health care delivery.

Prime Care Physicians, P.C.

This integrated group practice of cardiologists, primary care physicians, and radiologists employs such technologies as magnetic resonance imaging, three-dimensional cardiac ultrasound, and cardiovascular interventions, as well as behavior modification, in helping patients improve their quality of life.

PRIME CARE PHYSICIANS, P.C.

The caregivers of Prime Care Physicians, P.C., build strong doctor-patient relationships in an integrated group practice.

"Our goal," says Michael J. Gardner, M.D., the chairman of Prime Care Physicians, P.C., "is to treat our patients' health care needs with skill, expertise, and compassion."

Strength and energy unite people when they work together toward a common goal. In the case of Prime Care, that goal is to improve the quality of medical treatment by building strong doctor-patient relationships in an integrated group practice. Implementing that goal has made Prime Care a model of medicine and management among health care providers in upstate New York.

Doctors Harry C. Odabashian Jr. and David Brown founded Albany Associates in Cardiology in 1981. The firm became Prime Care Physicians, P.C., in 1997, when 14 prominent primary care physicians, who shared a common vision for improved quality of care, merged with the cardiologists. Prime Care provides comprehensive cardiology, radiology, inpatient medicine ("hospitalist"), and primary care services to more than 1,300 patients per day through its network of 80 physicians, 25 midlevel providers, and 350 nonmedical staff in 15 outpatient and 11 hospitals throughout upstate New York.

Prime Care's cardiology practice, which continues to be known as Albany Associates in Cardiology, is renowned throughout the region, often generating patient referrals from as far north as the Canadian border, from as far west as Utica, and from as far south as Poughkeepsie. Prime Care provides a full spectrum of cardiology services, from patients at risk for developing cardiovascular disease to patients who have end-stage heart disease. One of Prime Care's many successful programs is its Center for Preventive Medicine & Cardiovascular Health, which focuses on reducing cardiovascular risk, including altering nutritional and exercise habits through Prime Care's Cardiofit™ and Nutrafit™ programs. The center collaborates with selected restaurants in the Capital District to create Heart Healthy menu offerings, which enable patients who are at risk to enjoy dining out while still meeting the strict requirements of the Cardiofit and Nutrafit diets.

Prime Care uses advanced diagnostic modalities and therapeutic techniques. Prime Care is a pioneer in implementing protocols to rapidly diagnose acute and often life-threatening conditions and effectively treat these conditions with acute interventions leading to greatly improved patient outcome and resulting lifestyle. The group has effectively integrated its electrophysiology specialty—which focuses on diagnosing and treating arrhythmia with interventional procedures and devices such as automatic internal cardiac defibrillators—into its cardiology practice. It also uses noninvasive

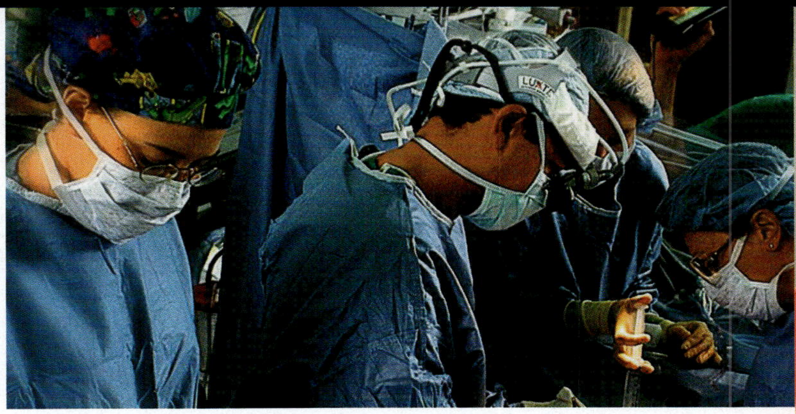

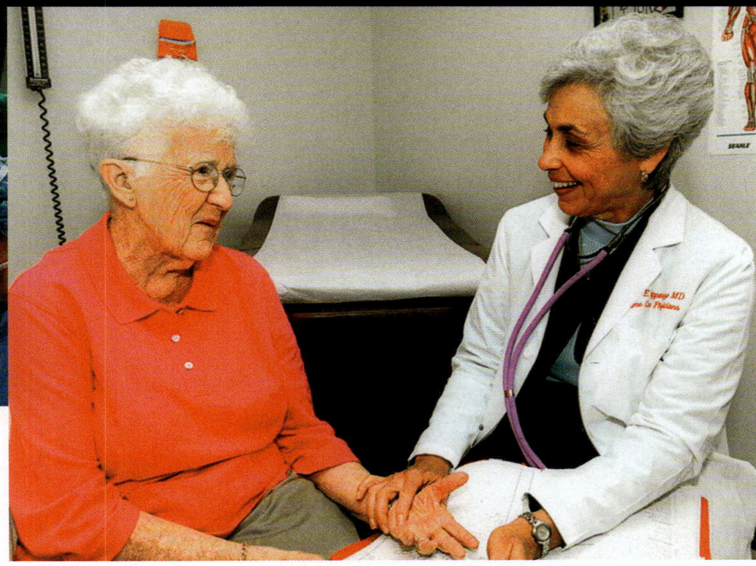

Far left and left: Prime Care physicians concentrate on focused and proactive care of their patients, allowing for cost-effective health management.

modalities, such as three-dimensional ultrasound and magnetic resonance imaging, to examine not only the anatomy but also the viability of the heart and other organ systems. In fact, Prime Care has made the use of clinical information technology a priority throughout its entire group. Physicians are provided with immediate access to a patient's clinical information via Prime Care's internally developed electronic medical record, Vertex®, and wireless technology.

Prime Care supports national and local causes, such as the American Heart Association, the American Diabetes Association, and the AIDS Council of Northeastern New York and provides lectures to physicians, other health care providers, and patients regarding the latest information on the prevention, diagnosis, and treatment of cardiovascular disease and other internal medicine–related conditions. Within the community, Prime Care provides health promotion screenings with various employer religious groups and also supports musical events and a local youth baseball team.

Prime Care has been recognized by the Denver, Colorado–based Medical Group Management Association (MGMA) as a Superior Performing group practice each year since 2001. According to John A. Lutz, Prime Care CEO, cost efficiency is a natural consequence of the group's focus on quality of care. By constantly evaluating the efficacy of clinical procedures—examining measurable indicators, such as risk factors for diabetes and cardiovascular disease, for instance—the group is able to provide proactive and focused care to its patients, thus allowing for more cost-effective health care. As a result, satisfaction rates are high for both patients and physicians. In addition to patient and physician recognition, Prime Care has been cited by outside organizations for its excellence in management. Prime Care was awarded a $100,000 Building Skills in New York State (BUSINYS) grant by the New York State Department of Labor in 2003 to promote staff and management development.

Prime Care operates at the leading edge of medical care. It is continually expanding its clinical research and patient outcomes programs in order to remain at the forefront of patient care.

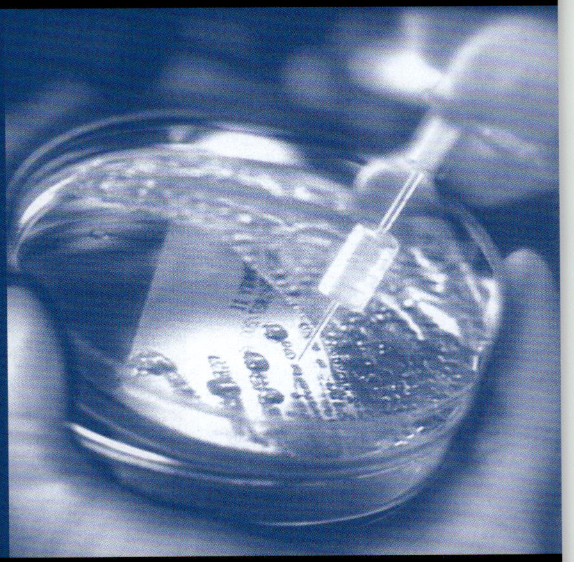

Pharmaceuticals & Biotechnology

SUNY Downstate Medical Center

Advancing its tradition of medical research, innovation, and service, SUNY Downstate Medical Center is creating the Advanced Biotechnology Incubator in the heart of Brooklyn—the city's first biotechnology incubator space in over a decade.

Right: SUNY Downstate Medical Center's Advanced Biotechnology Incubator in Brooklyn, New York, will provide 50,000 square feet of state-of-the-art space, accommodating 20 to 30 companies. Tenant firms will have access to SUNY Downstate's extensive facilities, research equipment, and world-class scientists—as well as the opportunity to provide internships to young investigators.

Biotechnology initiatives are projected to have a tremendous impact on economic growth and job creation in New York State in the 21st century. The industry holds extraordinary promise for New York City.

SUNY Downstate Medical Center's creation of the Advanced Biotechnology Incubator in the heart of Brooklyn is spurring the development of a vibrant community of technology companies and medical services.

The Downstate Advantage

This SUNY Downstate project is designed to help meet the high demand for affordable biotech incubator space in New York City. However, SUNY Downstate has a goal that is more ambitious: It intends to nurture a mutually beneficial, symbiotic relationship with biotech firms.

Firms leasing space in the SUNY Downstate Advanced Biotechnology Incubator will have access to the extensive facilities, research equipment, and scientists of SUNY Downstate—one of the eight world-class academic medical centers in the New York metropolitan area. In turn, these companies can provide educational and career opportunities for SUNY Downstate students. Firms locating at SUNY Downstate will be able to take advantage of the area's strong research institutions, its available pool of highly trained scientists, and its close access to New York City's capital markets.

SUNY Downstate's biotech initiative was well under way as of mid-2004, with phase one (11,000 square feet) of the project officially opened in June 2004 and phase two (13,000 square feet) scheduled for completion in fall 2004. When all three phases are complete, the incubator will offer 50,000 square feet of state-of-the-art laboratory space, accommodating from 20 to 30 companies. The incubator is part of a two-block biotechnology park adjacent to SUNY Downstate Medical Center.

ImClone Systems Incorporated, one of the state's largest biotechnology firms, is the park's anchor tenant and a model for success. SUNY Downstate has leased 13,000 square feet to ImClone to house a new division that is working on innovative treatments for cancer.

Growth Opportunities

In addition to the biotechnology incubator, SUNY Downstate is facilitating the development of biotechnology within New York City in other ways. For example, as the biotechnology firms that locate in SUNY Downstate's incubator grow, they will have the option of expanding into a wide range of low-cost industrial space in Brooklyn's Empire Zones—areas the state has designated for economic revitalization, with financial incentives for development and growth.

SUNY Downstate is aiding that growth by teaming with key Brooklyn organizations and companies in forming the Brooklyn Biotechnology Consortium. SUNY Downstate's consortium partners include the Brooklyn Economic Development Corporation, the Brooklyn Borough President's Office, Brooklyn Empire Zones, the Brooklyn Chamber of Commerce, the New York City Economic Development Corporation, the Empire State Development Corporation, the New York Biotechnology Association, Consolidated Edison Company of New York, KeySpan Corporation, and Pfizer Inc. The consortium's goal is to encourage technologies developed in New York City to stay in New York City by providing an affordable and supportive business and scientific environment. The Brooklyn Biotechnology Consortium has received strong support from federal, state, and local legislators, as well as the New York State Office of Science, Technology, and Academic Research (NYSTAR).

SUNY Downstate scientists have been responsible for some of the most important discoveries of the 20th century, such as the development of the heart-lung machine, suitcase dialysis, and the MRI. In 1998, SUNY Downstate distinguished professor emeritus Robert F. Furchgott, Ph.D., won the Nobel Prize in Medicine for his groundbreaking work on nitric oxide—work that is the basis for new drugs now being developed worldwide. And with the Advanced Biotechnology Incubator, SUNY Downstate will now apply its long tradition of research innovation and medical service on a much larger scale.

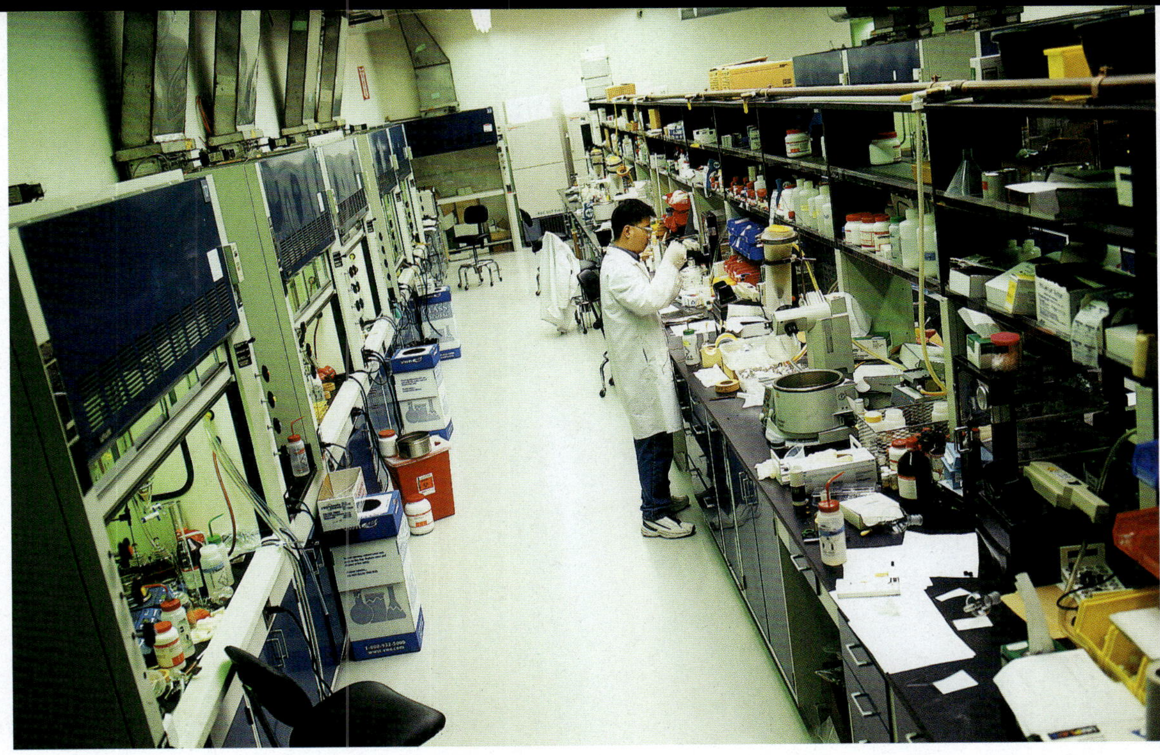

Left: The anchor tenant at the SUNY Downstate biotechnology park is the ImClone System division of small molecule compounds, which is developing innovative treatments for cancer.

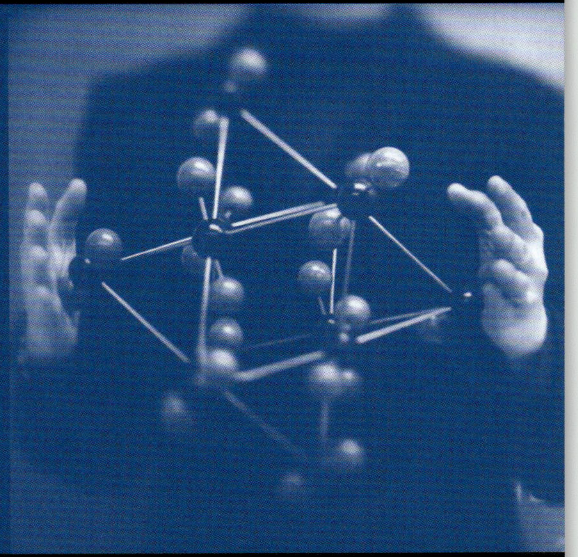

Education

Laboratory Institute of Merchandising

Academic excellence with a real-world focus is the core and unique strength of the Laboratory Institute of Merchandising—'The College for the Business of Fashion'—a fully accredited, cutting-edge private institution that has been nurturing innovative and business-savvy fashion leaders for more than six decades.

The Laboratory Institute of Merchandising educates its students in the business of fashion. Bachelor's degrees are offered in fashion merchandising, visual merchandising, and marketing.

Ideally located in the heart of the capital of the fashion world—New York City—the Laboratory Institute of Merchandising (LIM) is a one-of-a-kind college. For the past 65 years, this extraordinary institution has been educating and nurturing its students in the business of fashion. In addition to its rich and varied academic offerings, LIM offers students the opportunity to directly experience the daily rhythm and workings of the fashion industry. Given its proximity to trendsetting fashion houses, leading fashion manufacturers, and many of the world's most impressive retail enterprises, LIM provides its students with the distinct opportunity of being a part of the exciting environment they will enter upon graduation.

Overall, LIM's approach to educating its students is unique and highly successful. At LIM, students learn the business of fashion with programs in fashion merchandising, visual merchandising, and marketing through a creative and interactive approach that facilitates learning while motivating and inspiring students to meet their educational and professional goals. In-class instruction by professors who are leaders in their fields combined with on-the-job training ensures the success of LIM's graduates.

A Pattern for Success

Maxwell F. Marcuse, a pioneer in hands-on learning, advanced fashion education and made fashion history when he founded LIM in 1939. In 1962, Marcuse passed the torch to his son, Adrian G. Marcuse, who transformed LIM from a two-year non-degree-granting school to a college that offers two-year associate's degrees and four-year bachelor's degrees. Also under Adrian Marcuse's guidance, LIM became one of the first private colleges of fashion-related studies to be accredited by the Middle States Commission on Higher Education, the region's primary collegiate accrediting agency.

In 2002, Elizabeth S. Marcuse—following in the footsteps of her father and grandfather—assumed the presidency of this respected college. In addition to two generations of passed-on fashion and education wisdom, Elizabeth Marcuse's impeccable credentials include her positions as director of retail planning for Donna Karan and for Mamiye Brothers, Inc., and as a buyer for Lane Bryant, Montgomery Ward, and Macy's.

Today, the demand for the education that LIM offers has never been greater. The spring 2004 enrollment of more than 500 students broke all preexisting records. To accommodate this present and anticipated future growth, LIM recently expanded into a third campus location, added courses that deepen and strengthen its core curriculum, and hired 18 new professors. Recent additions to LIM's curriculum include courses in fashion styling, display graphics, and licensing.

Currently, LIM occupies two buildings in midtown New York City—a town house at 12 East 53rd Street and an office and class space at 226 East 54th Street. In 2004, LIM added a third location—the largest yet, with 25,000 square feet of space—at 216 East 45th Street. This additional location features a state-of-the-art library, an additional learning center, two new computer labs, and additional faculty and administrative office space.

Such expansions and growth ultimately support LIM's primary mission, "an education that works in the real world." LIM graduates—more than 90 percent of whom find positions within three months of graduation—have made and continue to make their mark on the fashion industry. LIM's alumni fill top positions at such prestigious companies as Coach, Perry Ellis, and Neiman Marcus.

A Global Presence

In the summer of 2004, LIM went global. Its two new study-abroad programs offer students the opportunity to study international fashion in Paris and London. This international presence is part of LIM's exciting vision for the future. Complementing its rich past and vibrant present, LIM's future plans include more bold yet strategic moves to keep the institute responsive to the needs of the marketplace.

All growth, however, will always be underscored by LIM's ongoing commitment to maintaining the warm, supportive, and personal learning environment that is the school's hallmark. "There will be more changes down the road, because LIM has to change to keep pace with the evolving fashion industry," states President Marcuse. "However, LIM will never lose sight of its special environment. Our intimate climate and emphasis on individual attention will continue to be our focus and strength."

Far left and above: An academic and experiential learning environment that is underscored by supportive relationships among and between students and faculty distinguishes the curriculum of the Laboratory Institute of Merchandising. Left: The creations of students are displayed in settings that complement the designs.

Brooklyn Law School

A vibrant intellectual community with a century-long tradition of teaching excellence, this renowned law school is highly regarded for its rigorous and innovative academic program, distinguished graduates, and an outstanding student body.

The Brooklyn Law School campus, with buildings designed by renowned architect Robert A. M. Stern, is ideally located for the study of law in one of the nation's busiest legal centers.

Photo: © Esto Photographics Inc.

Brooklyn Law School (BLS) is situated at the junction of the Brooklyn Heights Historic District, the Brooklyn civic center, and downtown Brooklyn, a location unrivaled for the study of law. Within a few blocks are some of the busiest federal and state courts, government agencies, and law offices in the nation. The surrounding residential neighborhoods of Brooklyn Heights, Cobble Hill, Park Slope, and Boerum Hill offer countless social and cultural amenities. Only minutes away is Manhattan, the financial, legal, and business capital of the world.

The focal points of the campus are a state-of-the-art academic building and a high-rise residence hall accommodating 360 students—opening in 2005—designed by the internationally acclaimed architect Robert A. M. Stern. The learning environment is supported by one of the largest and most advanced law libraries in the city, with over one-half million volumes. There are spacious student lounges and comfortable study areas. Throughout the building, there is broadband Internet access to full information resources. Within walking distance of the campus are eight more student residences in Brooklyn Heights.

The law school's most vital resource—its faculty—is the primary reason for its success and reputation. Studies have ranked the BLS faculty among the top 25 law school faculties in the nation for scholarly productivity and impact. The faculty has earned national and international reputations in the fields of evidence; torts; gender discrimination; human rights; and criminal, commercial, corporate, family, health care, products liability, intellectual property, information privacy, and international business law. The adjunct faculty includes many of New York City's leading judges, practitioners, and corporate counselors.

Faculty members bring to the classroom—and impart to their students—something more than textbook knowledge. Because they are active in shaping law and policy in the outside world, they are effective as teachers inside the classroom. The low faculty-to-student ratio ensures that professors are accessible to students in a way that few faculties are.

The student body of 1,500 is diverse and distinguished. In a typical entering class, students come from more than 30 states, a dozen foreign countries, and 175 undergraduate institutions. Many

students have advanced degrees and substantial work experience in other fields and professions prior to coming to law school. One-third or more of the entering students score among the top 10 percent in the nation on the LSAT, and nearly two-thirds receive undergraduate degrees at the most selective colleges and universities.

The law school's innovative and rigorous academic programs, including more than 200 elective courses, strike a balance between theoretical learning and lawyering skills. The goal is to help students cultivate the ability to think critically, to analyze problems creatively, and to recognize that no legal issue exists in a social, philosophical, economic, or political vacuum.

BLS's highly acclaimed clinical and professional skills curriculum offers students hands-on experience in more than a dozen areas of law. Students represent actual clients while mastering the art and craft of lawyering. The law school offers one of the largest externship programs in the country, placing hundreds of students each semester in law offices and judicial chambers. The school's Moot Court Program is among the best in the nation, consistently earning BLS students top honors in competitions.

Beyond the core curriculum, BLS sponsors several centers of excellence that enable faculty, students, and professionals from all over the country to collaborate in the study of cutting-edge legal issues. These centers, which sponsor high level symposia and academic conferences, and in some cases provide fellowships to distinguished students, are devoted to public-interest law; international business law; health law and policy; law, language, and cognition; and bankruptcy and commercial law. Also, students from the school's more than 30 student organizations sponsor dozens of forums at BLS each year in which luminaries from the corporate arena, law firms, public policy groups, government, and academia participate.

BLS offers many opportunities for interdisciplinary study. For those students who want to extend their studies further, the law school offers several joint master's/law degree options; summer study-abroad programs in Bologna, Italy, and Beijing, China; and an exchange program in Hamburg, Germany.

To make the transition from law school to the working world as successful as possible, the school's career center offers intensive, individual career counseling to students. Its On-Campus Interviewing Program attracts representatives of prestigious national and international law firms and government agencies to BLS to interview students for summer and permanent positions. The career center's aggressive job-development program identifies and opens new markets and opportunities. The employment statistics for graduates tell the whole story. The average annual placement rate has been 97 percent.

Brooklyn Law School's 16,000 alumni include leaders of premier law firms, government, business, academia, the judiciary, and public-interest organizations. They represent clients worldwide and maintain ties to BLS by mentoring, advising, and hiring the BLS graduates who follow in their footsteps.

Top left: A favorable student-faculty ratio and small seminar classes for many of the law school's 200-plus courses create a dynamic learning environment. Above: Students take full advantage of the library's large collection, abundant study rooms, and wireless access to the Internet. Bottom left: Nearby historic Brooklyn Heights offers popular spots for meeting, shopping, and dining and is an ideal residential neighborhood.

Photos: © Peter Olson and Ken Haas

Pace University

A private metropolitan New York university with a growing national reputation for offering students opportunity and the best teaching and learning in a student-centered environment, Pace is known for educating achievers who are engaged with critical issues both locally and globally.

Above: The Pace University New York City campus (foreground), with its signature tower, is located opposite City Hall Park in lower Manhattan, in the heart of the city's civic and financial center.

For almost 100 years, Pace University has upheld *Opportunitas* ("Opportunity") as both a motto and a promise to its students. Thousands of new Americans and first-generation college students have come to Pace over the years to receive a robust and practical education that provides access to the best jobs. Now, with a diverse and talented student body that is representative of the nation, and 100,000 alumni, most of whom live in metropolitan New York, Pace continues its legacy of providing opportunity by delivering a workforce with a superior education and strong connections to employers in business, industry, health care, education, government, and law.

Pace University's six campuses provide a wealth of learning opportunities in a number of different settings. The campus in lower Manhattan, in the heart of the civic and financial center of New York City, serves as an intellectual and cultural focal point for one of the city's most dynamic and vital areas.

Pace's modern Midtown Center at Fifth Avenue and 45th Street, only blocks away from Grand Central Terminal, offers graduate and undergraduate courses to goal-oriented people looking to advance their careers.

The Pleasantville campus, in mid-Westchester County, is set on 200 acres of rolling countryside where Pace offers a broad range of undergraduate degree programs in a stimulating collegiate environment. The Briarcliff annex, a short distance away, is the location of residence halls, recreational facilities, and administrative offices. The White Plains campuses, in the county's hub, are home to Pace Law School and a center for graduate courses in business, nursing, and computing.

At the Hudson Valley Center in New Windsor, Pace's Division of Adult and Professional Education and the schools of the university offer credit and noncredit programs, and customized professional corporate training programs.

The university's six schools and colleges offer a variety of academic programs and learning environments to more than 14,000 students. Dyson College of Arts and Sciences is home to Pace's innovative core curriculum, which is designed to promote active learning and strong faculty-student interaction. Stressing a firm foundation in writing, computing, and quantitative analysis, the core also has a civic engagement component that works to form leaders who will contribute to their communities and their world.

Pace's roots in the business world are deep. Founded as an accounting and business institute by the authors of the first widely accepted accounting textbooks, Pace continues its leadership in business education and has a reputation for producing graduates who are prepared to put theory into practice. Innovations such as the doctoral program of professional studies and the *e*.MBA—an online executive MBA that is truly convenient for executives—keep Pace's Lubin School of Business on the cutting edge of graduate schools of business.

Innovation is found throughout Pace. The School of Computer Science and Information Systems was the first of its kind in the nation, and its graduates are sought after by prime employers in the New York area. Recognizing the importance of international trade, the university purchased the World Trade Institute in 1997. Pace's World Trade Institute provides professional, comprehensive, and experience-based training for individuals, companies, and public agencies that operate in the global marketplace.

In 2004, the School of Education teamed up with the City of New York to found Pace High School. This innovative collaboration provides a training ground for sorely needed educators and an opportunity for some New York City school children to attend a small school. By educating nurses in both undergraduate and graduate programs, the Lienhard School of Nursing works to help alleviate the acute nursing shortage.

Exhibiting both innovation and a commitment to community service, Pace Law School leads the way in environmental law and is known for its clinical training. Through its Women's Justice Center, each year the law school assists more than 1,000 women and families who are survivors of domestic violence. The only law school in Westchester County, Pace Law School in White Plains is home to the New York State Judicial Institute, a center for education and research designed to enhance the quality of the courts.

Fully engaged on a local, national, and international level, Pace University is one of 10 founding institutions of Project Pericles, which fosters civic engagement as a key educational component. The Center for Downtown New York (CDNY), established at Pace after September 11, 2001, is a community partner for revitalizing lower Manhattan. CDNY has helped with rebuilding, public policy development, and fellowships for research on the events of September 11th. Additionally, the Pace Poll samples opinion on social, political, and economic issues, with students playing key roles in the polling process. Pace's social involvement extends to the natural world as well, in the work of the Pace Academy for the Environment.

Above: On Pace University's Briarcliff campus, Dow Hall houses the university's Center for Applied Ethics. Above, left: The Evelyn and Joseph I. Lubin Graduate Center is located on the Pace campus in White Plains. Left: The university's Pleasantville campus is home to the state-of-the-art Ann and Alfred Goldstein Health, Fitness, and Recreation Center.

The university's goals for its second century reaffirm a deep commitment to making the American dream a reality for an ethnically and culturally diverse student population. To this end, Pace grants $39 million in scholarships to academically promising students. The university also guarantees undergraduate tuition rates for up to five years.

As Pace prepares to celebrate its centennial in 2006, its reputation for civic engagement, innovation, and academics continues to reach new heights, setting the stage for an even stronger second century of education and opportunity.

For additional information, visit the university's Web site at www.pace.edu.

SUNY Cortland

Central to New York's education, this selective college emphasizes the liberal arts and teacher education at its main campus and Outdoor Education Center, while offering small class sizes, a bucolic setting, and graduate and undergraduate programs in a variety of professional fields.

SUNY Cortland students choose from among 70 dynamic academic majors. Top left: A professor and student examine plant growth as part of a classroom experiment. Left: Exercise science students measure human performance and endurance. Right: A student teaches at a local elementary school. Cortland is home to the largest comprehensive teacher education program in New York State.

Nestled atop one of the rolling hills in central New York's picturesque "City of Seven Valleys," the State University of New York College at Cortland was founded in 1868 as the Cortland Normal School. Cortland's earliest students included inventor and industrialist Elmer A. Sperry, who devised the gyroscopic compass; Alton B. Parker, the Democratic presidential nominee in 1904; and Nathan Miller, who was elected governor of New York in 1921.

The college's main campus in Cortland covers 191 acres and includes 30 traditional and modern buildings, from the stately brick Old Main building to its breathtaking $18 million Stadium Complex, heralded by *The New York Times* as "a new stadium worthy of a major university power." Fourteen of the college's structures are residence halls providing on-campus housing for approximately 3,000 students.

For more than 50 years, SUNY Cortland's historic Outdoor Education Center at Raquette Lake in the Adirondacks has fostered in its students a firsthand appreciation for environmental conservation and preservation, long before those concepts became fashionable. Camp Huntington, the jewel of the Outdoor Education Center, was the first of the "Great Camps of the Adirondacks" built by America's wealthy families in the late 19th century. The site is the birthplace of the distinctive Adirondack style of architecture.

SUNY Cortland science faculty and students greatly benefit from the college's other two adjunct campuses: the Hoxie Gorge Nature Preserve in Cortland County and the Brauer Memorial Geological Field Station on the Helderberg Escarpment near Albany. Additionally, Cortland boasts SUNY's oldest program for studying abroad and offers academic and work internship programs at more than 20 different locales in Europe, Asia, Africa, Australia, and Central and South America.

From its inception, Cortland has played a vital role in educating New York State's teachers. Today, that influence spans the nation. In 2004, more than half of the college's 7,500 undergraduate and graduate students were pursuing majors in teacher education. SUNY Cortland is home to the largest comprehensive teacher education program in New York State and the 22nd largest such program in the United States.

In 1948, Cortland became a charter member of the State University of New York, which has evolved into the nation's largest comprehensive university system. One of SUNY's 13 colleges of arts and sciences, Cortland offers undergraduate and graduate programs in the liberal arts and a variety of professional fields. The college remains committed to an all-inclusive curriculum, building on its traditional strengths in teacher education and physical education, and enhancing its high quality programs in the arts, humanities, and sciences.

For 136 years, quality teaching has remained the highest priority on the Cortland campus. The college prides itself on its small class sizes and its many opportunities for personalized professor-student instruction and research. SUNY Cortland students can chose among 70 majors and 44 minors within Cortland's three academic schools—Arts and Sciences, Education, and Professional Studies—and 26 academic departments.

Cortland's 54,000 living alumni have risen to the highest ranks of the educational, judicial, scientific, financial, business, and professional sports and entertainment fields. Cortland graduates reside in all 50 states and 40 other nations.

At Cortland, athletics are viewed as important to the educational mission of the college. With 14 women's and 11 men's teams, the Cortland Red Dragons collectively form one of the most extensive and successful NCAA Division III intercollegiate athletic programs. In 2002–2003, six Red Dragons teams finished in the national top 10, and 19 student athletes were named as all-Americans.

Whether students are in the classroom, in the laboratory, or on the playing field, SUNY Cortland strives to instill within them a sense of responsibility, an eagerness to help in the local community, and an awareness of the important role they must perform in an increasingly global society. The SUNY Cortland faculty, staff, and administration, together with dedicated alumni, work toward preparing Cortland graduates to make a difference in the lives of others.

Above left: Painter William West Durant, son of 19th-century railroad magnate Thomas Clark Durant, created what has become known as the Adirondack architectural style at Camp Pine Knot, the first of the "Great Camps of the Adirondacks," located at Raquette Lake, New York. Presented to SUNY Cortland in 1948, the historic complex of buildings has been carefully preserved by the college while three generations of its students have pursued courses at the unique Outdoor Education Center. Above right: Majestic Old Main houses the School of Arts and Sciences at SUNY Cortland, one of the most popular and selective campuses in the 64-school State University of New York system.

Hofstra University

Located in an idyllic suburban setting on Long Island, this private university offers advanced learning facilities enhanced by the latest technologies, faculty members with impressive credentials, and hundreds of athletic and cultural activities.

Right: Stuart Rabinowitz, president of Hofstra University, speaks with some members of the student community.
Far right: Business professor Linda Evans takes an opportunity to walk with students to class.

Progress is key at Hofstra University, located in Hempstead, Long Island, 25 miles east of Manhattan. Whether enhancing academics, elevating student services, or enriching the community through cultural presentations, Hofstra is "becoming known as a school on the move and as an institution that is constantly improving," says Stuart Rabinowitz, university president.

Hofstra is a private institution with impressively credentialed faculty members, state-of-the-art facilities, and a total enrollment of 13,300 students. Its rich academic menu offers 2,150 courses in 130 undergraduate and 140 graduate programs in liberal arts, the sciences and engineering, business, education, communications, and law.

The university also offers the innovative New College, the School for University Studies, Honors College, Saturday College, and the University College for Continuing Education.

The university traces its origins to William and Kate Hofstra. William Hofstra, of Dutch descent, was a millionaire several times over, dealing in lumber, wood pulp, and newsprint. When he died in 1932, he left his widow a considerable fortune. Before she herself died the following year, she specified that the bulk of the estate was to be used to create a memorial to her late husband. Hofstra University was founded in 1935 as that memorial.

Today, Hofstra attracts some of the world's brightest students, who hail from 47 states and U.S. territories and 78 countries. Freshmen entering the school in fall 2003 had an average SAT score of 1,130 and a grade point average of 3.1.

Hofstra holds 22 academic accreditations, including two prestigious accreditations from the Association to Advance Collegiate Schools of Business (AACSB International) for the Frank G. Zarb School of Business. Success is also evidenced by the number of prestigious fellowships, prizes, and grants that the faculty members win. Six faculty members in three years won fellowships from the National Endowment for the Humanities, ranking the university eighth nationally in receipt of these esteemed awards. Hofstra's faculty has included a MacArthur Fellow, Fulbright Scholars, and Guggenheim Fellows, as well as Pulitzer Prize and Emmy Award winners.

Faculty members also secure multimillion-dollar grants, including $11.5 million from the National Science Foundation to improve the teaching of middle-school mathematics. This grant "recognizes Hofstra's success as a national leader in education," Rabinowitz says.

The university fosters academic excellence by providing students and faculty with high-tech facilities and other amenities on its 240-acre campus. The *Princeton Review* ranked Hofstra as one of the most digitally connected campuses in the country. University leaders are committed to keeping computer laboratories and classrooms completely up to date and investing in new technologies.

In October 2003, the Hofstra community dedicated the school's newest gem, Hagedorn Hall. Home to the School of Education and Allied Human Services, the building has 20 classrooms and some 80 offices. Computers, VCR and DVD equipment, interactive whiteboards, cable television, and wireless network services fill the classrooms, which are designed to prepare Hofstra students to teach in the elementary and secondary schools of the future. Hagedorn Hall features a cybercafe, lounges, a curriculum and teaching library, and a digitized ticker flashing messages inside and outside of the building. A holographic screen in the lobby greets visitors and broadcasts information and images.

Hofstra hosts hundreds of cultural events each year and continually expands its facilities. Next to its John Cranford Adams Playhouse, a new academic building is under construction. It will house a 230-seat black box theater—a versatile, uncluttered performance space that focuses attention on the story, acting, and dialogue—plus backstage rooms for seminars, orchestra rehearsals, and music practices, as well as offices for the music, history, and journalism departments.

Additionally, a new soccer stadium has been donated by the New York Jets. The Hofstra Museum, which is accredited by the American Association of Museums, offers 12 exhibitions annually and features more than 65 pieces of outdoor sculpture. The university is an accredited member of the American Association of Botanical Gardens and Arboreta.

Hofstra offers more than 140 student clubs and organizations, 18 varsity sports, and seven theaters. Its proximity to Long Island's beaches adds to a pleasant environment, while neighboring New York City offers educational, cultural, and employment opportunities.

Hofstra's commitment to students, faculty, and facilities propels the university toward maintaining academic excellence. "We are continuing to make progress," says Rabinowitz, "in gaining for Hofstra the enhanced academic recognition and reputation it truly deserves."

Above left: The Hofstra Lions, who guard the entrance of the university, are part of the university's seal, which features the motto "Je maintiendray" (I stand steadfast). Hofstra's mascots, Kate and Willy, are also lions, and the teams are known as "the Pride." Above: Hagedorn Hall, a state-of-the-art building, is home to Hofstra's newly dedicated School of Education and Allied Human Services.

The City University of New York

The largest urban public university in the nation and one of its major academic research institutions includes 11 senior colleges and six community colleges, as well as a graduate school, law school, and school of biomedical education, with expert faculty members in every field.

Above: The student body of The City University of New York mirrors the broad diversity of the city itself.

The City University of New York (CUNY), founded in 1847, is the nation's largest urban public university, with 11 senior colleges, six community colleges, a graduate school, a law school, and a school of biomedical education. More than 450,000 students are enrolled in undergraduate and graduate degree courses or in adult, continuing, or professional education courses at campuses located in all five New York City boroughs. In fall 2003, 45 percent of all college students in New York City were enrolled at CUNY. Since the mid-1960s, CUNY has produced nearly 900,000 graduates. An estimated one-third of college-educated New Yorkers are graduates of CUNY.

Students

Located in cosmopolitan New York City, the CUNY student body mirrors the city's diversity with students from 167 different countries, among whom 119 languages are spoken, contributing stimulating perspectives to classroom discussions. CUNY students have won nationally competitive awards such as Marshall, Gates Millennium Scholars, Goldwater, and Rhodes scholarships and Fulbright, Mellon, Soros, Javits, and National Science Foundation fellowships.

Faculty

More than 80 percent of CUNY's senior college faculty hold the highest degrees in their fields. The full-time teaching faculty of over 5,800 includes world-renowned experts in virtually every field of human endeavor. CUNY Distinguished Professor at Lehman College Billy Collins served as U.S. Poet Laureate. Other CUNY faculty have won prestigious honors and awards in recognition of their contribution to education and scholarship. Included are Pulitzer Prizes, an Academy Award, MacArthur Fellowships, Guggenheim Fellowships, Carnegie Teacher of the Year Awards, and many other fellowships, honors, and grants. Faculty member achievements have been recognized by the American Academy of Arts and Sciences, the National Academy of Sciences, the American Association for the Advancement of Science, and others that salute scholarly excellence.

Research

With over 100 nationally recognized research centers, institutes, and consortia, CUNY is one of the nation's major academic research institutions. The New York Structural Biology Center at City College, opened in 2002 and operated by a CUNY-led consortium of 10 major medical research institutions in New York City, is a state-of-the-art facility for advanced biomedical research. Focused on magnetic resonance technology, the center houses the largest, most advanced cluster of high-field research magnets in the nation. The CUNY Institute for Macromolecular Assemblies, opened in 2003 at the College of Staten Island, builds on a base of research strengths in molecular biosciences at CUNY. In support of major research projects, during the 2002–2003 academic year CUNY faculty and staff members received $321 million in grants and contracts—a record annual amount for the university.

Academic Programs

CUNY offers approximately 1,400 academic programs, with more than 200 majors leading to associate and baccalaureate degrees, and more than 100 graduate degree majors, including graduate urban professional programs ranging from architecture to urban public health. Postsecondary education opportunities, from certificate courses to doctoral programs are offered at every level of the integrated CUNY system. Some baccalaureate and associate degrees can be earned entirely on weekends, to accommodate working adult schedules. Some university programs make courses available online via the Internet.

Honors Studies

The CUNY Honors College, established in 2001, enrolls the region's most academically talented students in a challenging honors curriculum that incorporates some of New York City's greatest cultural institutions, through seminars with leaders of museums, orchestras, and other institutions and the use of the "cultural passport," which offers admission to museums, concerts, operas, theaters, and more. Honors candidates are assisted by private funding, which helps provide full tuition, scholarships, laptop computers, cultural passports, academic expense accounts, and study abroad.

Campuses

Facilities at CUNY's 19 modern campuses throughout New York City include the traditional and the innovative. Its more than 280 buildings, on 23 million square feet of land, include state-of-the-art computer centers, science and language laboratories, performing arts centers, observatories, gymnasiums, and much more. The Baruch College Vertical Campus is the largest vertical campus in the city—approximately 800,000 square feet. The College of Staten Island's bucolic 204-acre, parklike setting is the largest college campus in New York City.

Libraries

CUNY includes more than 20 separate libraries that together contain seven million volumes, 30,000 periodicals, and thousands of microfilms, music scores, videotapes, and other materials. Students have access and borrowing privileges at all of the libraries and access to the vast resources of the New York Public Library.

Alumni

CUNY graduates include 11 Nobel laureates, placing CUNY among the nation's public universities with the highest such numbers. The university's outstanding alumni include the U.S. Secretary of State, a Supreme Court Justice, mayors, members of Congress, an astronaut, composers, writers, and inventors. More top U.S. corporate executives earned their bachelor's degrees at The City University of New York than at any other university in the country, according to a survey by Standard & Poor's.

Partners in Education

More than 40,000 high school students in over 200 New York City high schools are enrolled in College Now, a collaboration of CUNY and the New York City Department of Education. The program is aimed at improving the academic achievements of high school students and ensuring that graduating students are prepared to do college-level work. Qualified students can enroll in college classes and earn advance placement credit. Another 8,000 students are enrolled in CUNY-affiliated high schools.

The Teaching Opportunity Program is another collaboration of CUNY and the Department of Education. To address shortages in New York City schools of teachers for particular academic subjects, it recruits highly qualified graduates with baccalaureate degrees in these subjects who want to pursue a teaching career, including both recent graduates and others who wish to change careers. The program provides stipends and education awards, as well as special training, mentoring, and jobs in the New York City schools.

For more information, phone 800-CUNY-YES (800-286-9937); view CUNY-TV, City University Television, Cable Channel 75 in New York City, Sundays at 8 A.M. and 8 P.M.; or visit the Web site www.cuny.edu.

Above: CUNY's facilities include 19 modern campuses throughout New York City, with traditional and innovative styles. Shown here is the campus of Lehman College, in the Bronx. Above left: CUNY students have access and borrowing privileges at each of the university's 20 libraries. Left: Academics at CUNY are supported by state-of-the-art equipment and laboratories—such as this computer center—for all of the arts and sciences.

United Federation of Teachers

With headquarters in downtown Manhattan and offices in each borough, this 150,000-member trade union and professional organization works on behalf of teachers, students, and others in the New York City public school system, operating with the motto 'Teachers Want What Children Need.'

Above: The United Federation of Teachers works on behalf of New York City's public school system—the largest in the nation—which has a diverse body of 1.1 million students, among whom more than 100 languages are spoken. Here, some students collaborate on a classroom project.

The 150,000-member United Federation of Teachers (UFT), headquartered in downtown Manhattan, represents the professional men and women who teach the next generation, the 1.1 million children in New York City public schools. The students, among whom more than 100 languages are spoken, are taught by UFT members, who include 80,000 classroom teachers, 20,000 classroom paraprofessionals, as well as school psychologists, guidance counselors, and laboratory specialists. The UFT also has an active chapter of 50,000 retired teachers, many of whom serve as mentors to teachers and students and who may also attend any of the 500 courses offered each term in the UFT lifelong learning centers.

The New York City public school system is by far the largest in the nation, twice the size of the next largest (Los Angeles), and sports some of the most brilliant academic and cultural successes and faces some of the greatest challenges in education.

Elected the system's collective bargaining representative in 1961, the UFT has functioned as both a trade union and a professional organization since its inception. As a union, it negotiates comprehensive collective bargaining contracts covering wages and benefits with its employer, the City of New York and the New York City Department of Education. It maintains a sizable staff serving its members, pursuing grievances, and providing member health benefits ranging from eyeglasses to prescription drugs.

As a professional organization, it offers staff development and training to teachers in courses as diverse as classroom management, literacy, using theater in the classroom, and identifying child abuse. The UFT strongly supports and leads efforts to raise academic standards and strengthen instruction; reduce class size; create safer, more orderly schools; improve school facilities; and increase parent involvement in schools. As part of a long-term goal to provide teachers with the tools they need to perform their work in the classroom, the UFT, in affiliation with local colleges and universities, offers a full spectrum of workshops, conferences, and graduate-level courses to approximately 50,000 members annually.

The union's nationally acclaimed Dial-A-Teacher program offers homework assistance to more than 85,000 public school students and their parents every year in 10 languages: English, Spanish, Italian, Chinese, Korean, Russian, French, Haitian-Creole, Greek, and Hebrew. Parents also receive brochures that describe the importance of visiting their children's teachers regularly and ways they can help their children reach academic success. Further, the UFT hosts conferences designed to assist parents in understanding new, often complex, education policies and how these policies affect their children.

By 2000, the UFT had outgrown its three buildings around Gramercy Park at 260 Park Avenue South and searched for affordable quarters that would provide 400,000 square feet of office space, an auditorium to seat at least 1,000 people, and a technology infrastructure to serve a large and growing organization.

With the need to expand its services for members and the desire to participate in the revitalization and economic recovery efforts of lower Manhattan, the UFT relocated its headquarters to 50 and 52 Broadway in May 2003. It was the first major organization to expand into the downtown area after the tragic events of September 11, 2001. This decision reflects the courage of UFT members and the union's resolve to reaffirm in a substantial way its commitment to the city.

The union owns the 50 Broadway building, a 37-story art deco structure with 317,600 square feet of space. More than 50 commercial and nonprofit organizations lease space in this building, including the New York State AFL-CIO, New York State United Teachers, Amalgamated Bank, the American Liver Foundation, the League for the Hard of Hearing, the National Foundation for Jewish Culture, and the National Association of Social Workers. In addition, a significant investment was made in the renovation of the 52 Broadway building, a 19-story modern structure that houses most of the

union's departments that provide daily support to members. Together, the two buildings include 15,000 square feet of conference facilities—a generous accommodation that is unique in the lower Manhattan community. As a committed member of the community, the UFT makes space available to other unions, corporations, and community-based organizations for meetings and events.

Since 1961, the UFT has been the sole bargaining agent for the nonsupervisory educators who work at the city's 1,200 public school sites. It represents teachers, classroom paraprofessionals, school secretaries, attendance teachers, guidance counselors, psychologists, social workers, education evaluators, nurses, laboratory technicians, and adult-education teachers. In addition, the UFT represents teachers and other employees of several private and proprietary educational institutions. Further, the UFT represents the Federation of Nurses, which represents thousands of registered nurses and home health aides who are employed by various hospitals and agencies in New York City.

Historically, the UFT has recognized that the interests of school children and their teachers are inseparable, and the motto "Teachers Want What Children Need" became the rallying cry of every demonstration. The union also sees itself as a children's lobby—perhaps the single strongest children's lobby in the state—for education, health, antipoverty, and more. The UFT's aim is to make every school a safe place where learning takes place, where parents want to send their children, and where educators want to work.

As a member of the Campaign for Fiscal Equity (CFE)—a grassroots organization whose primary mission is to reform New York State's school finance system—the UFT has worked to compel the legislature to change what it deems an unfair funding formula that has deprived New York City public school children of adequate resources. The UFT has provided exemplary leadership and unlimited support to the stakeholders of public education—students, teachers, parents, and the community at large. The efforts of CFE over the years led to a lawsuit it filed in 1993 against the state. Consequently, in a landmark case that culminated in a victory in October 2003 for the members of CFE, New York's highest court issued a ruling directing the state, the legislature, the mayor of the City of New York, and the chancellor of the New York City Department of Education to come up with a fair and viable plan to correct the problem and change the current funding formula. The success of this CFE case exemplifies policy changes that have come about through UFT's commitment to the 1.1 million children who are entitled to and depend on a sound public education.

As a growing organization and a leader in the labor movement and education unionism, the UFT is contributing significantly to the revitalization of lower Manhattan. The union vows to continue to fight for the rights of its members, as well as the rights of every child in every school—particularly the right to a sound public education.

Top left: United Federation of Teachers (UFT) members participated in the 2004 Reading Summit, chaired by Randi Weingarten, president, in the organization's new auditorium at 52 Broadway. Above: More than 20,000 UFT members gathered outside City Hall in Manhattan in October 2003 to protest administrative policies that they considered flawed and a hindrance to teaching. Left: The UFT lobbies to make every New York City public school a safe, desirable place for learning. Shown here (counterclockwise) are students learning about real baby chicks, exploring topics in a Teens' Library, and pursuing the creative arts in a freehand drawing class.

State University of New York at Oswego

Situated on 700 scenic acres along the southern shore of Lake Ontario, the State University of New York at Oswego has a 143-year history of preparing students for productive and fulfilling lives.

Listed among the best northeastern colleges by the *Princeton Review,* the State University of New York at Oswego (SUNY Oswego) is a residential college on the shore of Lake Ontario in upstate New York that offers bachelor's and master's degrees in traditional arts and sciences as well as professional fields. About 8,500 students attend classes on the 700-acre campus, where delivering a learner-centered education is a priority.

Oswego has developed an undergraduate academic program built around a required core of courses focusing on fundamental skills and broad perspectives needed for lifelong success. In all, more than 100 programs of study offer an array of choices ranging from accounting to zoology, with abundant opportunities for internships and for study abroad.

The School of Education is the college's original cornerstone, founded by Edward Austin Sheldon in 1861. Oswego early on developed an international reputation for high quality teacher preparation. Today, the school is accredited by the National Council for Accreditation of Teacher Education (NCATE). The College of Arts and Sciences continues a liberal arts tradition even as it embraces innovations such as learning communities and interdisciplinary study. The School of Business occupies a state-of-the art facility and is accredited by AACSB International—the Association to Advance Collegiate Schools of Business.

Embracing a spirit of renewal, the college is in the midst of more than $100 million in building and renovations, the centerpiece of which is the new Campus Center. SUNY Oswego generates more than $200 million annually for the region, in addition to providing valuable educational and cultural contributions to the Central New York community.

Oswego faculty members have developed internationally respected research programs on the Great Lakes environment and computer software engineering. Additionally, the college's Education Center in southern Oswego County offers continuing education and workforce training.

Admission to Oswego is competitive. The college receives about 10,000 applications for 2,300 openings each year. A founding member of the State University of New York system, SUNY Oswego is accredited by the Middle States Association of Colleges and Schools.

For more information, visit the college's Web site at www.oswego.edu.

Top: "Gateway to Business" is one of many options in SUNY Oswego's distinctive freshman seminar program. Oswego has received national recognition for its array of programs that provide an engaging learning environment for first-year students. Bottom: SUNY Oswego sits on the shore of Lake Ontario. The rich Great Lakes environment is the subject of innovative research by Oswego faculty members.

St. Francis College

Located in the heart of historic Brooklyn Heights, this private college—'The Small College of Big Dreams'—offers undergraduate degree programs in the arts, sciences, and professions, providing students with a wealth of opportunities at an affordable price.

Founded by the Franciscan Brothers in 1858, St. Francis College is the oldest Catholic learning institution in the Diocese of Brooklyn. The college is located minutes from New York City, offering students an urban campus where the college's neighborhoods, and Manhattan itself, enhance the multicultural learning experience.

Academics form the cornerstone of students' experience at St. Francis College. Each student takes courses in the core curriculum, a set of studies designed to provide an intellectual foundation for further growth academically and professionally. After completing the core, students may choose from more than 40 majors, some in the liberal arts, others geared to specific professions. The college also offers an honors program for students of high achievement, and it awards numerous full and partial scholarships to students who have performed well academically.

Included in the college's long tradition of excellence in athletics is the founding, in 1901, of the men's basketball program, which was among the first in New York City. An NCAA Division I institution, St. Francis College today offers students the chance to play for any of 18 varsity athletic teams. The college's teams compete at some of the city's most well-known sports venues, such as KeySpan Park in Coney Island, home of the Brooklyn Cyclones, and the USTA National Tennis Center in Queens, the courts of the U.S. Open.

St. Francis College has a strong and impressive alumni network that puts students in contact with professionals in dozens of fields, including lawyers and judges, business executives, university presidents, and officers at major media organizations.

In 2003, the college opened the Anthony J. Genovesi Center, a 10,000-square-foot, state-of-the-art facility named in honor of the late Brooklyn assemblyman, which serves as a space for athletic competition, special events, community activities, and academic affairs. In spring 2004, St. Francis College broke ground on a new academic center building that will house a new library, computer facilities, a conference center, and interactive classrooms.

The college's Catholic-Franciscan heritage is central to life at St. Francis. All aspects of student life and learning are influenced by the Franciscan values of humility, tolerance, and compassion. The college encourages each member of its racially, ethnically, and religiously diverse student body to develop not only intellectually but spiritually as well.

Students of St. Francis College in Brooklyn Heights enjoy a multicultural urban campus setting just across the East River from Manhattan.

School of Visual Arts

Professional artists from such diverse fields as advertising, cartooning, computer art, design, film, fine arts, and illustration teach not only technical and aesthetic skills but also something intangible—what it takes to be a working artist in one of the toughest, yet most rewarding, arts markets in the world.

The School of Visual Arts (SVA) has been a vital part of New York's arts community for more than 50 years, educating artists who go on to make enduring contributions in a wide range of creative fields.

Each year, SVA attracts approximately 3,500 students from 45 states and 25 countries to New York. These young artists are taught by a faculty drawn from the state's top professionals in advertising, cartooning, computer art, design, film, fine arts, illustration, and photography, as well as scholars and historians. Students in the undergraduate and graduate degree programs learn their craft from people who are active in the very professions the students will join after graduation; the majority of SVA alumni live and work in New York State. SVA students gain more than skills; they also learn the invaluable lessons of what it takes to work and succeed in New York.

SVA is active in the state's cultural, educational, and financial life. Each year, the college's Office of Career Development helps place more than 250 students in for-credit internships at companies such as Calvin Klein, Inc.; Condé Nast Publications, Inc.; and Nickelodeon. They gain valuable experience in their chosen field while contributing to some of New York's most high-profile businesses. Students at SVA can prepare for careers in art education and art therapy, allowing them to bring their skills and creativity to New York State's public and private schools, hospitals, and universities. Among the college's unique classes is the Times Square Sign Workshop, in which computer art students create giant electronic displays on the Nasdaq headquarters building, at the center of the Crossroads of the World.

SVA's faculty of professional artists and its curriculum help students take advantage of being in one of the world's major arts centers. SVA and New York work together to help each generation of visual arts students become the next generation of visual arts professionals.

For additional information, contact the School of Visual Arts at 209 East 23rd Street, New York, NY 10010; phone: 212-592-2000 or 888-221-5782; or visit the college's Web site at www.schoolofvisualarts.edu.

The School of Visual Arts makes its home in the heart of Manhattan.

Photo: © Daniel Um/School of Visual Arts

Manhattan College

Situated on 22 beautiful acres in the Riverdale area of New York City, this top liberal arts college, founded by the Christian Brothers order of educators, offers students personal attention, small class sizes, and more than 40 major fields of study.

Photo: © Peter Finger

Left: Manhattan College is highly regarded by students who value personal attention from top educators. The college's scenic and historic campus serves as a pleasant learning environment.

Manhattan College was founded in 1853 by members of the Christian Brothers. This Catholic order of teachers began in 17th-century France with educational innovator St. John Baptist de La Salle. His pioneering of Lasallian education for the poor also helped elevate teaching as a profession as well as a religious vocation. Today, that tradition of commitment to social justice goes hand in hand with respect for individual dignity to create a "person-centered" education at Manhattan College.

With a faculty-to-student ratio of one to 13, the college offers students the personal attention and small class sizes that intensify the learning experience. The fact that 95 percent of faculty members hold advanced degrees contributes to the large number of Manhattan College graduates who go on to graduate work themselves. More than 3,200 students from 39 states and 60 countries are enrolled in five schools: arts, business, education, engineering, and science. In all, Manhattan College offers more than 40 major fields of study, with graduate programs available in education and engineering.

The school's high standards are acknowledged by *U.S.News & World Report*, which has placed Manhattan College in the top tier of schools in the Northeast. It is also one of only four comprehensive American colleges with chapters of the national honor societies Phi Beta Kappa, Sigma Xi, and Tau Beta Pi.

Manhattan College is also widely recognized for building leaders. One of them is a former mayor of New York City—Rudolph Giuliani, class of 1965. In fact, Standard & Poor's lists the school as third among the nation's liberal arts colleges in the number of graduates who go on to become corporate leaders.

Manhattan College enjoys the best of both urban and suburban advantages. The 22-acre campus, which has been featured in films and television commercials, overlooks Van Cortlandt Park in a pleasant community that is home to many of the city's prominent figures. Ready for exploration only a short subway ride away is Manhattan, one of the world's most vibrant metropolitan areas.

The horizons surrounding fortunate Manhattan College students are broad indeed.

For more information on Manhattan College, phone 800-MC2-XCEL (800-622-9235); or visit the college's Web site at www.manhattan.edu.

SUNY Downstate Medical Center

A world-class academic medical center, one of the eight in the New York metropolitan area, SUNY Downstate Medical Center is a vital source for education, training, research, and health care, with four colleges, an on-site teaching hospital, an advanced research center, and a new, state-of-the-art biotechnology incubator.

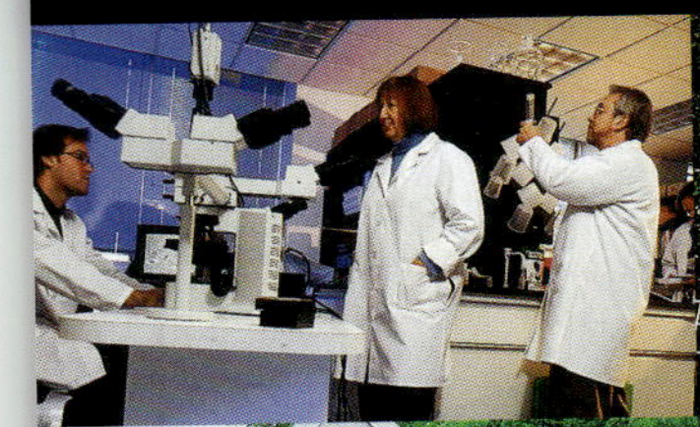

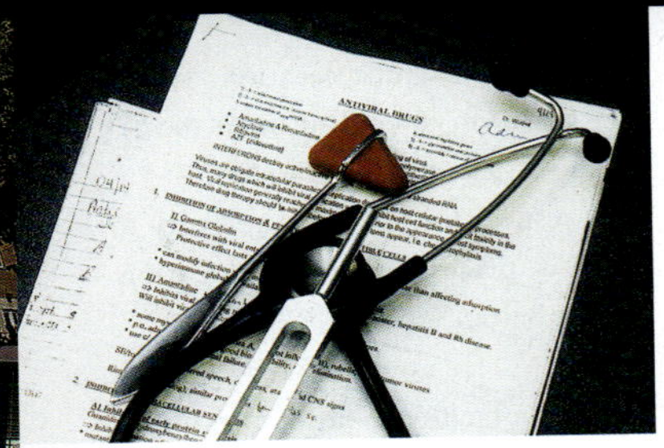

With four great colleges and one great teaching hospital, SUNY Downstate Medical Center is widely known for excellence in education, research, and health care. It is Brooklyn's only academic medical center.

SUNY Downstate Medical Center—part of the State University of New York's 64-campus system—has a long history of serving Brooklyn and New York State. The campus is a vital part of the Brooklyn community; one of its largest employers; and a critical source for education, research, and health care.

SUNY Downstate serves a distinct and diverse population of students. Many students are from Brooklyn and the New York City area. Numerous students are from economically disadvantaged backgrounds. Many are immigrants or children of immigrants just getting their start in American society. Over 40 percent of SUNY Downstate students are from under-represented minority groups.

The degrees granted by SUNY Downstate's four colleges include M.D., Ph.D., M.P.H., M.S., and B.S. degrees. Graduates win high marks for their clinical training—and for their academic acumen. Among SUNY Downstate's schools, programs, and facilities are:

- College of Medicine;
- College of Nursing;
- College of Health Related Professions;
- School of Graduate Studies;
- Master of Public Health Program;
- University Hospital of Brooklyn;
- Advanced Biotechnology Incubator.

The College of Medicine at SUNY Downstate ranks seventh nationally out of 125 academic medical centers in the number of alumni holding positions at medical schools and 11th in the number who are department chairs. The new Master of Public Health program is helping to find solutions to Brooklyn's health concerns.

The College of Nursing is one of the largest in the state, offering undergraduate degrees (including an innovative 15-month accelerated B.S. program) and master's degrees or certificate programs in every advanced nursing specialty.

In the College of Health Related Professions, six specialties—physical therapy, occupational therapy, midwifery, physician assistant, diagnostic medical imaging, and medical informatics—provide numerous options for interesting, high paying careers.

The School of Graduate Studies offers two career tracks—cellular and molecular biology and neural and behavioral sciences—as well as a unique collaboration in biomedical engineering with Polytechnic University.

With over $55 million in grants, SUNY Downstate shines in research. Its scientists have been responsible for some of the most important discoveries of the 20th century, such as the development of the heart-lung machine and magnetic resonance imaging (MRI). In 1998, distinguished professor emeritus Robert F. Furchgott, Ph.D., won the Nobel Prize in Medicine for his work on nitric oxide. And with the creation of the SUNY Downstate Advanced Biotechnology Incubator *(see pages 244–45)*, the school's graduates and faculty members are expected to play a significant role in the emerging biotechnology industry of Brooklyn and New York City.

For additional information, contact SUNY Downstate Medical Center at 450 Clarkson Avenue, Brooklyn, NY 11203; phone: 718-270-2446 for Student Admissions or 718-270-1000 for general information; or visit the Web site at www.downstate.edu.

Westchester Community College

As both an educator for tomorrow's workforce and a leading supporter for today's business—this successful college offers courses for credit and continuing education on its 218-acre main campus and at 11 extension sites and also creates special training programs for local companies.

With the highest student enrollment in its history, Westchester Community College, founded in 1946, has achieved unprecedented success in rising to the role it has today as an integral key to the lifeblood of Westchester County. The college's tremendous impact starts with its academic programs—hundreds of courses for credit and one of the largest Continuing Education units in the State University of New York (SUNY) system. Moreover, its standing in Westchester goes well beyond that of a typical community college and includes its role as a champion of local businesses. Although the broad economic impact of the institution cannot be precisely quantified, it is estimated by SUNY to be $150 million per year.

One key to the college's role in helping to fuel the region's economy is the large number of alumni who enter the Westchester County workforce. Many are graduates of the institution's wide variety of business programs, which range from accounting and marketing to international trade.

The college's 11,000 students enrolled in courses for credit enjoy the benefits of state-of-the-art resources—cutting-edge business laboratories, plentiful computers, and classrooms equipped with advanced technologies, such as interactive electronic whiteboards. Westchester Community College's main campus is on a spacious 218 acres in Valhalla, and it also operates 11 extension sites.

In addition to its role as an educator for tomorrow's workforce, the college also is a leader in supporting today's businesses. Its Professional Development Center (PDC) offers affordable custom-designed training programs for local companies of all kinds. One is the global reinsurer Swiss Re. Its manager of Learning and Development, Stefan Bolli, says, "I was tremendously impressed with the center's ability to create specialized business training. Our employees from Latin America needed assistance with English as a second language, and PDC prepared an in-house program, with amazing results."

PDC also offers courses for credit for employees of telecommunications services provider Verizon who are seeking associate degrees in telecommunications technology. In addition, Westchester Community College works in partnership with networking equipment provider Cisco Systems. The college is a certified Cisco Regional Training Academy, offering training in computer networking.

All in all—from the large number of courses for its students to special training programs for businesses—Westchester Community College remains an extraordinary, unique resource that helps keep the local economy healthy.

Left, top: Westchester Community College students confer with business professor Susan Cremins, who teaches in a laboratory using advanced wireless communications technologies. Left, bottom: Director of the college's Professional Development Center (PDC), Susan Burstein, standing, and members of the PDC advisory board discuss training programs being created for client businesses.

Real Estate, Development, & Construction Services

Forest City Ratner Companies

One of the nation's blue-chip commercial developers, Forest City Ratner Companies is impacting the New York City skyline with Class A office towers and exciting mixed-use projects built on time, on budget, and high-tech ready, bringing new life and new jobs to urban areas.

Forest City Ratner Companies is a leading developer of office and retail properties in the tri-state area. With 34 projects totaling over 12 million square feet and $3 billion in costs as of 2004, Forest City Ratner has developed more ground-up commercial projects in New York City over the past 15 years than any other New York firm. A full-service development company, Forest City Ratner, along with its subsidiary, First New York Management Co., employs more than 350 individuals with expertise in all facets of development, finance, land use, design, engineering, government approvals, construction, and building operations.

Based in Brooklyn, Forest City Ratner develops properties primarily for its own portfolio and a select group of users of Class A commercial office space. Beginning with the opening of Pierrepont Plaza in 1986 (at the time, Brooklyn's first new office building in 25 years), Forest City Ratner has developed, owned, and managed state-of-the-art office buildings for the most prestigious and demanding corporate tenants.

Forest City Enterprises

Forest City Ratner Companies is a subsidiary of Forest City Enterprises (FCE). A Cleveland, Ohio–based real estate development and management company, Forest City Enterprises thrives on creating long-term value. One of the largest publicly traded real estate firms in the United States, FCE has a portfolio of assets valued at more than $5.5 billion. Established over 75 years ago by the Ratner family, FCE is still controlled by the Ratners, who have always guided the direction and values of the company and its projects.

Core Capabilities of Forest City Ratner

Expert in New York City's Complex Development Process

Forest City Ratner is expert at planning, design, and construction in New York City's unique urban environment. Experience with complex and high-profile public/private projects has brought the company an exceptional understanding of the needs of community stakeholders and government groups in the development process.

High-Technology Development Specialists

Forest City Ratner is adept at identifying the needs of sophisticated tenants and their unique operations, and will work seamlessly with systems designers to provide buildings that are "high-tech ready." Few other development companies can replicate Forest City Ratner's expertise in building state-of-the-art facilities for specialized clients. In the construction of MetroTech Center and the New York Mercantile Exchange, Forest City Ratner set the standard for innovative design and construction in New York.

Consummate Negotiators

Forest City Ratner experts have the necessary skills to undertake and negotiate complex legal and financial agreements, from ground leases to construction management contracts. The Forest City Ratner negotiating team, supported by the company's in-house legal department, is able to quickly analyze and act, even under significant constraints.

Expeditious and On-Budget Developers

Forest City Ratner is able to quickly mobilize its team to gain a thorough knowledge of project costs and a detailed understanding of schedule feasibility. The company has an outstanding track record for delivering projects on budget and on schedule.

Demonstrated Ability to Secure Financing for Major Projects

Forest City Ratner's track record and strong relationships with major lenders give the company a significant advantage in securing project financing. Having been involved in several major mixed-use projects, the company also has developed an expertise in risk allocation for financing purposes.

Portfolio Highlights

MetroTech Center

Forest City Ratner's flagship development, MetroTech Center, is a $1 billion, seven million-square-foot office and academic development in downtown Brooklyn. Started in 1988, the 14-building complex is now fully developed and houses blue-chip tenants including J.P. Morgan Chase, Bear Stearns, Morgan Stanley, Goldman Sachs, KeySpan Corporation, and WellChoice, Inc., as well as the Brooklyn campus of Polytechnic University and the headquarters of the New York City Fire Department. MetroTech has played a pivotal role in the revitalization of downtown Brooklyn. In addition to the 22,000 jobs it has brought to the area, it provides a vibrant public space—enhanced by cultural and entertainment programs—in its 2.3-acre Commons.

In 2003, Forest City Ratner completed Fifteen MetroTech, a 19-story, 653,000-square-foot office tower designed by architect Cesar Pelli. Fifteen MetroTech was the first new commercial office building developed in New York City after the September 2001 terrorist attacks. The building opened to its primary tenant—Wellchoice, Inc., one of the largest health care insurers in New York State —just 19 months after breaking ground.

Atlantic Terminal

Atlantic Terminal is an office and retail complex located in downtown Brooklyn that opened in 2004. The 10-story, 400,000-square-foot office building sits above a four-story, 375,000-square-foot retail shopping center, and both are situated above the newly refurbished Atlantic Terminal transit hub, the largest such hub in the boroughs, where 10 subway lines and the Long Island Rail Road converge. The Bank of New York occupies 320,000 square feet of office space on eight floors. The retail mall, anchored by Target, houses an array of stores and restaurants, including Daffy's, DSW Shoe Warehouse, Bath & Body Works, Children's Place, and Red Lobster.

New York Times Building

In early 2004, construction began on the New York Times Building, a 52-story, 1.6 million-square-foot office building rising on Eighth Avenue at 41st Street in Manhattan. The New York Times Company is a co-owner of the building and will occupy the lower 28 floors; Forest City Ratner owns the upper portion, which will be leased to premier office tenants. Designed by internationally acclaimed architect Renzo Piano, this iconic tower will be a dramatic new presence on the New York City skyline.

Atlantic Yards

In January 2004, Forest City Ratner announced plans for Atlantic Yards, a large-scale, mixed-use development containing Class A office space, neighborhood-oriented retail stores, and thousands of units of affordable, middle-income, and market-rate housing. The main attraction of the planned project would be an 800,000-square-foot arena for the New Jersey Nets with architecture by Frank Gehry, making Atlantic Yards a new destination for New York City.

Opposite page: Developed by Forest City Ratner, this hotel, entertainment, and retail complex on 42nd Street reflects the excitement and creativity of New York City.
Above left: The New York Times Building, a bold new addition to the Manhattan skyline, has 52 stories—the first 28 floors for The Times and the upper floors for Forest City Ratner, for premier tenants.
Above center: Forest City Ratner's Fifteen MetroTech, a 19-story office tower at MetroTech Center in downtown Brooklyn, was the first office building developed in New York City after September 11, 2001.
Above: MetroTech Center is home to prestigious tenants such as Bear Stearns and J.P. Morgan Chase.

Syska Hennessy Group, Inc.

This top-ranked, award-winning engineering firm has shaped the skylines of the Empire State, the nation, and the globe with distinctive buildings and complexes that range from the United Nations Headquarters in New York City to the United States Courthouse and Federal Building in Islip, New York.

Above: For the United Nations Headquarters in New York City, Syska Hennessy Group designed the original electrical, mechanical, and sanitary systems and now is upgrading the four million-square-foot complex.

A national and international leader in engineering, technology, consulting, and construction, Syska Hennessy Group, Inc.—with its headquarters in New York City—has been a partner in progress with its home state for more than 75 years. Established in 1928 by two forward-looking mechanical engineers, Adolph G. Syska and John F. Hennessy, the firm was among the first to specialize in the mechanical and electrical systems at the core of 20th-century structures. Just as this firm was in the vanguard of a technological revolution at the turn of the 20th century, it remains at the forefront of industry solutions, innovations, and technologies for the 21st century.

Syska Hennessy Group, with a second headquarters in California, comprises 14 offices nationwide and a staff of over 500 experts who provide services throughout the world. The firm's list of clients is a who's who of the world's leading corporations and institutions, including the Port Authority of New York and New Jersey, Bank of America Corporation, Cablevision Systems Corp., Verizon, and the federal General Services Administration. Prominent structures and projects such as the Ellis Island restoration, Lincoln Center for the Performing Arts, the Jacob K. Javits Convention Center, the Chrysler Building, and the National Gallery of Art in Washington, D.C., are just a few of Syska Hennessy Group's notable accomplishments.

Think Better Outcomes™, Think 'Green'

Consistency in growth and success is a testament to this firm, which has never engaged in "business as usual." Creative solutions and industry innovations are imperatives of Syska Hennessy Group corporate vision and daily work. The company's experience is focused on the highly technical market sectors of education, energy, government, health care, entertainment, pharmaceuticals and research, communications, financial services, real estate, and aviation. Its major public-space projects include aquariums, convention centers, resort hotels, and sports venues.

Syska Hennessy Group also excels at direct-to-owner projects and team-basis projects with more than a few of the world's leading architects.

In many cases, Syska Hennessy Group's Science and Technology Group has written the book—or in this case, the software—that addresses industry-wide deficiencies and offers innovative new approaches—the Think Better Outcomes™ series. Syska Hennessy Group's Outcome CV™ outlines commissioning and validation processes to get clients to market faster. Outcome SRM™ delineates a security program that seamlessly incorporates people, technology, and operations. And the new Outcome E²C™, a fast-track construction solution, delivers robust engineered systems.

Syska Hennessy Group is also a leader in the creation of technically sophisticated, energy-efficient buildings. In December 2003, for the Natural Resources Defense Council (NRDC)—a national nonprofit organization of scientists, lawyers, and environmental specialists dedicated to protecting public health and the environment—Syska Hennessy Group's Sustainable Design team created the NRDC's new headquarters in Santa Monica, California. This 15,000-square-foot, Class A office building, incorporating only recycled or recyclable materials and other green innovations, achieved the highest certification to date for a U.S. building in the LEED (Leadership in Energy and Environmental Design) rating system's Platinum designation. The NRDC building has been acknowledged by the U.S. Green Building Council, which developed the LEED program, as a model of mainstream sustainable design and construction for other building projects to emulate.

Awards and Accolades

For such excellence and innovation, Syska Hennessy Group garners numerous awards every year. In 2004 alone, the firm won two National Awards, from Associated Contractors of America and from Associated Builders and Contractors, as well as the Marvin M. Black Award for Excellence in Partnering, for the construction of the new United States Embassy office building in Istanbul, Turkey. Many other industry groups, as well as publications, including the New York Association of Consulting Engineers, the Construction Management Association of America, the Illuminating Engineering Society of North America, the National Trust for Historic Preservation, and *California Construction* magazine, have similarly honored the work of Syska Hennessy Group.

Keeping a keen eye on the future, Syska Hennessy Group continues to deliver integrated service solutions as it partners with clients to plan, design, build, and operate technically superior facilities. "From our employees to our clients and shareholders, we create and evolve environments where everyone succeeds," says John Hennessy III, professional engineer and chairman of the board. "In turn, our nontraditional approaches and solutions transcend clients' expectations and increase the reward-to-effort relationship."

Left: Syska Hennessy Group provided engineering design services for the award-winning, 700,000-square-foot United States Courthouse and Federal Building in Islip, New York, working closely with architect Richard Meier & Partners.

Bette & Cring Construction Group

Building on a 40-year record of successfully completed projects, Bette & Cring combines its passion for excellence with state-of-the-art methods and proven skill to create industry-specialist teams whose supreme commitment and expertise make Bette & Cring an upstate New York contractor of choice.

Right: Bette & Cring Construction Group provided general construction services for this connector walkway at the Governor Nelson A. Rockefeller Empire State Plaza, in Albany, New York.

Begun in 1999 as a spin-off of a prosperous, family-owned construction management and contracting firm, Bette & Cring Construction Group has quickly established itself as a leading provider of construction services in upstate New York. The company, based in Latham, New York, already has many local projects to its credit in a range of fields and annual sales of more than $125 million. With its partner, real estate developer First Columbia, also based in Latham, Bette & Cring offers expertise in all aspects of planning, building, financing, and operational management for a wide range of real property projects.

The roots of the Bette family of companies are deep in the local construction industry. Barry & Bette, Inc., was founded in 1973 by Michael Bette, primarily to do heavy construction for highways and bridges. In 1983, the company diversified under the name Barry, Bette, & Led Duke (BBL) into real estate development and construction.

In 1998, Michael Bette's company had grown to become the largest construction services firm and the fourth largest privately held company in the Albany capital region, had added offices in other states, and was consistently ranked, in terms of revenue, in the top 100 of *Engineering News-Record*'s Top 400 Contractors list and among its Top 100 Construction Managers.

In 1999, BBL spun off several operational units to Bette's son Matthew Bette, in partnership with his brother Peter Bette and Harold Cring, and the Bette & Cring Construction Group was created. At the same time, BBL also spun off its development division, and from it First Columbia was formed by another Bette son, Kevin. Today, First Columbia is operated by Kevin, Christopher, and Mark Bette, in close alliance with Bette & Cring.

Development Services

Bette & Cring specializes in highways and industrial construction, health care facilities and offices, multifamily housing, schools, and commercial offices. It offers full services, including design-build, site work, concrete and masonry, structural steel erection, and carpentry. First Columbia provides all needed development services, from market research, planning, feasibility studies, and financing options to regulatory compliance, architecture, engineering, and property management. Together, the partner companies offer complementary expertise from a single source, helping to streamline even the most complex project.

The partnership of Bette & Cring and First Columbia is contributing to many New York communities, especially in the upper Hudson Valley, a growing center of high-technology manufacturing. New York International Plaza, in New Windsor, adjacent to Stewart International Airport, is a 260-acre, mixed-use campus featuring corporate offices, the Hudson Valley World Trade Center, hotel and convention facilities, retail stores, an E-commerce business incubator, and a university. The complex's infrastructure provides immediate communications capabilities, including broadband, advanced digital subscriber line (ADSL), local- and wide-area computer network (LAN and WAN), and more. One facility in the complex, the Medical Center of New Windsor, is an example of the many health care facilities developed by Bette & Cring and First Columbia.

Another development by Bette & Cring and First Columbia is Century Hill Plaza, in Latham, a state-of-the-art office park slated to total 300,000 square feet. In the park's buildings, tenants—some of them Fortune 500 firms—include New York Life, St. Paul Fire & Marine Life Insurance, the New York State School Boards Association headquarters, and BlueShield of Northeastern New York.

Also in Latham is Bette & Cring and First Columbia's Riverhill Center, located on a spacious campus overlooking the Mohawk River and convenient to Albany International Airport. The center is planned as a high-tech office complex of four buildings, incorporating advanced physical plant features, such as fiber optics.

Bette & Cring and First Columbia are also developing Slingerlands Crossing, an office park in Bethlehem. The complex is planned as three structures centering on the Slingerlands Medical Arts Building.

Construction Services

With offices in Watertown and New Windsor in addition to its Latham headquarters, Bette & Cring is well positioned to provide the highest quality construction services to clients throughout New York. For Benedictine Hospital in Kingston, it is building on its traditional strengths with the design and construction of a three-story, 35,000-square-foot cancer treatment center that will offer the region state-of-the-art radiation therapy. For another client, the $30 million Avila Independent Housing facility, it provided turnkey design, construction, and development services.

It is no wonder that, in 2003, *The Business Review* ranked Bette & Cring among the top five of the Area's Largest General Contractors and one of the top 15 of the Area's Largest Privately Held Companies.

For more information: for the Bette & Cring Construction Group, phone 518-213-1010; or visit the firm's Web site at www.bettecring.com; for First Columbia, phone 518-213-1000; or visit the company's Web site at www.firstcolumbia.com.

Top: Michael Bette (seated, center) started the Bette companies in 1973; with him are his sons (from left) Christopher, Peter, Kevin, Matthew, and Mark. Peter and Matthew are among the partners of Bette & Cring; Kevin, Christopher, and Mark operate First Columbia. Above: The Slingerlands Medical Arts Building is in the Slingerlands Crossing office park, which is being developed in Bethlehem, New York, by Bette & Cring and First Columbia.

Tishman Construction Corporation

The first name behind many of the most architecturally innovative buildings in New York and the nation is Tishman, whose landmark construction projects include Century City in Los Angeles, Florida's EPCOT Center, the original New York City World Trade Center complex, and now the 1,776-foot-high Freedom Tower.

Above: Built by Tishman—**The Westin New York at Times Square** (left), with 863 rooms, features avant-garde design; **4 Times Square**, the 1.6 million-square-foot Condé Nast headquarters (right), owned by the Durst Organization, also houses NASDAQ and other major companies.

For more than a century, the history and spirit of New York City has been intertwined with the history and work of the Tishman Construction Corporation, one of the few remaining American-owned major construction firms based in New York. Upon completion by 2009 of Freedom Tower at the World Trade Center site, Tishman Construction—in collaboration with famed architects Daniel Libeskind and David M. Childs, of SOM, and developer Larry Silverstein—will have given physical expression to the indomitable spirit of freedom that defines New York City and America. At 1,776 feet, this tapering skyscraper will be among the world's tallest buildings.

Tishman Construction is also building Ground Zero's new 7 World Trade Center, the forerunner of "an environmentally sensitive city within a city that is attuned to nature as well as the real estate market" (*The New York Times*, "At Ground Zero, Rebuilding With Nature in Mind," January 20, 2004). The extensive green guidelines for rebuilding the World Trade Center structures set new standards for New York and the world. "We're talking about building an environmentally sensitive city. That has never been done before," says Daniel R. Tishman, chairman and CEO of Tishman Construction and CEO of Tishman Realty & Construction Co., Inc., the original owner/builder company, founded in 1898.

Having a wide-ranging background in real estate development, planning, design, and construction—along with a particularly strong emphasis on environmental sustainability and energy conservation—Tishman has been personally in charge of such progressive buildings as the headquarters of Condé Nast Publications at 4 Times Square; the technologically advanced headquarters building of Reuters Americas and its subsidiary Instinet at 3 Times Square; the Louis Vuitton North American headquarters tower, at 19 East 57th Street; and The Westin New York at Times Square. As a New York native, Tishman is perhaps most proud of his firm's involvement in the restoration of venerable Carnegie Hall, a project led by his father, John Tishman.

State of the Art, Science, and Business

Founded by Daniel Tishman's great-grandfather Julius Tishman, Tishman Realty & Construction Co., Inc.—still headquartered in New York City and active nationwide—encompasses Tishman Construction and numerous affiliates. Tishman Interiors Corporation excels at interior fit-outs, modernization, and renovation. Tishman Technologies Corporation specializes in data and telecommunications infrastructure and facilities, intelligent-building systems, and installations demanding operations 24 hours a day, seven days a week. The Tishman Realty Corporation is a private-sector developer, while Tishman Urban Development arranges public/private ventures. Tishman Real Estate Services provides strategic corporate real estate planning, tenant and landlord representation, and property management. The Tishman Hotel Corporation is expert in hotel asset and property management,

Photos: Far left, © Norman McGrath; left, © Andrew Gordon

brokerage, and investment banking worldwide. Notably, Tishman Realty & Construction is one of the only organizations in the industry with its own research affiliate, the Tishman Research Corporation. "The objective is to keep our organization on the leading edge of every discipline we offer," Daniel Tishman says.

Tishman Construction is responsible for the construction of more than 400 million square feet of base building and interior space of every size and type of facility worldwide—office, hotel, residential, retail, medical, educational, entertainment, recreational, and institutional. Tishman Construction's total value of construction under contract in 2004, for its own accounts and for third-party clients, is approximately $4 billion.

First in Industry Firsts

Tishman Construction's contributions to the building industry include many firsts in building technology and development. The company has pioneered the use of unattended, high-speed, electronically controlled elevators; aluminum-and-glass curtain walls; modern fire-safety and energy-management systems; automatic, energy-saving lighting systems; and many more innovations that have become industry standards. In its construction management capacity, Tishman Construction features a professional and diversified staff of architects and estimators; preconstruction and construction managers; mechanical, electrical, and civil engineers; and scheduling and cost-control specialists. This staff of 800 provides Tishman Construction's clients with personal consultation and guidance in all phases of a building project.

Because of such in-house resources, the scope of the company's experience, and its continued leadership in the industry, Tishman Construction Corporation brings the most current methodologies and technologies to every project. "For the present and future, we will continue to set ourselves apart," says Daniel Tishman. "In order to do that, we always stay focused on our clients' needs. It is our aim to be the best—not the biggest—full-service construction and real estate company in the United States."

Top row, from left: Tishman's **E Walk** in Times Square, a public/private venture, is an entertainment, retail, and restaurant complex. **The Impala** is one of Tishman's residential projects; the firm has built housing since 1898. **Freedom Tower**, at the World Trade Center site, is being built by Tishman Construction for Silverstein Properties in collaboration with the Port Authority of New York and New Jersey. For **One Bryant Park**, for the Durst Organization and Bank of America, Tishman is construction manager.
Far left: The new **7 World Trade Center** is being built by Tishman, which also built the original 7 World Trade Center.
Left: For **745 Seventh Avenue**, for Morgan Stanley and Rockefeller Group Development Corporation, Tishman Construction, Tishman Technologies, and Tishman Interiors handled base building, technology/telecommunications infrastructure, and major interior space construction.

Photos, this page: Top row, from left, © Philip Greenberg; © Norman McGrath; © Jock Pottle/Esto; © dbox studio for Cook + Fox Architects; bottom row, from left, © Advanced Media Design Inc.; © Norman McGrath

Civil Technologies and Engineering, P.C.

These experienced construction and design professionals use innovative strategies to create functional, cost-effective buildings that also are aesthetically pleasing and safeguard the Hudson Valley's natural beauty.

The Civil Technologies and Engineering (CTE) expansion of the Nortrax facility (right) in Beacon, New York, was completed ahead of schedule and under budget using the design-build method of contract delivery. Design-build, one of CTE's most popular services, enables construction of certain areas of a project to take place while others are being reviewed and approved, saving time and money.

Civil Technologies and Engineering, P.C. (CTE) provides comprehensive architectural and engineering services to commercial, residential, and municipal clients. Given the company's roots in construction, its team of multidisciplined experts, and its use of state-of-the-art technologies, CTE develops and oversees projects from beginning to end—which ensures a savings in time and money for clients.

CTE was established in 1990 by Eugene D. Ninnie, P.E., whose family roots in the construction industry stretch back 90 years in the Hudson Valley. Mr. Ninnie personally brought more than 10 years of construction experience and 12 years of design experience to his forward-thinking firm. He founded CTE to apply practical field experience to the design process and bridge the gap between construction drawings and specifications with what can be practically and economically produced in the field.

In building his company, Mr. Ninnie established a "family" of engineers, planners, and designers, each of whom has many years' experience in the construction industry. With this experience and CTE's use of modern computer applications and hardware, the company provides functional and cost-effective designs for any size project. This practical side of building and design is not normally found with other such firms.

Enhancing the Quality of Life

In developing its projects, CTE is also mindful of the environmental and aesthetic, as well as business, aspects of each project. For example, as the engineering firm for several Hudson Valley municipalities, CTE designs and maintains local infrastructures while safeguarding the valley's natural beauty. In addition, CTE provides restoration and rehabilitation services to local historical buildings, thus preserving the rich history of the Hudson Valley.

And CTE, conveniently headquartered in Wappingers Falls, New York, helps support Hudson Valley's economics and job market. Using local labor, CTE completed a facility expansion design-build project for Nortrax, a construction equipment retailer, enabling Nortrax to rethink its company strategy and relocate its regional headquarters from New Hampshire to Beacon, New York, bringing new jobs to the state.

Photo: © Royalty-Free/CORBIS

Hospitality

New York City Marriott Hotels

New York City's distinctive, award-winning Marriott hotels provide a complete range of amenities and services for business and leisure travelers, from the business-minded Courtyard by Marriott hotels to the luxurious Rihga Royal–New York, a JW Marriott Hotel.

Above: At the New York Marriott Marquis, in the heart of Times Square, is the Atrium Lounge.

New York City's distinctive, award-winning Marriott hotels provide a complete range of amenities and services for leisure and business travelers, from the business-minded Courtyard by Marriott properties to the luxurious all-suite Rihga Royal–New York, a JW Marriott Hotel.

Each year, millions of visitors come to New York City. They come to see Broadway shows and the Statue of Liberty, stroll through museum galleries and gardens, shop in boutiques and major department stores, or sip cappuccinos downtown. Wherever their adventures take them, they will find a Marriott hotel close at hand.

Located in the heart of Times Square and Broadway's bustling theater district, the 49-story **New York Marriott Marquis** is one of the largest Marriott hotels in the world. This landmark hotel, designed by John Portman, features numerous architectural earmarks, including a dramatic 37-story atrium with 12 glass-enclosed elevators. All 1,946 guest rooms and suites are spacious and comfortably appointed, and many offer a view of Times Square. The hotel's Marquis Fitness Center is a glass-enclosed, 4,000-square-foot space that appears as a floating light box midway over the atrium, providing an exciting setting for a full workout, as well as panoramic views of Times Square and midtown Manhattan. The hotel houses the 1,600-seat Marquis Theater, a premier Broadway musical house. Gourmet diners enjoy several restaurant choices, including: The View, New York's only revolving-rooftop restaurant; JW's Steakhouse, with an award-winning wine list; and Katen Sushi Bar. Classic cocktails are served at the elegant Atrium Lounge, and in the Broadway Lounge, guests can relax while looking out over the lights of Broadway.

Adjacent to the Marriott Marquis in the center of Times Square is the **Renaissance New York Hotel Times Square**. This 26-story high-rise houses 305 guest rooms and suites, a cardiovascular and weight-training room, and a luxurious lobby. The hotel's art deco–style lounge, The Bar, features a raised circular bar, plush furnishings, and nightly live musical entertainment. Foley's Fish House, an 80-seat restaurant with a spectacular bird's-eye view of Times Square, serves a wide-ranging selection of seafood brought in fresh from Foley's New England fishermen.

Across town, within walking distance of Rockefeller Center, the Museum of Modern Art, and shops on Fifth Avenue, is the **New York Marriott East Side**, located on Lexington Avenue at 49th Street. Beautifully restored, this stately hotel, originally the Shelton Towers and later, Halloran House, dates back to 1924 and was designed by architect Arthur Loomis Harmon, who collaborated on the design of the Empire State Building. The hotel's elegant ambiance is marked by rich wood paneling, marble floors, oriental rugs, and mahogany furnishings. Its 643 guest rooms and suites, fully refurbished in charming contemporary style, are tastefully decorated and impeccably maintained. Diners enjoy American fare at the hotel's Shelton Grille, where breakfast, lunch, and dinner are served in a gracious, relaxing atmosphere.

For guests desiring a location in lower Manhattan, the **New York Marriott Financial Center** awaits. This 504-room hotel in the heart of the Wall Street district received a major renovation in 2001 for its guest rooms, main lobby, and lobby bar—now called "85 West." While guest rooms have a traditional European ambiance, the sparkling new lobby can be described as classic modern. Most of the guest rooms and suites have sweeping views of the Hudson River. The hotel's health club, complete with indoor swimming pool, is available to hotel guests. The Marriott Financial Center became the first Marriott hotel to form a partnership with a name chef when it opened its fashionably popular

restaurant Roy's New York, in 1999. Chef Roy Yamaguchi is known as the father of Hawaiian Fusion cuisine, and this is his only restaurant in New York City. The Marriott Financial Center offers easy access to Wall Street, the South Street Seaport, Ellis Island and Statue of Liberty ferries, SoHo, Greenwich Village, Little Italy, and Chinatown.

Opened in 1998, the **New York Marriott at the Brooklyn Bridge**, located at 333 Adams Street, was the first new hotel construction in New York City's most populous borough in nearly 70 years. This upscale, full-service hotel affords guests easy access to the numerous sightseeing destinations in lower Manhattan—just across the landmark Brooklyn Bridge—and in historic Brooklyn. Recommended Brooklyn attractions include the Brooklyn Heights Historical District, the Brooklyn Museum of Art, the Brooklyn Botanic Garden, the Brooklyn Academy of Music, the Brooklyn Children's Museum, and Prospect Park. The Brooklyn Marriott has 376 modern guest rooms, including 21 suites, and an 8,000-square-foot, state-of-the-art fitness center with a 75-foot lap pool. Historic Brooklyn memorabilia, on loan from the Brooklyn Historical Society, are displayed at the hotel's Archives Restaurant.

Marriott opened its first luxury hotel in New York, the **Rihga Royal–New York, a JW Marriott Hotel**, in March 2001. This all-suite hotel, with 500 guest suites, is located in the heart of midtown Manhattan and offers some of the most outstanding views of the city. Its richly designed suites are frequented by scores of celebrities and entertainment industry personalities. Halcyon is the hotel's signature restaurant, where media moguls engage in the power breakfast scene.

In 1998, the opening of two Courtyard by Marriott hotels signaled the entrance into Manhattan of Marriott's leading hotel brand designed to meet the needs of business travelers. The 244-room **Times Square South Courtyard by Marriott**, located at 114 West 40th Street, was the first new hotel to be built in the garment district since 1970. The 308-room **Manhattan Midtown East Courtyard by Marriott**, located at 866 Third Avenue, is a conversion of the former Macmillan Publishing Company building. In 2000, Marriott opened the **Jersey City–Newport Courtyard by Marriott**, located across the Hudson River on the Jersey City, New Jersey, waterfront. The hotel is situated in the heart of Newport Centre, home to the many corporate businesses that have moved across the Hudson, and offers easy access to Manhattan via train and ferry service.

For the business traveler who needs to be close to the city's airports, Marriott offers two hotels at LaGuardia Airport and one at John F. Kennedy International Airport. The 436-room **New York Marriott LaGuardia** and the 288-room **LaGuardia Courtyard by Marriott** are both located directly across Grand Central Parkway near the airport. The 166-room **JFK Courtyard by Marriott**, which opened in June 2001, is a short, five-minute ride from the airport's terminals. All three hotels offer van service to and from airport terminals.

For additional information on New York City Marriott hotels, visit the Web site www.nycmarriott.com; for all Marriott hotels, visit www.marriott.com.

Above: Among Marriott's New York City hotels are, from left, the Renaissance New York Hotel Times Square, the New York Marriott at the Brooklyn Bridge, the New York Marriott East Side, the New York Marriott Financial Center, and the Rihga Royal–New York, a JW Marriott Hotel.

The Crowne Plaza Hotel

The Crowne Plaza Hotel in White Plains, New York, provides finely appointed guest rooms and suites with exceptional amenities and services, as well as state-of-the-art event spaces for meetings and elegant social occasions.

In the Crowne Plaza lobby at the main entrance, brass, copper, and steel come together in this dramatic sculpture, which is suspended from the skylights.

The Crowne Plaza Hotel in White Plains, New York, has earned a reputation for providing superior service to business and pleasure travelers alike. Built in 1985 in downtown White Plains, the Crowne Plaza has 14 floors that include 401 elegantly appointed guest rooms and two suites, and 17,000 square feet of flexible meeting and event space.

Providing exceptional service has long been a cornerstone of the hotel's mission, and the Crowne Plaza White Plains is the winner of the prestigious Quality Excellence award. Key to the hotel's outstanding service is its long-standing staff, many of whom have been with the hotel since it opened.

Historically, the hotel has maintained an average occupancy of 85 percent. Individual and group business travelers fill the hotel during the week. On weekends, the hotel is the place to be for leisure travelers attending social functions. In addition to its corporate and leisure clientele, the hotel has hosted notable groups such as the Professional Golf Association (PGA) and the Ladies Professional Golf Association (LPGA).

Crowne Plaza's guest rooms are especially luxurious thanks to a 2002 renovation that added numerous features, such as marble bath facilities. All rooms include such amenities as a coffeemaker, refreshment center, hair dryer, iron and ironing board, business desk with ergonomically designed desk chair, two telephone lines including a data port, and an in-room safe.

Guests looking for added luxury can take advantage of the Club Level. The Club Level offers the privacy of keyed access, nightly turndown service, bathrobes, and access to the Club Lounge. The lounge provides a complimentary continental breakfast and evening cocktails and hors d'oeuvres. The club's suites feature spacious living and dining rooms with bedrooms on either side.

All guests can enjoy hotel facilities such as the indoor swimming pool and whirlpool spa, as well as a private-access fitness center that is open 24 hours per day. Fenimore's Bistro serves a variety of delicious dishes for breakfast, lunch, and dinner. The Sunday brunch and Saturday night prime rib buffet are favorites among local patrons. A private dining

room accommodates up to 30 people, and room service is available daily until midnight. Guests also will find more than 60 great dining opportunities within walking distance of the hotel.

The Crowne Plaza Hotel's transportation service is extensive, providing guests with rides to and from local businesses, shops, and restaurants within a seven-mile radius. The hotel's vans also shuttle guests to and from the Westchester County Airport.

Crowne Plaza is a lavish venue for events, from corporate conferences to weddings, bar and bat mitzvahs, and reunions of all types. A full-time support team of catering and conference managers is available to assist with the planning of business meetings and special occasions, and a banquet manager is on duty to provide personal service throughout all functions.

The hotel's meeting and banquet event space of 17,000 square feet accommodates groups of up to 800 people. Seventeen meeting rooms include a boardroom with a beautiful, handcrafted oak conference table and 16 ergonomic leather chairs. The New Rochelle Ballroom accommodates up to 800 people for meetings and up to 600 for dining. Hosts may choose from a variety of menus, or the hotel's trained catering experts can create a special menu.

Crowne Plaza conference facilities feature technologically advanced audiovisual equipment. Meeting rooms are equipped with in-room climate controls, category 5 shielded cable with multiple port capabilities, and high-speed Internet access. The hotel's in-house audiovisual department offers a comprehensive range of equipment and services, including microphones, slide projectors, VCRs, LCD computer-display lecture facilities, modem connections and high-speed ISDN lines, webcasting, and satellite communication networks for worldwide videoconferencing capabilities. Secretarial, fax, and copying services are available in the hotel's business center.

Its state-of-the-art facilities are a testament to the Crowne Plaza White Plains commitment to provide exceptional service and value to all of its guests, whether visiting for business or for pleasure.

Above left: The hotel's guest rooms, completely renovated in 2002, incorporate warm tones in an elegant and modern design. Above: The Mamaroneck Boardroom provides an intimate setting for executive meetings.

Jacob K. Javits Convention Center of New York

Since it opened in 1986, the 'Marketplace for the World'® has hosted more than 2,500 trade shows, conventions, and special events, including the New York International Auto Show and the National Boat Show, and brings in more than a billion dollars a year in business for the state and the city.

The Jacob K. Javits Convention Center of New York, the city and state's premier convention center and trade show venue, is a lightsome jewel on Manhattan's West Side.

A stunning, $486 million asset to New York State and New York City, the Javits Center, "Marketplace for the World"®, is the state and city's premier, world-class convention and trade show facility.

Around the world, in an industry worth $94 billion a year, mention Javits Center and professionals know immediately that you are talking about one of the major success stories of recent New York history. The Javits Center is owned and operated by New York State and, under a mandate from George E. Pataki, the state's governor, a topflight professional staff has made Javits one of the most sought-after trade show, convention, and special event venues in the United States.

Since it opened in 1986, Javits has hosted more than 2,500 trade shows, conventions, and special events, plus more than 600 commercial photo shoots, parts of such popular television series as *Law & Order,* and even scenes from such major motion pictures as *The Peacemaker,* with Nicole Kidman and George Clooney, and *The Manchurian Candidate,* with Meryl Streep and Denzel Washington.

In the 1970s, there was a definite need for a much larger trade show and convention facility than the New York Coliseum. The industry was growing enormously, and city and state officials began looking for a larger venue. They found one on Manhattan's West Side.

Jacob K. Javits spent 32 years in Washington, D.C., representing the state. A moderate Republican, Javits had a long and honorable record of public service, working with Fiorello LaGuardia when LaGuardia was the city's mayor; serving as state attorney general for three years; as U.S. representative of New York's 21st District for eight years; and as a U.S. senator from New York for 24 years.

The Javits Center hosts an average of 140 events a year. Most are major trade shows and conventions attracting about 2.5 million visitors annually. Among the giant shows are the New York International Auto Show, the National Boat Show, the twice-yearly International Gift Fair, the National Retail Federation conference and exhibition, and a variety of other trade events, from computers to fashion.

Javits today is turning away almost as much business as it accepts. Its 2004 and 2005 major show calendar is nearly completely filled, and the center is booking events into the year 2020 and beyond, which is why there is a tremendous need for Javits to expand. The center generates more than a billion dollars a year in business for the state and the city, which means about $100 million in tax revenues. Estimates indicate expansion could nearly double such financial success.

No matter what the future brings, New York can be justifiably proud of a beautiful and extremely successful asset. The Javits Center is, and will continue to be, the "Marketplace for the World"®.

Photo: © Gayle Gleason

Photo: © James Leynse/CORBIS

Corporate Housing

Marriott ExecuStay

Temporary Housing With a Familiar Name℠, Marriott ExecuStay features luxury studio, one-bedroom, and two-bedroom apartments—all with high-speed Internet access, fully equipped business centers, state-of-the-art fitness centers, and much more—at convenient locations throughout New York City.

The corporate apartments at the Marriott ExecuStay Chelsea offer ample, elegant spaces for business and personal use.

Marriott ExecuStay provides ideal corporate-housing solutions in one of the most exciting cities in the world—New York. Marriott, a familiar brand to New Yorkers, features hotels located throughout the metropolitan area. Marriott ExecuStay's temporary-housing apartments are spacious, well-appointed, and central to the business and entertainment districts of this great city. In addition, through Marriott's virtual inventory program, Marriott ExecuStay suites can be located just about anywhere an apartment is needed in New York City.

Nationwide, Marriott ExecuStay is well known for providing high levels of comfort and service. With just one phone call, a fully furnished, customized, and serviced apartment can be set up and ready to be moved into anywhere in the United States.

Always at Home with Marriott ExecuStay

The many benefits and amenities of Marriott ExecuStay apartments include the following:

- True apartment living with more space and privacy than a hotel room;
- An affordable solution for longer-term stays;
- Marriott Rewards® points that are redeemable for hotel stays, frequent-flier miles, and more;
- One easy-to-read monthly invoice for all expenses;
- Friendly customer service.

From the little things that matter to going above and beyond guests' expectations, Marriott ExecuStay anticipates and addresses every need. For stays of 30 days or longer, Marriott ExecuStay is an easy choice.

Marriott Rewards® with Every Stay

Marriott Rewards members earn two-and-a-half points for every dollar spent during stays of 30 days or more. As points accumulate, so do the chances of relaxing and enjoying a vacation at any one of more than 2,300 Marriott hotels worldwide. With more than 60 countries and more than 300 additional rewards to choose from, Marriott truly offers something for everyone.

In New York City, Marriott ExecuStay's exciting choices include the newly opened Marriott ExecuStay Aurora, located in elegant Murray Hill; the Marriott ExecuStay Chelsea, located in hip-and-happening Chelsea; and luxury apartments conveniently located around the city.

The Marriott ExecuStay Aurora: See the Light

The Marriott ExecuStay Aurora stands tall and shines over a vibrant city life. Surrounded by awe-inspiring sights, critically acclaimed restaurants, and contemporary cafés, the Aurora, located in the Murray Hill section of midtown Manhattan, is as much a starting point for adventures as it is a quiet retreat.

With its proximity to the Grand Central Terminal, Manhattan's great dining establishments, Bryant Park (terrific for reflective walks), and world-class shopping (for faster paced sprees), the Aurora is singularly electric.

Inside, the Aurora features 126 studio and one-bedroom apartments, with high-speed Internet access and convenient washer and dryer units. The facilities also offer a state-of-the-art fitness center, a fully equipped business center, 24-hour security, and a concierge.

Countless guests put their trust in Marriott's one-stop solution for temporary housing to lay the groundwork for a restful and productive stay at the Aurora. Backed by 77 years of Marriott hospitality and lodging experience, Marriott ExecuStay Aurora makes the transition to New York City an easy one by providing high levels of quality and service.

The Marriott ExecuStay Chelsea: Where It's At

The Marriott ExecuStay Chelsea, located in the heart of Chelsea, is convenient to the bustling Garment District as well as to hip, hot nightspots. No place in New York is far from the Chelsea, because it sits near eight major subway lines. And Chelsea is the happening area of New York. Once known more for factories than culture, the area has experienced a major face-lift in recent years and welcomed the arrival of art galleries, new museums (the Eyebeam is noteworthy), and great theaters. With major loft conversions, Chelsea also encompasses wonderful residential blocks, and many of its streets feature sidewalk cafés and bistros.

The Chelsea boasts 205 extraordinary studio, one-bedroom, and two-bedroom apartments. Like the Aurora, the Chelsea is pet friendly and there are several dog walks in the area (great places to meet New Yorkers). Two roof terraces with exhilarating city views, a fully outfitted health club with the latest equipment, a communal laundry, 24-hour security, and a concierge round out the amenities of the Chelsea. Numerous supermarkets and more than 300 fine restaurants are within walking distance of the Marriott ExecuStay Chelsea.

For additional information about Marriott ExecuStay, phone 800-877-2800 (toll-free) or 212-953-5707; or visit the company's Web site at www.execustay.com.

Above and center: The Marriott ExecuStay Chelsea offers a central location and fine amenities, such as a state-of-the-art fitness center. Far left: The Marriott ExecuStay Aurora, located in the Murray Hill neighborhood of midtown Manhattan, provides guests with comfortable, well-appointed surroundings.

Retail Market

Trans World Entertainment Corporation

With nearly 1,000 specialty music and video stores in 47 states, the District of Columbia, Puerto Rico, and the U.S. Virgin Islands, the Trans World Entertainment Corporation—headquartered in Albany, New York—defines the current state of entertainment retailing as well as the future of this booming market sector.

Robert J. Higgins, chairman and CEO of Trans World Entertainment Corporation, founded the company in 1972 in Albany, New York, and then guided and expanded it into one of the strongest specialty entertainment retailers in the United States.

Renowned as one of the largest specialty music and video retailers in the United States, Trans World Entertainment Corporation owns a playlist of stores with widespread name recognition. The company's impressive portfolio includes the freestanding Wherehouse Music, Coconuts Music & Movies, Strawberries, Spec's, CD World, Second Spin, Streetside Records, Planet Music, and Saturday Matinee stores; three e-commerce sites; and the groundbreaking, mall-based FYE–For Your Entertainment brand. These stores, typically 3,500 to 45,000 square feet, offer a wide-ranging selection of CDs, DVDs, prerecorded audio- and video-cassettes, electronics, and related accessories, and have been setting records every year as major employers and financial leaders. Collectively, total sales for 2003 (the latest available fiscal year) exceeded $1.3 billion.

"We are very pleased with our consistent sales and earnings results," says Robert J. Higgins, Trans World's founder, chairman, and CEO. "Comparable store sales continue to increase. These results reflect our increasing market share in video and other entertainment categories. They also reflect the strength of our FYE–For Your Entertainment brand, our position as a total entertainment destination, and our ability to capitalize on opportunities resulting from industry consolidation. At a time when many of our peers are struggling, we are able to post earnings that exceed expectations through improved gross margin in all major product lines and by implementing expense and cost controls."

Making Entertainment History

Established in 1972 as the Trans World Music Corporation in Albany, New York, where the company remains headquartered, Trans World rose quickly to become a major entertainment entity. During the first 10 years, capitalizing on the booming mall phenomenon, Trans World debuted 38 stores. In 1986, the company went public (NASDAQ: TWMC). By 2001, Trans World united its mall-based portfolio and retail Web site under the FYE–For Your Entertainment brand name to create a consistent, cross-channel experience for its customers. In the process, Trans World redefined and revolutionized entertainment retailing.

With something for everyone, Trans World's freestanding retail units are located in strategic locations across the nation. The corporation's Coconuts Music & Movies stores, located in high-traffic freestanding shopping centers, offer competitively priced products. The massive Planet Music store, with more than 31,000 square feet of selling space, caters to music enthusiasts. The Strawberries stores, with an average of 3,000 square feet of selling space, offer the range of specialty music products, while Spec's appeals to serious entertainment enthusiasts. Wherehouse Music, a mostly West Coast chain, presents the latest in music, movies, games, and electronics and a wide selection of used titles. The Saturday Matinee stores provide a wide range of movies, DVDs, and games.

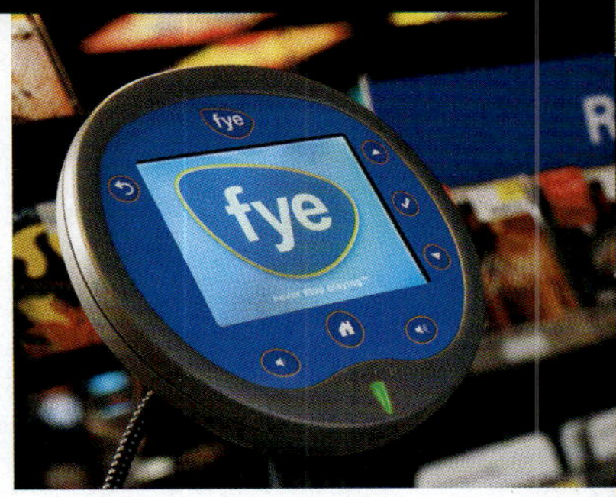

The Future of Entertainment

Setting the stage for the future of entertainment retailing is Trans World's exciting FYE–For Your Entertainment brand, which unifies the corporation's entire mall portfolio of more than 650 units in prime locations nationwide. *Interactive, ubiquitous,* and *customer-centric* define the FYE–For Your Entertainment concept. With a related Web site, FYE creates a powerful, consistent, cross-channel experience. A broadband digital platform links every FYE store, enabling immediate innovations. This cutting-edge technology also provides the infrastructure for future applications, including the digital delivery of products, t-commerce (television-based e-commerce), and m-commerce (mobile e-commerce). With such proprietary in-store technologies, advanced Customer Relationship Management (CRM) techniques, and a complete experiential- and research-based understanding of its customers, FYE positions the entire corporation for continued growth and success.

Through three decades of industry changes and challenges, Trans World Corporation has led as a pioneer and emerged as a leader. "We expect to continue to improve our comparable store sales results through a combination of improved releases in music, continued growth in DVD products, and the further development of our business initiatives," says Higgins. "Continued efforts by the music industry to reduce piracy will further drive more consumers back to the stores and increase sales. For the present and future, we will continue to leverage on our improving sales and capitalize on growth opportunities in the marketplace, while remaining focused on reducing the cost of doing business. We will also continue building the FYE brand, through marketing and technology strategies, to position FYE as a premier entertainment destination."

Trans World's FYE–For Your Entertainment stores offer an interactive, inspiring shopping experience, featuring in-store technologies such as the FYE listening-viewing station (above left) and other customer-driven initiatives.

Transportation

Metropolitan Transportation Authority

A public-benefit corporation chartered by New York State, the Metropolitan Transportation Authority operates the subways, buses, railroads, bridges, and tunnels that provide transit for a population of 14.6 million people in New York City, Long Island, southeastern New York, and Connecticut.

New subway cars continue to improve service on MTA New York City Transit.

The Metropolitan Transportation Authority (MTA) network links the diverse parts of New York, enabling residents and visitors to get where they want to go swiftly and at reasonable cost. MTA services give the region efficient, environmentally sound travel alternatives to gridlocked streets and highways. The mobility provided by the MTA helps ensure New York's place as a world center of finance, commerce, culture, and entertainment.

The size and scope of the MTA is immense. Its network—the subways and buses of MTA New York City Transit, the commuter rail lines of MTA Long Island Rail Road and MTA Metro-North Railroad, the buses of MTA Long Island Bus, the bridge and tunnel crossings of MTA Bridges and Tunnels, and the construction management of MTA Capital Construction—is North America's largest, providing more than 7.5 million rides every weekday, while its bridges and tunnels carry nearly 880,000 cars, trucks, and buses. Peter S. Kalikow, MTA chairman, notes that the MTA operation is so extensive that "in three days, our mass transit operation moves more riders than Amtrak does in a year. In 11 weeks, we move more people than the airlines in a year. And in two and a half years, we move the equivalent of every man, woman, and child on the planet."

But the greatest value of the MTA lies in its beneficial impact on the New York region's economy and quality of life. New York ranks near the top among the nation's best cities for business, *Fortune* magazine has written, because it has "what every city desires. A workable mass transit system."

Out of the Past

Mass transit by rail in and around New York City is nearly as old as the steam locomotive itself. The New York & Harlem Railroad (one of the predecessors of Metro-North) was chartered in 1831, while the Long Island Rail Road was created three years later. The Big Apple's first subway opened in October 1904 when the Interborough Rapid Transit Company inaugurated its first route in Manhattan, charging a nickel for a ride. The system grew rapidly, reaching into the Bronx less than a year later, Brooklyn in 1908, and Queens in 1915. The motor bus has nearly as long a history, having first plied the streets of Manhattan in 1907. Responding to the growth of automobile traffic, the city created the Triborough Bridge Authority, which eventually became Bridges and Tunnels, in 1933.

The network came together in 1968 when the MTA was formed to oversee the operations of New York City Transit, the Long Island Rail Road, and Bridges and Tunnels. Long Island Bus was added in 1973, a newly formed agency that took over the operations of 10 failing bus companies in Nassau County. In 1983, the commuter rail service of Penn Central, serving the northern suburbs in New York State and western Connecticut, came under the auspices of the MTA as Metro-North Railroad. Capital Construction was added in 2003 to oversee the first major expansion of the system in over five decades.

Into the Present

Back in the 1970s, after decades of neglect and disinvestment, the MTA's

infrastructure was collapsing. Ridership was falling. Graffiti-covered trains, high crime, and declining reliability threatened the core of New York's regional transportation—and its prosperity.

In 1982, the MTA began to rehabilitate its transit network through a series of capital programs—the largest public transportation rebuilding effort in national history, investing over $40 billion in the past 20 years.

Maintenance facilities have been overhauled, track has been rehabilitated, stations are cleaner, and subways and buses are graffiti-free. New rolling stock makes the system more reliable and comfortable.

The MTA Capital Program also provides significant economic benefits to the region. MTA projects directly provide jobs to thousands of New Yorkers, creating an annual average of 21,000 private-sector jobs, $1.1 billion in wages, $100 million in state and local tax revenues, and $2.5 billion in economic activity.

The MTA's technological innovations, MetroCard® automated fare collection and E-ZPass℠ electronic toll collection, revolutionized fare and toll payment. MetroCard brought free transfers between subways and buses; multiride bonuses; and weekly, monthly, and daily transit passes, reducing the cost of public transportation for the first time. E-ZPass transformed local and regional highway travel, dramatically shortening toll lines and reducing pollution.

On to the Future

While the MTA's primary role is to provide transportation that is effective, flexible, inexpensive, and safe, the attack on the World Trade Center made it clear that the MTA has a much greater role to play as a key part of the region's emergency transportation network. The prompt response of MTA employees immediately after the attack ensured that no customer or employee was injured, and it was the ability of the MTA to quickly reestablish service that enabled millions to return home that afternoon and evening. The MTA is now working to improve its ability to move vast numbers of people during emergencies and is paying particular attention to system security.

The MTA is also working to expand its network. In the pipeline are East Side Access to bring the Long Island Rail Road into Grand Central Terminal, the Second Avenue subway, a subway extension from Times Square to the far West Side, the Fulton Street Transit Center, and South Ferry Terminal. A new agency, MTA Capital Construction, is managing these major projects.

"These new services will dramatically enhance commercial, economic, residential, and cultural development of New York City and the region," says Katherine N. Lapp, MTA executive director.

Across the MTA network, the commitment to maintaining all subways, buses, locomotives, rail cars, track, stations, bridges, and tunnels in a state of good repair makes commuting easier for millions of riders.

Energy

Plug Power

Through a global network of strategic partnerships, this leader in fuel cell technology researches and develops methods of reducing costs and enhancing product performance and market viability while creating next-generation sources of clean, reliable, and sustainable energy.

Right: At the Long Island Power Authority's substation in West Babylon, New York, are Plug Power fuel cells, which are connected to the supplier's electric grid. The installation is part of a program to foster the development and application of clean technologies for generating power.

One of the challenges to be faced in the 21st century is the development of clean, sustainable energy that can be distributed efficiently and affordably to consumers and businesses around the world. On the cutting edge of developing innovative energy technology is Plug Power. Headquartered in Latham, New York, with offices in Washington, D.C., and the Netherlands, Plug Power (Nasdaq: PLUG) is a global leader in the design, development, and manufacture of proton exchange membrane (PEM) fuel cells.

The fuel cell may be to 21st-century technology what the battery was to the 20th century—an indispensable means of supplying energy for commercial and industrial use, from cell towers to remote offices and from cordless telephones to public transportation systems. A fuel cell provides continuous direct current (DC) electrical power. A fuel cell's principal fuel source is hydrogen, which can be extracted from widely available fuels such as natural gas and propane. With proper applications, this visionary technology might help provide a solution to such problems as California's rolling blackouts of 2001 and the Northeast's crippling power outages in the summer of 2003.

Plug Power, a leader in fuel cell technology, was founded in 1997 as a joint venture between Detroit, Michigan–based DTE Energy, a diversified energy services company, and Albany, New York–based Mechanical Technology Incorporated, an early developer of fuel cells. Plug Power is focused on a number of objectives. Its goals in the short term include enhancing product performance and market viability, providing a solution for critical backup power needs at a competitive price, improving manufacturing and integration processes, and building strategic relationships with clients and partners. The company's long-term goals include delivering energy that is clean, reliable, and sustainable.

In the few years since its inception, the company has established three platforms—GenSys™, GenCore®, and GenSite™—to meet demands for on-site generation of energy. GenSys offers on-site systems for applications requiring continuous power. The GenSys platform has led to numerous offshoots, including GenSys™ 5P, the company's first product fueled by liquefied petroleum gas (LPG). GenCore provides standby, emergency, and uninterruptible power supply (UPS) for backup of mission-critical applications across a wide range of outdoor conditions. GenSite provides pure, compressed hydrogen gas at the point of use. Its industrial uses include generator cooling and metals processing.

Plug Power has developed a global network of strategic partners to assist in the research and development of fuel cell technology. Located in the United States, Europe, and Asia, these partners play an active role in the design, manufacture, distribution, and service of the company's products. These key partnerships include Celanese AG; DTE Energy; Engelhard Corporation; GE; Honda R&D Co., Ltd., of Japan; and Vaillant GmbH. Through these alliances, Plug Power continues to lay a firm foundation for the accelerated adoption and commercialization of on-site energy products.

Plug Power and Honda R&D co-created a prototype for the Home Energy Station, a fuel cell system that provides electricity and heat to homes while also providing hydrogen to power a fuel cell vehicle. In 2003, a successful demonstration of the prototype took place at the Honda R&D America facility in Torrance, California. In 2004, the two companies agreed to begin phase two of the project: the creation of a next-generation prototype of the Home Energy Station, with Honda R&D of Japan funding Plug Power's development costs.

The importance of this project is underscored by Roger B. Saillant, Ph.D., Plug Power president and chief executive officer, who says, "It is becoming more and more evident that the Home Energy Station could become a critical element in the emerging hydrogen economy."

As part of its ongoing strategy, Plug Power is engaged in discussions with state and federal governments to increase funding for research and development, provide tax incentives, and create a favorable regulatory infrastructure that will become a foundation for widespread adoption of distributed power generation. Since its inception, Plug Power has been awarded grants and received funding from the New York State Energy Research and Development Authority, the U.S. Department of Energy, the U.S. Department of Defense, and the National Institute of Standards and Technology to advance stationary fuel cell development.

A farsighted leader in the energy field, Plug Power focuses on a triple bottom line—the economic, social, and environmental benefits associated with generating and distributing clean, reliable, sustainable energy. From the CEO to employees across the company, Plug Power participates in community programs and charitable organizations. For instance, the company helps to support the Regional Food Bank of Northeastern New York, with employees performing volunteer work both during business hours and on weekends for fund-raising activities such as benefit barbecues. This commitment to the well-being of the community is just one aspect of Plug Power's ultimate objective: finding ways to make producing and distributing clean, sustainable power on a global scale compatible with living life on a human scale.

Above: This Honda–Plug Power prototype Home Energy Station at the Honda R&D America facility in Torrance, California, is a fuel cell system that can power both a home and vehicles. It generates heat and electricity for the house and hydrogen for fuel cell vehicles.

Cherbo Publishing Group

Cherbo Publishing Group's business-focused, art book–quality publications celebrate the vital spirit of America's past, present, and future.

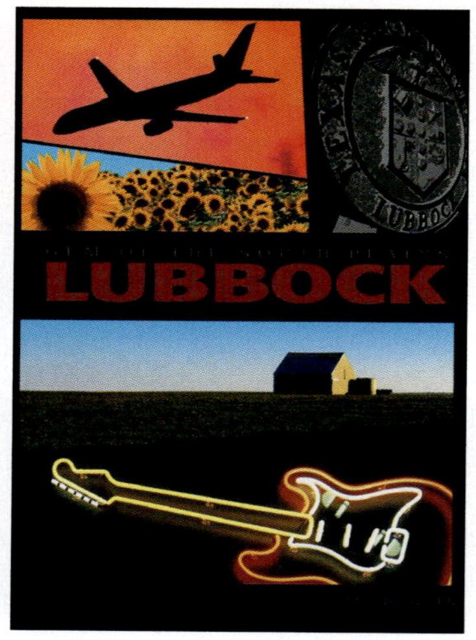

Cherbo Publishing Group, Inc. (CPG) is North America's leading publisher of books for commercial, historical, civic, and trade associations. CPG products offer informative content, imaginative design, and quality materials and manufacture. From concept to completion, all publications are produced in CPG's facility using state-of-the-art equipment.

"Cherbo Publishing Group is a growing, privately held corporation with a talented staff and modern facilities," says company president, Jack Cherbo. "These assets, along with a professional sales and marketing team and a sophisticated network of suppliers and contractors, are part of CPG's recipe for success."

Jack Cherbo, a pioneer in the custom publishing industry, and Elaine Hoffman, CPG executive vice president, took Cherbo Publishing Group private in 1993. The company was formerly a division of Jostens, Inc., a Fortune 500 company and the world's largest maker of school yearbooks and class rings. Today, CPG is based in Encino, California, and has regional offices in Philadelphia, Minneapolis, and Houston.

American Industries, American Ingenuity

CPG publications—most of which are created in collaboration with a sponsoring agency—pay tribute to America's extraordinary business acumen and continuing legacy of innovation. These publications range from regional, architectural, preservation, and special-interest books to state/regional business reports.

One of CPG's newest ventures is the Architectural series, beautifully illustrated books that celebrate the work of visionaries. Handsomely designed, these books demonstrate how city legislators, planners, designers, builders, and others have changed the urban landscape. Likewise, the Preservation & Smart Growth series illustrates the ways individual cities have managed to blend conservation efforts with structural growth.

CPG also publishes regional books that spotlight the country's most affluent and fastest growing metropolitan areas. Each book provides an in-depth look at a region's economic climate and industrial strengths.

CPG business reports highlight the economic advantages of individual cities or regions, while special-interest publications celebrate anniversaries or special occasions for corporations, organizations, and professional and trade associations.

For more information about these and other new projects, or to find out how CPG can help you celebrate a special occasion or showcase your company or organization, contact Cherbo Publishing Group at (800) 854-9880 or visit www.cherbopub.com.

Select CPG Publications

State/Regional Series

AMERICA & THE SPIRIT OF ENTERPRISE
Century of Progress, Future of Promise

ARKANSAS *The Natural State of Enterprise*

CALIFORNIA *Golden Past, Shining Future*

CONNECTICUT *Chartered for Progress*

DUPAGE COUNTY, ILLINOIS
Economic Powerhouse

INDIANA *Crossroads of Industry and Innovation*

LUBBOCK, TEXAS *Gem of the South Plains*

MARYLAND *Anthem to Innovation*

MICHIGAN *America's Pacesetter*

MISSOURI *Gateway to Enterprise*

NORTH CAROLINA *The State of Minds*

OKLAHOMA *The Center of It All*

PENNSYLVANIA *Keystone of the New Millennium*

UPSTATE NEW YORK *Corridor to Progress*

WASHINGTON *New Discoveries, New Frontiers*

Commemorative Series

CELEBRATE ST. PAUL
150 Years of History

BUILD IT & THE CROWDS WILL COME
Seventy-Five Years of Public Assembly

THE EXHIBITION INDUSTRY
The Power of Commerce

THE NATIONAL RURAL LETTER CARRIERS' ASSOCIATION
A Centennial Portrait

THE NEW YORK STATE ASSOCIATION OF FIRE CHIEFS
Sizing Up a Century of Service

VISIONS TAKING SHAPE
Celebrating 50 Years of the Precast, Prestressed Concrete Industry

State/Regional Business Reports

MINNESOTA REPORT 2004

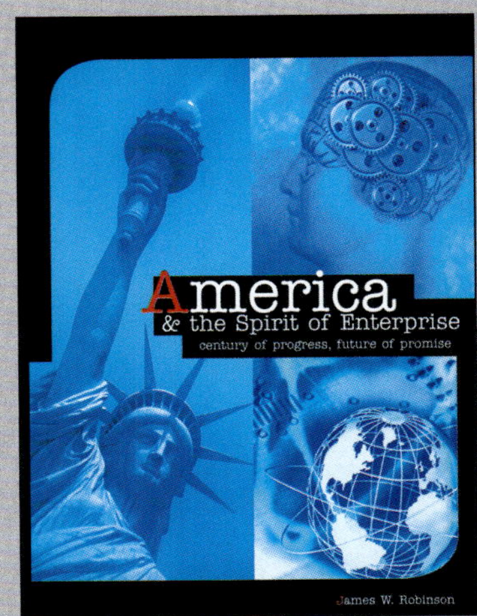

Bibliography

"About Chautauqua." Chautauqua Institution. <www.ciweb.org/history.html> (2004).

"Advanced Research Centers (ARCS)." New York State Office of Science, Technology and Academic Research. <www.nystar.state.ny.us/arcs.htm> (2003).

"Advance Publications, Inc. Company Profile." Yahoo Finance. <biz.yahoo.com/ic/40/40006.html> (2003).

"Agricultural News." New York Agriculture Statistics Service, February 2003. <www.nass.usda.gov/ny> (2003).

Allen, Frederick. *Only Yesterday.* New York: Harper and Row, 1931.

Alterio, Julie. "Missouri Company Buys Stake in New Roc City." New York Journal News, October 30, 2003. <www.nyjournalnews.com/newsroom/103003/a013nrcapelli.html> (2003).

"Analysis of Local Exchange Service Competition in New York State." New York State Public Service Commission, 2001.

"Annual Report." New York Building Congress, 2003.

Barton, Bruce. *The Man Nobody Knows.* New York: Collier Books, 1925.

"Beaches & Parks." Long Island Convention & Visitors Bureau and Sports Commission. <www.licvb.com/beaches_and_parks.cfm> (2003).

Block, Valerie. "Stitch in Time Buoys Brooklyn Firms." *Crain's New York Business,* September 27, 1999.

Bobby Reiss, interview with author. New York, November 2003.

Bridger, Chet. "Breaking New Ground." *The Buffalo News,* September 24, 2003. <www.bnmc.org/news/377263774884268.html> (2003).

Browning, E. S. "Investors Take Good News and Run With It." *Wall Street Journal,* June 17, 2003.

Brunner, Borgna, et al, eds. *Time Almanac 2004.* Needham, Mass.: Pearson Education, Inc., 2003.

"Buffalo TV Market Ranking Falls Three Places." *Business First,* August 20, 2001.

"The Business Services Industry Cluster in New York State." Empire State Development, April 2001. <www.nylovesbiz.com/NYS/_Home_To_Business/Industry_Clusters/business_services.asp> (2003).

"CB4 Just Loves Skyscrapers." Hell's Kitchen Online, December 3, 2001. <hellskitchen.net/develop/index.html?x=31> (2003).

"Centers of Excellence." Empire State Development. <www.nylovesbiz.com/High_Tech_Research_and_Development/centers_for-excellence.asp> (2003).

"Centers of Excellence." New York State Office of Science, Technology, and Academic Research. <www.nystar.state.ny.us/coes.htm> (2003).

"Cluster Update: Biomedical." Empire State Development, July 2001. <www.nylovesbiz.com/NYS_Home_To_Business/Industry_Clusters/biomedical.asp> (2003).

"Cluster Update: Industrial Machinery and Systems." Empire State Development, November 2001. <www.nylovesbiz.com/NYS_Home_To_Business/Industry_Clusters/industrial_machinery.asp/IndustrialMachineryUpdate.pdf> (2003).

"Cluster Update: Materials Processing." Empire State Development, July 2002. <www.nylovesbiz.com/NYS_Home_To_Business/Industry_Clusters/material_processing.asp/materialsprocessingupdate0800.pdf> (2003).

"Cluster Update: Optics and Imaging." Empire State Development, August 2002. <www.nylovesbiz.com/NYS_Home_To_Business/Industry_Clusters/optics_imaging.asp> (2003).

"Cluster Update: Transportation Equipment." Empire State Development, June 2002. <www.nylovesbiz.com/NYS_Home_To_Business/Industry_Clusters/transportation.asp> (2003).

"The Communications and Media Services Industry Cluster in New York State." Empire State Development, April 2001. <www.nylovesbiz.com/NYS_Home_To_Business/Industry_Clusters/communication_media.asp> (2003).

Crain's New York Business Book of Lists 2003. <www.crainsny.com/businessList.cms> (2003).

Crain's New York Business 2003 Market Facts. <www.crainsny.com/marketFacts.cms> (2003).

"Crop Profile: Cabbage and Other Crucifers in New York." The Pesticide Management Education Program at Cornell University, 2003. <pmep.cce.cornell.edu/fqpa/crop-profiles/cabbage.html> (2003).

"Crop Profile: Labrusca Grapes in New York." The Pesticide Management Education Program at Cornell University, 2000. <pmep.cce.cornell.edu/fqpa/crop-profiles/labruscagrape.html> (2003).

"Crop Profile: Onions in New York." The Pesticide Management Education Program at Cornell University, 2003. <pmep.cce.cornell.edu/fqpa/crop-profiles/onion.html> (2003).

"Crop Profile: Sweet Corn in New York." The Pesticide Management Education Program at Cornell University, 2003. <pmep.cce.cornell.edu/fqpa/crop-profiles/swcorn.html> (2003).

"Crop Profile: Vinifera and French Hybrid Grapes in New York." The Pesticide Management Education Program at Cornell University, 2000. <pmep.cce.cornell.edu/fqpa/crop-profiles/vinifera&french.html> (2003).

"The Distribution Industry in New York State." Empire State Development, March 2001. <www.nylovesbiz.com/NYS/_Home_To_Business/Industry_Clusters/distribution.asp> (2003).

Drury, Tracey. "WNY Poised to Enter Bioinformatics Arena." *Business First,* July 29, 2002.

Dunlap, David W. "Time Goes Forward on Plan for Tower on Eighth Avenue." *New York Times,* December 14, 2001. <www.wirednewyork.com/forum/topic.cgi?forum=4&topic=11> [cited December 14, 2001] (2003).

"Edgar Allen Poe." *American Master's* series, Public Broadcasting System. <www.pbs.org/wnet/americanmasters/database/poe_e.html> (2004).

"Empire State Manufacturing Survey." Buffalo Branch, Federal Reserve Bank of New York, June 2003. <www.ny.frb.org/research/regional_economy/mfg_survey/6_2003> (2003).

"Entertainment Properties Trust Acquires Interest in New Roc City." Entertainment Properties Trust (press release), October 28, 2003. <www.eprkc.com/press/2003/EPRKC_10_28_03.pdf> (2003).

"Ethan Allen Furniture's Boonville Division." Rome (N.Y.) *Daily Sentinel,* November 2, 1998.

"The Financial Services Industry Cluster in New York State." Empire State Development, April 2001. <www.nylovesbiz.com/NYS_Home_To_Business/Industry_Clusters/financial_services.asp> (2003).

"The Food Processing Industry Cluster in New York State." Empire State Development, April 2001. <www.nylovesbiz.com/NYS_Home_To_Business/Industry_Clusters/food_processing.asp> (2003).

"Forbes Inc. Company Profile." Yahoo Finance. <biz.yahoo.com/ic/44/44195.html> (2003).

"Fortune 500." *Fortune,* August 14, 2003.

"The Four Seasons Restaurant." Online Highways. <www.ohwy.com/ny/t/toensrra.htm> (2003).

Friedlander, Blaine, Jr. "CU Food Experts Judge New York State's Best Milk, Cheese Producers." *Cornell Chronicle,* August 31, 2000. <www.news.cornell.edu/Chronicle/00/8.31.00/milk-cheese-judge.html> (2003).

Goldbaum, Ellen. "Bioinformatics Center Moves Forward." *Reporter,* Division of University Communications, University at Buffalo, January 24, 2002. <www.buffalo.edu/reporter/vol33n14/f1.html> (2003).

Goldberger, Paul. "Spiffing Up the Gray Lady." *The New Yorker,* January 7, 2002. <www.wirednewyork.com/forum/topic.cgi?forum=4&topic=11> [cited January 4, 2002] (2003).

"GoSki New York." GoSki.com. <www.goski.com/resorts/rusany/newyork.htm> (2003).

"Governor Announces Florian Wireless to Create 350 New Jobs." New York State Office of the Governor (press release), July 22, 2001. <www.state.ny.us/governor/press/year02/july22_02.htm> (2003).

"Governor Announces $230 Million Long Island Center of Excellence." New York State Office of Science, Technology and Academic Research (press release). <www.nystar.state.ny.us/pr/02/press25-02.htm> (2003).

"Governor: BAE Systems to Expand, Create New Jobs on Long Island." New York State Office of the Governor (press release), March 21, 2002. <www.state.ny.us/governor/press/year02/march21_1_02.htm> (2003).

"Governor Breaks Ground on New Best Buy Distribution Center." State of New York Governor's Office for Small Cities (press release), June 17, 2002. <www.nysmallcities.com/press/june17_02.htm> (2003).

"Governor: Buffalo Firm to Expand Operations, Create New Jobs." New York State Office of the Governor (press release), November 18, 2002. <www.state.ny.us/governor/press/year02/nov18_2_02.htm> (2003).

"Governor, Industry Announce Buffalo Center of Excellence." New York State Office of the Governor (press release), December 6, 2001. <www.state.ny.us/governor/press/year01/dec6_01.htm> (2003).

"Governor Pataki: Ethan Allen to Create 125 Jobs in Boonville." State of New York Executive Chamber (press release), October 29, 1998. <www.nylovesbiz.com/press/1998/ethanal.html> (2003).

"Governor Pataki: Kmart Will Invest $120 million in NYS." New York State Office of the Governor (press release), April 5, 2001. <www.state.ny.us/governor/press/year01/april5_01.htm> (2003)

"Governor Pataki Makes Series of High-Tech Announcements." State of New York Executive Chamber (press release), September 23, 2002. <www.nylovesbiz.com/press/press_display.asp?id=27> (2003).

"Governor Pataki: National Pipe & Plastics, Inc. Expands Operations." Governor's Office of Regulatory Reform (press release), March 15, 2002. <www.gorr.state.ny.us/gorr/03_14-02-EmpireZone-Brome.htm> (2003).

"Governor Pataki Unveils New $1 Billion High-Tech/Biotech Plan." New York State Office of the Governor (press release), January 3, 2001. <www.state.ny.us/governor/press/year01/jan03_3_01.htm> (2003).

"Governor: Target to Purchase Kmart Distribution Center." New York State Office of the Governor (press release), April 14, 2003. <www.state.ny.us/governor/press/year03/april14_3_03.htm> (2003).

"Governor: Wal-Mart Picks Johnstown for Distribution Center." State of New York Executive Chamber (press release), August 26, 1998. <www.nylovesbiz.com/press/1998/walmart.html> (2003).

"Governor: Wal-Mart to Create 1,000 New Jobs in New York State." New York State Office of the Governor (press release), July 31, 2002. <www.state.ny.us/governor/press/year02/july31_02.htm> (2003).

"Green Living in Battery City Park." Lower Manhattan.info, April 18, 2003. <www.lowermanhattan.info/news/green_living_in_battery_86127.asp> (2003).

"G-III Apparel Group Ltd. (GIII)." Yahoo Finance. <finance.yahoo.com/q/is?s=GIII&annual> (2003).

Hacker, Louis, and Mark Hirsch. *Proskauer.* Tuscaloosa, Ala.: University of Alabama Press, 1978.

"Harbor Footwear Group Ltd." *Newsday.* <www.newsday.com/business/ny-toppri-harborfootwear.story> (2003).

Healy, Edward. "Buffalo Niagara's Heritage Trail." *Going Places,* March/April, 2002. <www.aaasouth.com/previous_issues/mar_apr_02/niagara.asp> (2003).

Herman, Eric. "Designs on Times HQ." *New York Daily News,* December 14, 2001.

"HMO Phone Numbers, Service Areas, and Accreditation Status." In *2003 New York Interactive Consumer Guide to HMOs,* State of New York Department of Insurance and State of New York Department of Health. <www.nyshmoguide.org/HmoAdditionalInfo.asp> (2003).

Hood, Clifton. *722 Miles.* New York: Simon and Schuster, 1993.

"InformationWeek 500 2003." *InformationWeek.* <www.informationweek.com/956> (2003).

Ip, Greg. "Manufacturers in New York State Report An Increase In New Orders." *Wall Street Journal,* June 17, 2003.

Jackson, Kenneth, ed. *The Encyclopedia of New York City.* New Haven: Yale University Press, 1995.

"J. Walter Thompson (US)." Adbrands.net. <www.adbrands.net/us/jwt_us.htm> (2003).

"Kobayashi's Speedy Gluttony Rattles Foes." Associated Press, Rochester, N.Y.: July 4, 2001.

Kreinin Souccar, Miriam. "Broadway Sales Hit New High." *Crain's New York Business,* week of June 1, 2004. <www.crainsny.com/news.cms> (2004).

Kumar, Sarath P. "Midas' Touch." *The Week,* August 10, 2003. <www.the-week.com/23aug10/life11.htm> (2003).

Lange, Alexandra. "Queens Modern." *New York,* June 17, 2002.

"Largest Trade Publishers, 2002." *Publishers Weekly,* June 16, 2003.

"Lifetime Entertainment Services Company Profile." Yahoo Finance. <biz.yahoo.com/ic/47/47291.html> (2003).

"Lockheed Martin Systems Integration–Owego, Owego New York." U.S. Environmental Protection Agency. <www.epa.gov/performancetrack/apps/pdfs/sum/lockheedowego.pdf> (2003).

Meyer, Corky. "The Best WW II Fighter." *Flight Journal,* August 2003.

"Nanotech Moves the Future to a New Level." *The Guardian,* July 28, 2003.

"Nanotechnology—Definition." About.com. <physics.about.com/library/dict/bldefnanotechnology.htm?terms=nanotechnology> (2003).

"New York—Best Destination for Fish and Wildlife Recreation!" New York State Department of Environmental Conservation. <www.dec.state.ny.us/website/dfwmr/huntfish.html> (2003).

"New York Retains First Place As the City Most People Would Like to Live In or Near." The Harris Poll number 50, September 3, 2003. <www.harrisineractive.com/harris_poll/index.asp?PID=399> (2003).

"New York's Radio City Music Hall Recaptures Its Past." National Trust, October 18, 2000. <www.nationaltrust.org/news/docs/20001018_award_nyradiocity.html> (2004).

"Niagara Falls: History of Power." Thunder Alley. <www.iaw.com/~falls/power.html> (2003).

Ó hAnluain, Daithí. "Reaching through the Net to Touch." *Wired,* July 3, 2003.

"Pataki Announces $200 Million Bioinformatics Center for Buffalo." *Business First,* December 6, 2001.

"Pennsylvania Communications Company Expanding into Steuben County." *Business First,* July 24, 2002.

Philipkoski, Kristen. "Bio Gets Big Blue's Big Bucks," Wired.com. <www.wired.com/nes/technology/0,1282,38295,00.html> (2003).

Phillips, Matthew. "Montgomery County Hopes Firms Will Target Business Park." *The Business Review,* June 6, 2003.

"Proskauer Rose Goetz and Mendelsohn." In *The Encyclopedia of New York City,* Kenneth Jackson, ed. New Haven: Yale University Press, 1995.

"Publishers Weekly 2002 Bestsellers." *Publishers Weekly,* March 24, 2003.

Rasmussen, Aaron. "Saratoga Springs, New York." *New York,* March 24, 2003.

"Renzo Piano to Design New York Times Building." Associated Press, Rochester, N.Y.: October 13, 2000.

"Research, Development, and Outreach Centers." New York State Office of Science, Technology, and Academic Research. <www.nystar.state.ny.us/research.htm> (2003).

Rich, Motoko. "Aiming to Be the Next Big Amenity." *New York Times,* November 13, 2003.

Rothman, Ellen. *Hands and Hearts.* New York: Basic Books, 1984.

Salamone, Salvatore. "Blue Gene Is Cool for 2006." *Bio-IT World,* July 15, 2003.

"Schenectady, New York Industrial History: The General Electric Company." The Schenectady Digital History Archive, Schenectady County Public Library. <www.schenectadyhistory.org/ge/index.html> (2003).

"Schumer, Clinton Secure $32.5 Million for Schweizer Aircraft for Unmanned Aerial Vehicles." U.S. Senator Charles E. Schumer, New York (press release), September 25, 2003. <www.senate.gov/~schumer/SchumerWebsite/pressroom/press_releases/PR02055.html> (2003).

"Shares Surge as New York Factory Report Fuels Optimism." *New York Times,* June 17, 2003.

Simmons, Mark. "Madison Square Garden: A Sports Haven." AskMen.com. <www.askmen.com/sports/business/59_sports_business.html> (2003).

"Skadden, Arps, Slate, Meagher and Flom." In *The Encyclopedia of New York City,* Kenneth Jackson, ed. New Haven: Yale University Press, 1995.

Slayton, Robert. "The House That Ruth Built." *New York Archives,* no. 3 (spring 2004): 18-20.

———. *Empire Statesman.* New York: The Free Press, 2001.

"Southwestern Suburbs Top List of Fastest-Growing Cities." *New York Times,* July 11, 2003.

"Special Report: Agency Report." *Advertising Age,* April 21, 2003.

"State Electricity Profiles: New York." U.S. Department of Energy/Energy Information Administration. <www.eia.doe.gov/cneaf/electricity/st_profiles/new_york/ny.html> (2003).

"Strategically Targeted Academic Research (STAR) Centers." New York State Office of Science, Technology, and Academic Research. <www.nystar.state.ny.us/stars.htm> (2003).

Strouse, Jean. *Morgan.* New York: HarperCollins/Perennial, 1999.

Thompson, Glen. "Optimism Reigns at Unveiling of Times Tower Design." GlobeSt.com, December 14, 2001. <www.wirednewyork.com/forum/topic.cgi?forum=4&topic=11> [cited December 14, 2001] (2003).

"Time Inc. Company Profile." Yahoo Finance. <biz.yahoo.com/ic/43/43661.html> (2003).

"2003 New York Agricultural Statistics Annual Bulletin." New York Agricultural Statistics Service. <www.nass.usda.gov/ny/Bulletin/2003/an2002.html> (2003).

Valigra, Lori. "Touch Technology." *Christian Science Monitor,* July 24, 2003.

"The Wall Street Journal Announces New Integrated Print and Online Sales and Marketing Initiatives." Business Wire, November 3, 2003. <www.businesswire.com/webbox/bw.110303/233075695.htm> (2003).

Weiss, Lois. "On Real Estate." New York Post, December 12, 2001. <www.wirednewyork.com/forum/topic.cgi?forum=4&topic=11> [cited December 13, 2001] (2003).

Whyte, William. *City.* New York: Doubleday, 1988.

Williams, Stan. "Ask the Expert: In Simple Terms, What Is Nanotechnology?" CIO.com. <www2.cio.com/ask/expert/2002/questions/question865.html?CATEGORY=119&NAME=Innovation> (2003).

The Web sites of the following organizations were also consulted for this book.

adage.com, Adirondack Trust Company, Albany International Airport, Albany Molecular Research, Albany NanoTech, Altria Group, American International Group, Antigenics, Arkwin Industries, Arrow, Associated Builders and Contractors, Associated New York State Food Processors, Associated Press, Astoria Federal Savings, Avone, BAE Systems, Barrons Educational Series, Bausch & Lomb, BBDO, BBL, Benderson Development, Bertelsmann, BH Aircraft, Bloomberg, Brooklyn Chamber of Commerce, Buffalo Philharmonic Orchestra, Canandaigua Wine, CardWorks, Carrier, Cazenovia College, Center of Excellence in Environmental Systems, Citigroup, cityguidemagazine.com, CMP Media, Columbia University, Con Edison, Conference Center Niagara Falls, CONSTANTIN Group, Constellation Brands, Cornell University, Cornell University Agricultural Experiment Station, Corning, Credit Suisse, The Culinary Institute of America, Curtis Instruments, Deloitte Touche Tohmatsu, Dow Jones, Dresser-Rand, Editor & Publisher, The Egg, EJ Footwear, Ellicott Development, empireblue.com, Empire State Building, Empire State Development Corporation, Energy East, epodunk.com, Ernst & Young, Eyetech Pharmaceuticals, Fairmont Hotels & Resorts, The Farmers' Museum, Federal Reserve Bank of New York, Fenimore Art Museum, First Albany, Forbes, Fortune, Frontier, Garment Industry Development, GBX, Glimmerglass Opera, GORP, Grant Thornton, greatlakes-seaway.com, G-III Apparel Group, Harden Furniture, Hardy Holzman Pfeiffer, heritage.dupont.com, Hill & Knowlton, hipusa.com, Hobart and William Smith Colleges, Hodgson Russ, Hoover's, Hunter Mountain, IBM, IBM Research, Israel Discount Bank of New York, Jacques Moret, Jamestown Business College, J. P. Morgan Chase, Kodak, Korn/Ferry, KPMG, Lockheed Martin, L-3 Communications, Madison Square Garden, Mamiye Brothers, MapInfo, Marsh & McLennan, Martin Benefits Consulting, MasterCard, McCadam Cheese, McCann, McGraw-Hill, Mediacom, Merrill Lynch, Metropolitan Life Insurance, Metropolitan Transportation Authority, Monadnock Construction, Moody's, Moog, Mount Sinai Hospital, Mount Sinai School of Medicine, nanoindustries.com, National Baseball Hall of Fame and Museum, National Nanotechnology Initiative, National Pipe & Plastics, newroccity.com, News Corporation, New York Building Congress, New York-Presbyterian Hospital, New York State Agricultural Experiment Station, New York State Association of Convention and Visitors Bureaus, New York State Association of REALTORS, New York State Builders Association, New York State College of Ceramics at Alfred University, New York State Department of Economic Development, New York State Department of Labor, New York State Department of Transportation, New York State Electric & Gas, New York State Thruway Authority, New York Stock Exchange, The New York Times, New York University, New York Wine & Grape Foundation, Nexia Biotechnologies, Nixon Peabody, NLX, Nomura Group, Northrop Grumman, nyscanalbusiness.com, Ogilvy Public Relations, Olean Business Institute, Olympic Regional Development Authority, Oxford Health Plans, Pall, Penguin Group (USA), Perfect Fit Glove, Pfaudler, Pfizer, Photocircuits, Plastics Technology, Port Authority of New York and New Jersey, Practicare Medical Management, Prestolite Electric, Proskauer Rose, realtor.org, Rensselaer Polytechnic Institute, Rochester Gas & Electric, Rockefeller University, Roswell Park Cancer Institute, Ruder Finn, Rudin Management, Scholastic, Schweizer Aircraft, Sensis, Shearman & Sterling, simonsays.com, Sirius Radio, Skadden Arps Slate Meagher & Flom, Skanska, skanskausa.com, The Solaire, Solomon and Solomon, State University of New York, State University of New York at Buffalo, State University of New York at Canton, State University of New York Maritime College, Syska Hennessy Group, United Nations, United States Military Academy at West Point, University at Buffalo Center of Excellence in Bioinformatics, University at Buffalo Virtual Reality Laboratory, Upstate Farms Cooperative, U.S. Department of Housing and Urban Development, Vassar College, Vornado Realty Trust, Watson Research Center, Welliver McGuire, Whiteface Mountain, White Osterman & Hanna, WoltersKluwer, Zogby, zyvex.com/nano

Index

Index

Index

Index

Index

n y s

New York State

prime mover

cherbo publishing group, inc.

Typography

Principal faces used:
Helvetica, first designed by Alfred Hoffmann and Max Miedinger in 1957; Adobe Garamond, designed by Robert Slimbach in 1989, which was derived from previous designs by Claude Garamond, Jean Jannon, and Robert Granjon; and Scala Sans, designed by Martin Majoor in 1993.

Hardware

Macintosh G5 workstations, digital color laser proofing with Xerox Docucolor 12, digital imaging with Creo EverSmart Supreme.

Software

QuarkXPress, Adobe Illustrator, Adobe Photoshop, Adobe Acrobat, Microsoft Word, Eye-One Pro by Gretagmacbeth, Creo Oxygen, FlightCheck.

CTP, Printing, and Binding

Performed by Friesens of Altona, Manitoba, Canada, and Neche, North Dakota, USA.

Paper

Text Paper: #80 Garda Gloss.
Bound in Rainbow® recycled content papers from Ecological Fibers, Inc. Dust Jacket: #100 Sterling-Litho Gloss.